W9-CJH-213

MUSCLE CAR

Mighty Machines that Ruled the Road

JOHN GUNNELL

©2006 Krause Publications

Published by

An Imprint of F+W Publications

700 East State Street • Iola, WI 54990-0001
715-445-2214 • 888-457-2873

Our toll-free number to place an order or obtain
a free catalog is (800) 258-0929.

Library of Congress Catalog Number: 2006922213

ISBN 13-digit: 978-0-89689-313-9

ISBN 10-digit: 0-89689-313-8

Designed by Kara Grundman

Edited by Brian Earnest

Printed in China

DEDICATION

This book is dedicated to the great automotive free-lance photographers who have helped me capture the images of the muscle car era for so many years, in this book and others, especially Brad Bowling, Mike Carbonella, Henry Austin Clark, Jr., Tom Glatch, Jerry Heasley, Tom Jevcak, Milton Gene Kieft, Phil Kunz, John Lee, Daniel Lyons, Doug Mitchel, Jonathan Stein and Nicky Wright.

— *John Gunnell*

Contents

Introduction

When carmakers took the gloves off, an armada of legendary machines were born

Oldsmobile altered the American automotive landscape with its '49 Rocket 88. This big-engined/small-bodied factory hot rod was amazing. In addition to inspiring the first rock n' roll song—Ike Turner's "Rocket 88," the 88 has been called the "first muscle car."

In this book, we aren't going back quite that far. Our aim is to give you a rundown of what we consider to be the top 10 muscle cars. If you agree with our picks, you'll probably love the book because we think alike. If you disagree with our choices, you'll also love the book because you're showing us that you care about muscle cars. And debate is healthy.

Muscle cars are cars factories modified to go faster and look hotter than the grocery-getter cars they're based on. The years between 1964 and 1972 are considered the "Muscle Car Era," even though some people trace the roots of the movement back to the Rocket 88. And even after '72, there were a few models that lingered to keep the muscle car spirit alive.

Chevy's mid-'61 release of the Impala Super Sport was the catalyst for a muscle car explosion. By '63, Ford's legendary 427-powered Fairlane-bodied T-Bolts were tearing up drag strips. Then came the GTO. Sired by a DeLorean and nurtured by a team of "Young Turk" engineers at Pontiac, this option package for the mid-sized Tempest snuck out the back door of the factory to "light 'em up" on Woodward Avenue. Jim Wangers promoted the GTO as a factory rod and sold so many copies that GM forgot it had rules against such a car.

Ford and Mopar created their own "great pretenders." One-upmanship to the max followed with one company after another "supersizing" the competition's latest supercar. Chevy launched the SS 396 and Z/28. Dodge took the fast track with its Charger fastback, quickly offering the legendary "Street Hemi." Ford's Fairlane jousted with the GTO using a 7-liter lance. Hot Mustangs carved their own muscle niche until GM's F-Car combo came along.

Plymouth's mid-sized Belvedere launched a Satellite and GTX before hitting its stride with the rascally Road Runner. Buick and Olds—GM's used-to-be-go-fast cars—found themselves losing sales to their A- and F-body cousins. These premium marques never got an F-car, but both found neat A-body answers to their problem. The Skylark-based Buick GS was a glitterier go machine with a few

Jerry Heasley

more cubic inches. The Olds 4-4-2 was simply one of America's most awesome muscle cars. It won constant praise from the car magazine road testers.

During '67-'68, high-po sports compacts basked in the limelight. The Mustang engine bay grew enough to swallow big-block V-8s. The Camaro SS 396, Mustang SCJ 428 and Formula 400 Firebird were wild and wooly street racers that appealed to young buyers on a budget.

It wasn't long before mid-sized supercars like the Endura-nosed GTO and Ford Torino began to look more like their pony car counterparts. Then, Plymouth introduced the bargain-basement '68 Road Runner to inspire clones like the GTO Judge and Ford Falcon-Torino.

The late '60s brought more big 400-plus-cube V-8s. By corporate edict, GM brands dropped fuelies and multi-carb setups. Mopar did the opposite with its "Six Pack." New Ram-Air systems were devised to keep power levels high. Chrysler and Ford picked these up, too. Even AMC joined the game with several hot new models and power teams.

Mopar's "Winged Warriors"—the Plymouth Superbird and Dodge Daytona—shook the superspeedways, while Z/28s and Boss Mustangs shook the streets. Dodge and Plymouth entered the pony-car parade with a new Challenger and a reconstituted Plymouth 'Cuda. Chevy's Chevelle got a neat-but-not-drastic restyling and some massively strong engine options. Mopars throughout the range of mid-size and sports-compact cars were offered with Hemi V-8s. These turned out to be rarities and great investments.

If the muscle car niche was going to die, it was going out smokin'. The 455 Hurst/Olds, Buick GSX Stage 1, Trans Am 400 H.O., LS6 Chevelle SS 454, Plymouth GTX 440 Six-Pack, Boss 429 Mustang, Cougar CJ-R, Hemi 'Cuda, Hemi Superbird, Hemi Charger S/E and Ram Air IV Goat were '70 models that did 13-second quarter-miles at over 100 mph!

AMC joined the fray around '68 and hung in until the bitter end. As a small, struggling outfit, AMC had to depend on wild creativity to run in a neck-to-neck sales race. Its AMX 401, Rebel "Machine" and Hurst SC/Rambler were great budget-priced performers.

"Insurance companies gave the muscle cars one last kick, raising rates so high that young drivers torned to Pintos and Vegas."

Muscle Car

With the '71 swing to unleaded gas, high performance began to fizzle out. By '72, high-octane V-8s gave way to low-compression versions. Insurance companies gave the muscle cars one last kick, raising rates so high that young drivers turned to Pintos and Vegas.

By 1974, it was clearly "all over" for anything but lick-'em-stick-'em muscle cars. These were factory *customs*, but they were not factory hot rods. A couple had big-cube V-8s, but with smog equipment and two-barrel carbs. They could hardly get out of their own way. "Sayanora Supercar" said one magazine writer in a memorable lament.

Tom Glatch

Jerry Heasley

Camaro

Chevrolet's Mustang hunter
proves worth the wait

1967 - 1974

1967

When Lee Iaccoca and his "whiz kids" at FoMoCo introduced the Mustang, they caught The General with his pants down. It was a double-whammy sort of situation, too. GM had no car to compete head-to-head with the Mustang. In addition, the "Stang" had stolen away a sporty-car market niche that the Corvair had started to carve out. With the lengthy new-model development times in effect back then, there was nothing GM could do but watch the Mustangs go by for almost three years.

By 1966, the pages of buff books were filled with sketches of Chevrolet's Mustang-type car. It was code named "Panther" back then. Most of the sketches just slightly resembled the pony car that came to be, but towards the end, a few of them were nearly dead-on accurate representations of the showroom Camaro. They depicted a car that was curvier, smoother and more aggressive-looking than the Ford product. The accompanying stories pointed out that the Panther's engine bay was large enough to accommodate big-block V-8s.

■ *Just 602 first-year Z28s were built, making survivors like this Ermine White and black example nice collector prizes.*
Mike Mueller

1967   1968   1969   1970   1971   1972   1974

1967: New Camaro debuts with V-6 or V-8 engines and RS, SS (with 396 power), and Z/28 (with 302 engine) trims.

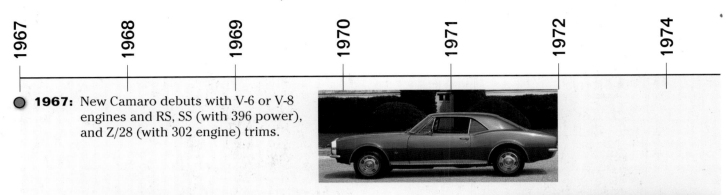

1968: The now-famous Houndstooth cloth made its debut on this model along with astro ventilation. Camaro SS offered two distinctive hoods: one for the 350 engine and one for the 396. 235,147 Camaros were produced.

1969: Special COPO and Yenko versions available with 427 power.

1970: Major redesign with European styling and new 350 engine for Z28.

1971: Chevrolet becomes the first automaker to build 3 million cars and trucks for one model year. A total of 114,643 of those were Camaros.

1972: Shortened production year. The last year of the big-block engine.

1974: Federal bumper impact standards facilitated a major facelift. New extruded aluminum bumpers graced the front and rear.

The Camaro finally made the scene on September 26, 1966 as Chevrolet's Mustang clone. "Camaro is band-box new by Chevrolet and a freshly styled example of how fine an exciting road machine can look," said the company's sales catalog, which described it as "a go as well as show machine." The Camaro offered "wide stance stability" and "big-car power." It came as a Sport Coupe or as a convertible.

All Camaro models could be *personalized* with extras. There was the base six-cylinder version with bucket seats and carpets, the Rally Sport version with "hideaway" headlights and the high-performance-oriented SS350 with its "bumblebee" stripes and powerful V-8 engines. Buyers could add a custom interior, various engines and transmissions and accessories like vinyl roofs and rally wheels. Those who wanted to customize their Camaro further could team some of the factory extras with others to create juicy combos like an RS/SS.

The Camaro rode a 108-inch wheelbase, the same used by the Mustang. Its overall length was 185 inches, an inch longer than Ford's pony. Where the Mustang offered six engines, Camaro initially offered seven. They included two sixes, a pair of 327-cid V-8s, one hi-po version of the 350 V-8 with 295 hp and a pair of Turbo-Jet 396 V-8s, one with 325 and the other with 375 hp.

■ *Distinct badging identified the first SS Camaros.* Mike Mueller

The L30 Turbo-Fire V-8 327 was rated at 275 hp. It had hydraulic valve lifters and a Rochester four-barrel carburetor.
Tom Glatch

An added option introduced in December 1966 was the first Camaro Z/28. This was a very special car engineered as a sedan racer for Trans-Am competition. Under its hood was a high-output small-block V-8 with a special cam, solid valve lifters, an aluminum "tuned-inlet" manifold, a baffled oil pan and all kinds of special features and chrome-plated parts. To go with the heated-up engine, the Z/28 had all heavy-duty underpinnings, quick steering and special tires. The Z/28 got up to 60 mph in seven seconds flat and ran the quarter-mile in 14.8 seconds at 96 mph. No wonder the Z/28 was selected to pace the 1967 Indy 500—it had the stuff to stay out ahead of the Indy racing cars of the day on parade laps.

The 327- and 350-powered cars were slower than a Z/28, while the SS 396 version was faster from 0 to 60, but a bit slower in the quarter-mile. Like the

Mustang, part of the Camaro's popularity was based on its appeal to a wide range of people. The six-cylinder models had the style and looks without the higher price tag, while the V-8s attracted everyday drivers, sports-car buffs and drag racers.

With total production of 220,906 Camaros, the new '67 model was a great start towards something big. The Camaro became a cultural icon with roles in television series such as "Charlie's Angels" and "Betwitched." The Chevy F-car also thrilled fans at race tracks across the nation. During the muscle-car era, it would pass through two major styling "generations" reshaping its character for enthusiasts of different times.

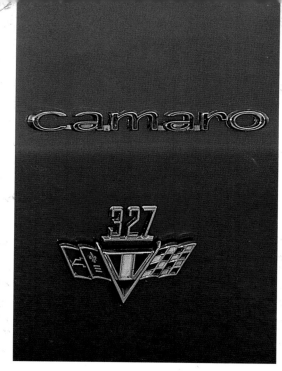

■ *The fender badging announced the power plant of this 1967 Camaro RS.* Tom Glatch

■ *An Ermine White Camaro SS convertible was chosen to lead the 1967 Indy 500.*

■ *The fat hood and deck lid stripes were first seen on the 1967 Z/28s. The stripes have since been permanently linked with the early Z cars.*
Mike Mueller

■ *All of the 1967 Z/28s were coupes.*

"Like the Mustang, part of the Camaro's popularity was based on its appeal to a wide range of people."

■ *It wasn't hard to guess why the Camaro Rally Sport was so well received in its first year. Like all the Camaros, it had clean, sporty styling, some serious power train options (this one carried the L48 350-cid V-8 with a Rochester four-barrel) and a very reasonable price tag.*

Tom Glatch

■ For buyers serious about driving a fast-moving ragtop, a 396-powered '67 Camaro was a pretty attractive option. The Royal Plumb '67 example here is a rare beast today. In the background is a 1969 Pace Indy Pace Car. Tom Glatch

■ As first-year muscle cars go, the 1967 Z/28 has to be near the top of the list. Jerry Heasley

Muscle Car

1968

At first glance the '68 Camaro looked like a '67. There were not many sheet metal changes, but plenty was going on under the skin and there was a subtle, but significant body style revision. The '68 had no "butterfly" windows. The new "vent-less" side windows were hailed as a major styling advance, but those of us who grew up with what GM called "ventipanes" will miss those vent windows forever. They did a good job of cooling interiors before A/C was popularized and they also made riding in a car a lot less stuffy experience. We have to admit, though, that messed-up hair could be one negative side effect.

The '68 Camaro also had front and rear side marker lights designed to meet new safety regulations dictated by a meddling Uncle Sam. There were also engineering refinements that Chevy said were "designed to keep the '68

■ *When Don Yenko Sportscars of Canonsburg, Pennsylvania, got hold of a 1968 Camaro SS, the result was budget-priced supercar. Yenko created the Super Yenko Camaro by stuffing a 427, 435- or 450-cid V-8 under a Corvette "stinger" hood and giving the cars some other go-fast parts. Somewhere between 54 and 100 of these cars were built. The exact number is subject to debate.*

Phil Kunz

Camaro the finest car in its field." A lot of the added goodies were located under the hood and beefed up the Camaro's muscular attributes.

The base Camaro used a 230-cid six, while the 327-cid remained base V-8. A 350-cid V-8 became standard in the Camaro SS. The Turbo-Jet 396-cid V—which made it into just over 5,500 SS Camaros in '67—was the factory's hot one. Some owners took their '68 Camaros to performance dealers like Don Yenko, Fred Gibbs, Motion Performance or Nickey Chevrolet to have the factory engine replaced with a big-block 427. Not counting these "aftermarket" 427s, there were 10 engines in all and eight were V-8s with horsepower ratings from 210 to 375.

Glamour was a strong point of the '68 RS package and husky performance was the calling card of the SS option. Cars with the 396 engine had a black-finished rear body panel. Also returning was the Z/28 with its 290-hp small-block V-8. With the good press it got in '67 (*Car and Driver* called it the "most responsive American V-8 we've ever tested") and a full year of selling, the Z/28 gained a bigger following. It was ordered by 7,199 buyers this year. The '68 Z/28 managed to cop the year's Trans-Am championship, as well as the NHRA World Finals title.

As a "street racer," the Camaro Z/28 was the darling of the buff books and three of the "big" car magazines put it to the test in '68. At this time, the magazines were so competitive that they strived to outdo each other in testing cars. It was if they believed that the magazine that drove a car the fastest would wind up with the most subscribers. *Road & Track* recorded a 6.9-second 0-to-60 time for the Z/28 and a 14.9-second quarter-mile run with a terminal speed of 100 mph. That indicated it was a tad faster than the '67 version. *Car Life* came up with 7.4 seconds for 0 to 60, but 14.85 seconds for the quarter-mile with a trap speed of 101.4 mph.

Car and Driver did something a little different and tested a Camaro that had been "tweaked" against a Mustang with similar upgrades. The Camaro registered a 5.3-second 0-to-60 time and a 13.77-second quarter-mile at 107.39 mph. We are not sure which magazine had the highest number of readers in '68, but we're guessing that Camaro owners liked *Car and Driver* best!

On the bottom line, 1968 was a good year on top of a good year for the Camaro. Overall model-year sales of the Chevy's new "pony car" rose by 15,000 units, a feat for any second-year car. On top of that, the Camaro expanded its muscle car acceptance level with several new engine options. It also proved itself a winner in several forms of motor sports. The Camaro forced Ford to take a shoe stretcher to the Mustang and widen its engine bay for big-block power. That fact alone made it clear that Chevy had bit the Ford pony car like a super-sized horsefly.

■ *This car was the only 1968 Z/28 convertible made. It sported a white convertible top. The white seats and door panels of this one-of-a-kind car made for a stunning interior combination.*

"The Camaro expanded its muscle car acceptance level with several new engine options."

1969

These were the good old days when The General could do nothing wrong and Chevrolet was really on the ball with the Camaro in '69. Muscular-looking new sheet metal made the car a killer as far as cosmetics went. The somewhat squarer body had a longer, lower and wider look with flattened wheel housings and sculptured side panels. The header panel, the front valance, all four fenders, both doors, both rear quarter panels and the rear beauty panel were all completely redesigned to look more aggressive. The grille was more angular and the tail lights were wider units with triple lenses instead of two. The back-up lights were moved from under the bumper into the center tail light lens.

Styling details varied again according to which Camaro "model option" was ordered. The Rally Sport had the headlights hidden behind tri-slotted "grilles" and big "RS" letters in the center of its blacked-out grille. The performance-oriented SS package featured a very cool-looking hood with chrome simulated intake ports. "hockey-stick" body striping, fat tires and wheels. "SS" grille letters and body badges, a 350-cid 300-hp V-8 and other extras that gave it a "hot" image. The RS and SS packages could be blended together to create an RS/SS model.

■ *The 1969 COPO Camaros were products of the Central Office Production Order system that allowed dealers to get their hands on some really fast cars from the factory. It is believed about 1,015 of these cars were produced. They featured L28 396-cid/325-hp engines that were tweaked and combined with various option packages. Yenko Chevrolet and several other dealers wound up handling these iconic muscle cars.*

Jerry Heasley

An RS/SS convertible with a 396-cid Turbo-Jet V-8 paced the Indy 500. It was the second time in three years that a Camaro served as the Official Pace Car for the classic race. Chevy did not sell pace car replicas in 1967, but 1969 was a different story. Experts say 3,675 of the Z11 Indy pace Car convertibles were made, along with a few hundred hardtops that featured a somewhat similar (and very rare) Z10 Indy Sport coupe package. Both the Z11 and the Z10 are among the most desirable Camaros to own today.

Back for the third year in a row was the Z/28 option for the sport coupe with power disc brakes and a four-speed manual gearbox. The engine was again a very special 302-cid small-block V-8 that put 290 hp on tap. The '69 Z/28 engine featured four-bolt mains with nodular iron caps, a high-rise aluminum intake, solid lifters, a special 30/30 lash cam, aluminum impact-extruded pistons and large-port heads. Due to its high exposure—especially by Roger Penske's "Sunoco" Camaros—on race tracks, the Z/28 drew 20,302 orders. In April, a rear deck lid spoiler was made a mandatory option for the "Z-car."

"Muscular-looking new sheet metal made the car a killer as far as cosmetics went."

Camaro 1967–1974

■ *With a red-hot 427-cid V-8 under the hood, the COPO Camaros were in the elite class of muscle cars in 1969.*

Mike Mueller

Chevrolet temporarily nicknamed the '69 Camaro the "Hugger." One advertisement showed a Frost Green SS coupe wearing a Hugger license plate. Chevy even had a Hugger Orange paint color for those who really wanted to turn heads. The name did not really stick and was rarely heard after 1970.

Another 1969 innovation was the COPO (Central Office Production option) 427 Camaro. The factory COPO system was set up to order large fleets of cars with special equipment such as taxicabs, squad cars and salesman cars. In 1968 a number of Chevrolet dealers that played to the performance market began stuffing Chevrolet's biggest V-8 into the Camaro. They knew the 427 would fit fine, since it was the same outward size as the factory available 396.

Some dealers like Fred Gibb, of Illinois, were doing quite a few big-block engine swaps into Camaro and it was expensive. Gibb talked to Chevrolet's performance guru Vince Piggins and used the COPO system to order a batch of 50 cars with factory-installed aluminum-block 427s. Designated COPO 9560 ZL1s,

■ *A total of 69 ZL1 Camaros were built in 1969 to make the ZL1 engine legal for NHRA drag racing. The legendary cars with aluminum engines were some of the fastest machines produced during the muscle car glory days of the 1960s and early '70s. All were RS models outfitted with power brakes and steering, racing mirrors, tachometers, blackwall tires, dual exhausts with resonators and a list of other goodies.*
Jerry Heasley

"The Camaro hadn't quite taken over the Mustang in popularity, but it was getting closer to that goal each year."

■ *The SS convertible got the nod as the Indy Pace Car in 1969.*   Tom Glatch

■ *The aluminum 427 hiding under the hood of a handful of ZL1 Camaros gave the bow tie crowd something to brag about at the drag strip.*   Mike Mueller

The all-black interior and manacing black-sidewall tires with body-matching rims seemed a perfect match for the ZL1's race track personality.

■ *The unique hood bulge and SYC emblem on the hood are trademarks of the famous Super Yenko Camaros. These cars carried a base price of $3,895.*

Mike Mueller

Gibbs planned to sell the cars as drag racing cars. By the time the order was finished, other dealers ordered an additional 19 cars. Dealer Don Yenko, of Canonsburg, Pennsylvania, ordered another batch of 201 factory 427 Camaros with the cast-iron L72 engine. The Yenko or "SYC" (for Yenko Sports Cars) models were built under COPO 9561. An undetermined amount of additional cars, for other dealers, were built under COPO 9561. The Yenko cars had special graphics to make them stand out.

By the end of 1969, Chevrolet racked up its third year in a row of climbing sales for Camaros. Model-year production peaked at 243,085 cars. The Camaro hadn't quite taken over the Mustang in popularity, but it was getting closer to that goal each year.

■ *With unique segmented hood louvers, hockey stick striping, front lip and rear deck lid spoilers, and lots of other cool styling cues, the Camaro SS from 1969 could hold its own in any factory muscle car beauty contest.*
Doug Mitchel

■ *The 1970 1/2 Z28 was a radically different machine, at least on the outside, from its predecessors.* Mike Mueller

1970

The 1970 Gen II Camaro came only as a two-door hardtop—usually referred to simply as the "coupe"—and it was all new from one end to the other. The body was longer, lower and wider, although the wheelbase was unchanged from the first generation. A strike postponed its debut until mid-1970. As a result, some dealers sold '69 models and '70s. A couple of dealers were even sued for doing so.

Luckily, the late arrival was a big hit. Its smooth, Euro-style appearance hit the bulls-eye with the public and car magazine writers alike. Some compared the look of The General's new F-cars to that of Italy's Maserati. As before, a number of "model options" were offered. These were option packages that Chevy promoted as if they were separate models. They started with the base coupe. The Rally Sport (RS) package was designed to add sportiness, flash and luxury. The Super Sport (SS) was the street muscle car. The Z28 (the slash between the letter and numbers was dropped from the badge) was the small-block built-for-racing car.

The RS included a different grille and front end treatment with left and right front bumpers on either side of the grille replacing the standard full-width front bumper. It all had a body-color grille frame molded of a resilient plastic material. The SS had a 350-cid 300-hp V-8 and heavy-duty underpinnings. The Z28 changed to a 350-cid engine, but it was a special one—essentially the four-bolt-mains Corvette LT1—that churned out 360 hp. It did 0 to 60 in less than 6 seconds and the quarter in 14.2.

The low-slung, road-hugging Camaro chassis got a number of impressive improvements this year. Front disc brakes were introduced as a new optrion. The wheel hub and disc rotor were of a new integral cast design. Power brakes were available. Wider front and rear treads contributed to better stability and road handling. Variable-ratio power steering was offered for the first time to provide better road feel.

■ *The famous split grille on the front of the second-generation Camaros was part of the Rally Sport package. These unique front ends could also be found on SS and Z28 models that had more than one option package. This RS was outfitted with the Z28 wardrobe.* Jerry Heasley

The '70 Camaro also had a larger and sturdier front stub frame with better front suspension geometry. The rear suspension was redesigned to improve both comfort and handling. The ride was claimed to be 30 percent softer than in previous Camaros, thanks to new lower-rate multi-leaf springs. New rear spring bushings reduced lateral movement so the car "rocked-and-rolled" less than before. The Z28 had 15-inch wheels and the other models had 14s. Bias-ply tires were standard but the SS and Z28 got wider white-letter tires as part of their packages.

Factory power offerings included a single (250-cid) in-line six this year, plus six V-8s. The 307-cid/200-hp engine was the base V-8. The 350-cid V-8 came in 250-, 300- (SS) and 360-hp (Z28) versions. Two versions of a new 402-cid V-8 (still promoted as a "396") were also offered. This engine had a 4.126-inch bore compared to the real 396's 4.094 inches. It was available with 350 or 375 hp. A few cars had solid-lifter 454s stuffed into them by specialty dealers like Motion Performance in Baldwin, New York, but these were no longer factory built. Baldwin Motion added the "aircraft carrier" big block, along with outside exhausts and special body graphics.

■ *The familiar Z28 badge was found at the base of the deck lid in 1970.*

Jerry Heasley

■ *The 1970 SS option package went on 15,201 cars. It carried a blacked-out grille, a 300-hp Turbo-Fire 350 V-8, racing mirrors, SS identifications, and other nifty styling details.*

Jerry Heasley

Due to the delayed start of production, the gorgeous new Camaros had only a half a season to sell, so the production total of 124,901 cars seemed very low compared to the numbers the Gen I cars generated. No one knew that things were going to get worse, before they got better. The Camaro was headed for a rough period in the early '70s, but the troubles had nothing to do with the design or engineering of the product itself, which were great.

1971

If you want to make your '70 Camaro a '71, all you need to do is find a Vega in a junkyard and swap bucket seats. Well, that's a simplification, but not a huge one. Chevy also gave the '71 steering wheel a cushioned center hub and changed some small items. But the alterations were not the type that hit you over the head. The reality was that automakers were so busy trying to make their cars conform to new safety and pollution rules that no one had time to update things in the looks and muscle departments.

At midyear, the Camaro front end was modified to accept suspension and steering parts from "big" Chevys. The company also swapped the old forged steering knuckles for nodular iron castings. The front tread was widened to go along with these changes.

There were new body badges and new exterior paint colors. A new type of thinner windshield glass was also used. Camaro engines were re-tuned so that they could be run on low-lead or no-lead gasoline. They had lower compression ratios—and power ratings. To downplay the horsepower numbers even more, The General started using the net horsepower system, although '71 engines were rated both ways. One less engine was availablefor Camaros, too.

For '71, the base Camaro with a V-8 was still priced below $2,900—at least without options. Of course, most Camaros left the assembly line with plenty of extras tacked on them. The RS model option retailed for $179 and included an array of features similar to the same 1970 package. Ditto for the SS package priced at $314—although the high-performance car did have 30 less "ponies" under the hood than in 1970. The Z28 Special Performance package retailed

"The Camaro was headed for a rough period in the early '70s, but the troubles had nothing to do with the design or engineering of the product itself ..."

for $787 for Camaros with a V-8 and either a four-speed manual or THM transmission. A pair of wide hood stripes, a ducktail-style spoiler and bright red "Z28" badges made the race-bred coupe seem like a nasty Chevy to tangle with. No doubt, a few Mustang owners backed down from stoplight stompers on looks alone. The Z28 was a smooth, handsome muscle car!

In the underhood department, there was only one inline six, the 250-cuber with 110 nhp and 140 hp (Author's note: I guess you could say "ghp" for gross horsepower, but I've never seen that used). The 307 was base V-8 with 140 nhp or 200 hp. Also available was a 350-cid engine with 165 nhp and 245 hp. Base engine in the Camaro SS was a 350 with 210 nhp and 270 hp. The hot version of the 350 used in the Z28 produced 275 nhp and 330 hp. That was as good as it got, although it was 30 gross hp less than the '70 Z28 engine. The 402 (a.k.a. 396) was also back again in just one version with 260 nhp and 300 hp.

A very typical three-speed manual transmission was standard equipment in most models, but a floor-shifted four-speed gearbox was a mandatory option in the SS and Z28 models. Actually, both wide- and close-ratio four-speeds were available. Powerglide automatic transmission was optional in six-cylinder-powered cars. Turbo-Hydra-Matic was optional equipment with V-8s.

Unfortunately, the 1971 Camaro didn't bask in the glory of Chevrolet Motor Division's first three-million-vehicle (including trucks) sales year. Its production actually dropped by over 50 percent to 114,630 units. Contributing to the drop was a United Auto Workers strike that lasted from mid-September to November 22. The government and insurance companies were making it very hard to own a performance car and the Camaro was losing much of its market appeal.

1972

"THE END IS NEAR!" That's what the handwriting on the wall said about the future of muscle cars late in 1971. September 23rd brought the showroom introduction of a new Camaro, but changes were in the "spot-the-five-things-different-in-this-photo category." The standard grille had a coarser mesh to it (but the RS grille was unchanged). A new steering wheel was seen, new interior door panels with map pockets were used, "wet look" vinyl tops were introduced and the four-speed manual transmission came with a push-down style lock-out button.

Chevrolet's muscular pony car (as well as that of the Pontiac Firebird) was said to be in danger after a labor strike at the Camaro assembly plant in Lordstown, Ohio, created massive problems. When the UAW members walked out, they left many partially built Camaro and Firebirds sitting on the assembly lines. By the time the union dispute was settled, these unfinished cars were unfit

"A pair of wide hood stripes, a ducktail-style spoiler and bright red 'Z28' badges made the race-bred coupe seem like a nasty Chevy to tangle with."

■ *The Z/28 remained largely unchanged for 1972, still retaining the new rounded look of the '71s and familiar wide stripes and deck lid spoiler.* Dan Lyons

for public sale under new federal safety standards. General Motors was forced to scrap them and almost did the same with the entire F-car program.

Chevrolet's engineering director Alex C. Mair put on his boxing gloves and punched it out with corporate bigwigs to keep the F-cars in the model lineup. He ultimately triumphed and his efforts paid off in spades—just a few years later—when Camaros and Firebirds went on to achieve record sales. In fact, they became GM's "darling cars" of the otherwise pretty much unexciting late-'70s. Mair was rewarded by being appointed general manager of the Truck and Coach Division of General Motors in 1972. Then, four years later, he would go on to become general manager of Pontiac Motor Division. Unfortunately, that gig didn't go as well.

Standard equipment on the '72 Camaro again included power front disc brakes and steel inner-door guardrails, as well as all other General Motors safety features including all-vinyl upholstery, bucket-style rear seat cushions, carpeting, a cigar lighter, Astro-Ventilation, E78-14 bias-belted black sidewall tires and a three-speed manual transmission with floor shifter. The base engine was a 307-cid small-block V-8 with a 170-hp rating (and all the ratings were now "net horsepower" numbers).

The Camaro SS package included a 350-cid/200-hp V-8, dual exhausts, bright engine accents, power brakes, special ornamentation, hood insulation, F70-14 white-lettered tires, 14 x 7-inch diameter wheels, a black-finished grille insert, hide-away wipers with black arms and "SS" emblems and was priced at $306. Optional in SS models was the LS3 version of the "396" (402-cid) engine with 240 nhp. Chevrolet built 6,522 cars with the SS option and only 970 SS 396s.

The Camaro RS package added a special black-finished grille with a rubber-tipped vertical center bar and resilient body-color grille frame, independent left and right front bumpers, license plate bracket mounted below the right front bumper, parking lights with bright accents molded on the grille panel, hide-away headlights, bright window, hood panel and body sill moldings, body-colored door handle inserts, RS emblems (deleted when the SS package was also installed), an RS steering wheel medallion, bright-accented tail lights and bright-accented back-up lights. It cost $116.

"In short, (the 1972) was not your father's Camaro, which was probably a whole lot faster."

A rare package in '72 was the Z28 group, which seemed to be losing favor with enthusiasts. Thanks to critical articles in magazines like *Road & Track*, everyone knew the Z-machine was no longer prepped to go racing right off the showroom floor. The $770 model option still included a solid-lifter 350 with an aluminum intake manifold, but it was considerably choked up with a 9.0:1 compression ratio. The advertised output was just 255 nhp. According to *Motor Trend*, the four-speed Z28 took 7.7 seconds to move from 0 to 60 mph and needed 15.2 seconds to get down the quarter-mile with a speed of 86.6 mph through the traps. In short, it was not your father's Camaro, which was probably a whole lot faster. Only 2,575 Camaro Z28s were made. Total model-year production of all '72 Camaros came in at 68,651.

1973

If you liked "steel bumper" Camaros, the '73 model was the last one you could buy off the showroom floor. To meet new federal bumper standards, Chevy was planning a change to resilient plastic bumpers. Of course, no one knew that when the cars were new and the last shiny-bumper cars didn't exactly pull buyers into the showroom. Business did climb, but only to the

■ *The Type LT, or "luxury touring" model, joined the Camaro lineup in 1973 and helped fill the void left by the departed SS models.*
Jerry Heasley

level of 96,752 cars being built. That was about a one-third increase over '72, but still well under the six-figure numbers the first Camaros had racked up. The General and the bow tie boys could not have been overwhelmingly happy, but they had no idea that it was the start of a positive trend.

Underlining the erosion of the muscle car niche was the introduction of a new Type LT for the "girly men" of the day. This was no option package—it was officially a separate model, which probably meant that Chevy was hoping to sell lots of them. The Type LT had chrome rocker moldings, Rally rims, hidden wipers, woodgrained trim and other fancy stuff. Fortunately, it could still be optioned up with some muscle, but everyone knew that Chevrolet had something else in mind for the LT. The initials were supposed to mean "Luxury Touring," but "Lady's Transportation" would do, too!

Hey, there's nothing wrong with the concept. My girlfriend had a first-year LT. Linda loved it and kept it for a lot of years and a lot of miles. She joined a Camaro club and even put on Camaro shows. It was her hobby car. It was fun. And the base 350 was plenty enough engine for her needs. But then, she had no desire to take her LT drag racing.

The real drag racing Camaro—the SS—was gone. Dropped. Deleted. Eliminated. Vanished. Banished? That's right—no Super Sport this year. However . . . you could start checking boxes on the long-as-your-arm options list and get your '73 LT pretty close to what the previous SS had been—as long as you didn't want the 402 (a.k.a.) 396 Turbo-Jet V-8. You couldn't have that engine. It was long gone as well.

The Rally Sport package was still around—now strictly as an option. You could add it to a Type LT for $97 or to a base Sport Coupe for $118. The RS gave you the grille with the finer-mesh insert and the split bumpers—one on each side of the grille. Another possibility was combining the RS stuff with the still-available Z28 Special Performance package. However, with its low $502 price tag, you just knew that the 1973-style Z28 content wasn't quite what it used to be in the good old days.

The hot Z28 got a new Holley four-barrel, but the old aluminum intake was replaced with a cast-iron type. Solid lifters gave way to hydraulic lifters, too. Net

"Underlining the erosion of the muscle car niche was the introduction of a new Type LT for the 'girly men' of the day."

horsepower was advertised as 245. Chevy also replaced the neat cast-metal Z28 emblems on the rear body panel with foil type stickers. *Car and Driver* found it possible to get the Z28 up to 60 mph in 6.7 seconds. Quarter-mile performance was reported as 15.2 seconds at 94.6 mph. Actually, that was pretty darn close to what the 302-powered Z28 did back in 1967 (7.0 seconds for 0 to 60 and 14.8 at 96 mph in the quarter). Model-year production of '73 Camaro Z28 coupes was 11,574 cars.

■ *By 1974, the Z28 was not nearly as muscular as it had been but, like the rest of the Camaro lineup, it was still a decent seller.*

1974

Some folks say the muscle car era ended in 1972, and others say it lasted through 1975. For the Camaro, a natural breaking point is 1974. At the time, it seemed like that year would be the finale for the Z28. As things turned out, it wasn't the end, but the fact that Chevy tried to drop the model spoke volumes about its view of the performance market circa '74. Hot Camaros would return in '77.5 and beyond, but the formula was somewhat different than in the "dust-and-glory" days.

■ *This original, unrestored survivor provides a good look at a vintage '74 Z28 interior, complete with a manual four-speed and an 8-track player. The steering wrap is not a factory item.*
Jerry Heasley

The '74 Camaro had a facelift and a new butt. The new "shovel-nosed" front had an egg-crate grille. Both of the revised end pieces incorporated stronger, impact-absorbing aluminum-faced bumpers that satisfied Uncle Sam and the insurance man. The new bumpers, though sturdier in design, were actually lighter in weight. However, the complete bumper system, with all its elaborate hardware, added nearly 200 performance-robbing pounds to the basic Camaro.

Engine options started with the same 250-cube six, which carried a 100-nhp rating. A 350-cid 145-nhp engine replaced the "307" as base V-8. Also available were 160- and 185-nhp versions of the 350, plus the Z28 type 350. The latter gained a breakerless HEI ignition system. It was again advertised as a 245-nhp option.

There were three series and only one body style. Camaro, Camaro Type LT and Camaro Z28 sport coupes ranged in price from just below $3,000 to just below $4,000. The LT had a host of luxury features as standard equipment. The

CAMARO YEAR-BY-YEAR SPEC'S

1967

Engine	Bore/Str.	Comp. Ratio	CID	BHP	WT.	W.B.	O.L.	Width	HT
I6	3.875 x 3.25	8.50	230	140 @4400 *	2,910	108.0	184.7	72.5	51.4
V-8	4.001 x 3.25	8.75	327	210 @ 4600 +	3,070	108.0	184.7	72.5	51.4

* Optional 250 CID, C.R. 8.50, BHP 155 @ 4200.
+ Optional 327 CID, C.R. 10.00, BHP 275 @ 4800 up to 396 CID, C.R. 11.0, BHP 375 @ 5600.
Z/28 Coupe only: 302 CID, C.R. 11.00, BHP 290 @ 4400.

1968

Engine	Bore/Str.	Comp. Ratio	CID	BHP	WT.	W.B.	O.L.	Width	HT
I6	3.875 x 3.25	8.50	230	140 @ 4400 *	2,950	108.0	184.6	72.3	50.9
V-8	4.001 x 3.25	8.75	327	210 @ 4600 +	3,105	108.0	184.6	72.3	50.9

* Optional 250 CID, C.R. 8.50, BHP 155 @ 4200.
+ Optional 327 CID, C.R. 10.00, BHP 275 @ 4800 up to 396 CID, C.R. 11.00, BHP 375 @ 5600.
Z/28 Coupe only: 302 CID, C.R. 11.00, BHP 290 @ 4400.
COPO: 427 CID, C.R. 11.25, BHP 435 @ 5800.

1969

Engine	Bore/Str.	Comp. Ratio	CID	BHP	WT.	W.B.	O.L.	Width	HT
I6	3.875 x 3.25	8.50	230	140 @ 4400 *	3,005	108.0	186.0	74.0	51.6
V-8	3.87 x 3.25	9.00	307	200 @ 4600 +	3,135	108.0	186.0	74.0	51.6

* Optional 250 CID, C.R. 8.50, BHP 155 @ 4200.
+ Optional 350 CID, C.R. 9.00, BHP 255 @ 4800 up to 396 CID, C.R. 10.25, BHP 325 @ 4800.
Z/28 Coupe only: 302 CID, C.R. 11.00, BHP 290 @ 5800.
COPO: 427 CID, C.R. 11.25, BHP 435 @ 5800.
ZL1: 427 CID, C.R. 12.50, BHP 430 @ 5800.

1970

Engine	Bore/Str.	Comp. Ratio	CID	BHP	WT.	W.B.	O.L.	Width	HT
I6	3.875 x 3.53	8.50	250	155 @ 4200	3,166	108.0	188.0	74.4	50.5
V-8	3.87 x 3.25	8.50	307	200 @ 4600 +	3,278	108.0	188.0	74.4	50.5

+ Optional 350 CID, C.R. 9.00, BHP 250 @ 4800 up to 402 CID, C.R. 10.25, BHP 350 @ 5200.
Z/28 only: 350 CID, C.R. 11.00, BHP 360 @ 6000.

1971

Engine	Bore/Str.	Comp. Ratio	CID	BHP	WT.	W.B.	O.L.	Width	HT
I6	3.875 x 3.53	8.50	250	145 @ 4200	3,186	108.0	188.0	74.4	49.1
V-8	3.87 x 3.25	8.50	307	200 @ 4600 +	3,298	108.0	188.0	74.4	49.1

+ Optional 350 CID, C.R. 8.50, BHP 245 @ 4800 up to 402 CID, C.R. 8.50, BHP 300 @ 4800.
Z/28 only: 350 CID, C.R. 9.00, BHP 330 @ 4000

1972

Engine	Bore/Str.	Comp. Ratio	CID	BHP	WT.	W.B.	O.L.	Width	HT
I6	3.875 x 3.53	8.50	250	110 @ 3800	3,213	108.0	188.0	74.4	49.1
V-8	3.87 x 3.25	8.50	307	130 @ 4000 +	3,325	108.0	188.0	74.4	49.1

+ Optional 350 CID, C.R. 8.50, NHP 165 @ 4000 up to 402 CID, C.R. 8.50, NHP 240 @ 4400.
Z/28 only: 350 CID, C.R. 9.00, NHP 255 @ 5600.

1973

Engine	Bore/Str.	Comp. Ratio	CID	BHP	WT.	W.B.	O.L.	Width	HT
I6	3.875 x 3.53	8.25	250	100 @ 3600	3,205	108.0	188.0	74.4	49.1
V-8	4.00 x 3.480	8.50	350	145 @ 4000 +	3,435	108.0	188.0	74.4	49.1

+ Optional 350 CID, C.R. 8.50, NHP 145 @ 3600 and 350 CID, C.R. 8.50, NHP 175 @ 4400.
Z/28 only: 350 CID, C.R. 9.00, NHP 245 @ 5200.

1974

Engine	Bore/Str.	Comp. Ratio	CID	BHP	WT.	W.B.	O.L.	Width	HT
I6	3.875 x 3.53	8.25	250	100 @ 3600	3,413	108.0	195.4	74.4	49.2
V-8	4.00 x 3.480	8.50	350	145 @ 3800 +	3,670	108.0	195.4	74.4	49.2

+ Optional 350 CID, C.R. 8.50, NHP 160 @ 3800 and 350 CID, C.R. 8.50, NHP 185 @ 4000.
Z/28 only: 350 CID, C.R. 9.00, NHP 245 @ 5200.

Z28 featured a black-out style grille, body graphics and upgrades to both the drive train and the suspension system. Included among the Z28 decorations were three rather loud hood stripes with a large Z28 decal in front of them.

Radial tires were introduced, along with front brake pad sensors. An unpopular new safety feature was a seat belt interlock system that forced front passengers to buckle up before the car would start. While people today are conditioned to accept such intrusions upon their personal liberties, in 1974 they let up such a howl that Congress quickly stepped in and changed the law to eliminate the interlock system requirement. How we miss those days of a responsive electorate.

Unfortunately, people back then did not have enough clout to save the muscle car genre as well. It would be a decade or so before the Camaro started to look like a real high-performance car again—and even then it was a different kind of high-tech performance that looked good on paper, but didn't have quite the same "feel" as you got from the '60s and early '70s muscle cars.

PRODUCTION STATISTICS AND BREAKOUTS

1967 CAMARO PRODUCTION

Year	Body Code	Body Type	Engine Type	MSP Price	Model Yr. Prod.
67	STD37	2HT	6	$2,466	49,194
67	STD67	2CV	6	$2,704	4,570
TOTAL					**53,764**
67	STD37	2HT	8	$2,572	88,244
67	STD67	2CV	8	$2,809	9,795
TOTAL					**98,039**
STANDARD CAMARO GRAND TOTAL					**151,803**
67	DLX37	2HT	6	$2,561	4,329
67	DLX67	2CV	6	$2,799	715
TOTAL					**5,044**
67	DLX37	2HT	8	$2,667	53,998
67	DLX67	2CV	8	$2,904	10,061
TOTAL					**64,059**
DELUXE CAMARO GRAND TOTAL					**69,103**
ALL CAMARO TOTAL					**22,0906**

Note: 1967-1968 tables are from recently released General Motors 1955-1968 production data records.

1968 CAMARO PRODUCTION

Year	Body Code	Body Type	Engine Type	MSP Price	Model Yr. Prod.
68	STD37	2HT	6	$2588	37,263
68	STD67	2CV	6	$2802	2,756
TOTAL					**40,019**
68	STD37	2HT	8	$2694	131,373
68	STD67	2CV	8	$2908	13,294
TOTAL					**144,667**
STANDARD CAMARO GRAND TOTAL					**184,686**
68	DLX37	2HT	6	$2693	10,193
68	DLX67	2CV	6	$2907	757
TOTAL					**10,950**
68	DLX37	2HT	8	$2799	35,878
68	DLX67	2CV	8	$3013	3,633
TOTAL					**39,511**
DELUXE CAMARO GRAND TOTAL					**50,461**
ALL CAMARO TOTAL					**235,147**

Note: These are from recently released General Motors 1955-1968 Production data records.

1969 CAMARO PRODUCTION

Year	Body Code	Body Type	Engine Type	MSP Price	Model Yr. Prod.
CAMARO SIX					
69	STD37	2HT	6	$2,621	See notes
69	STD67	2CV	6	$2,835	See notes
CAMARO V-8					
69	STD37	2HT	8	$2,727	See notes
69	STD67	2CV	8	$2,940	See notes
ALL CAMARO TOTAL					**243,085**

PRODUCTION NOTES
165,2267 base Camaro hardtops were built
17,573 base Camaro convertibles were built.
37,773 cars had Rally Sport equipment.
36,309 cars had Super Sport equipment.
20,302 cars had the Z/28 option.
3,675 Indy Pace Car convertibles were built.
Approximately 200-300 cars had the Indy Sport Coupe option.
Numbers do not total 243,085 because some cars had multiple options.

1970 CAMARO PRODUCTION

Year	Body Code	Body Type	Engine Type	MSP Price	Model Yr. Prod.
CAMARO SIX					
70	STD87	2HT	6	$2,749	See notes
CAMARO V-8					
70	STD87	2HT	8	$2,839	See notes
ALL CAMARO TOTAL					**124,901**

PRODUCTION NOTES
100,967 base Camaro hardtops were built.
27,136 cars had Rally Sport equipment.
15,201 cars had Super Sport equipment.
8,733 cars had the Z/28 option.
Numbers do not total 124,901 because some cars had multiple options.

1971 CAMARO PRODUCTION

Year	Body Code	Body Type	Engine Type	MSP Price	Model Yr. Prod.
CAMARO SIX					
71	STD87	2HT	6	$2,758	See notes
CAMARO V-8					
71	STD87	2HT	8	$2,848	See notes
ALL CAMARO TOTAL					**114,630**

PRODUCTION NOTES
91,481 base Camaro hardtops were built.
18,404 cars had Rally Sport equipment.
18,287cars had Super Sport equipment.
4,862 cars had the Z/28 option.
Numbers do not total 114,630 because some cars had multiple options.

1972 CAMARO PRODUCTION

Year	Body Code	Body Type	Engine Type	MSP Price	Model Yr. Prod.
CAMARO SIX					
71	STD87	2HT	6	$2,730	See notes
CAMARO V-8					
71	STD87	2HT	8	$2,820	See notes
ALL CAMARO TOTAL					**68,651**

PRODUCTION NOTES
58,544 base Camaro hardtops were built.
11,364 cars had Rally Sport equipment.
7,532 cars had Super Sport equipment.
2,575 cars had the Z/28 option.
Numbers do not total 68,651 because some cars had multiple options.

1973 CAMARO PRODUCTION

Year	Body Code	Body Type	Engine Type	MSP Price	Model Yr. Prod.
CAMARO SIX					
71	STD87	2HT	6	$2,781	See notes
CAMARO V-8					
71	STD87	2HT	8	$2,872	See notes
ALL CAMARO TOTAL					**96,751**

PRODUCTION NOTES
52,850 base Camaro hardtops were built.
32,327 Type LT Camaros were built.
16,133 cars had Rally Sport equipment.
11,574 cars had the Z/28 option.
Numbers do not total 96,751 because some cars had multiple options.

1974 CAMARO PRODUCTION

Year	Body Code	Body Type	Engine Type	MSP Price	Model Yr. Prod.
CAMARO SIX					
71	STD87	2HT	6	$2,828	See notes
CAMARO V-8					
71	STD87	2HT	8	$3,040	See notes
ALL CAMARO TOTAL					**128,798**

PRODUCTION NOTES
88,243 base Camaro hardtops were built.
49,983 Type LT Camaros were built.
13,802 cars had the Z/28 option.
Numbers do not total 128,798 because some cars had multiple options.

PRICE GUIDE

Tom Glatch

Vehicle Condition Scale

6 — Parts car:
May or may not be running, but is weathered, wrecked and/or stripped to the point of being useful primarily for parts.

5 — Restorable:
Needs complete restoration of body, chassis and interior. May or may not be running, but isn't weathered, wrecked or stripped to the point of being useful only for parts.

4 — Good:
A driveable vehicle needing no or only minor work to be functional. Also, a deteriorated restoration or a very poor amateur restoration. All components may need restoration to be "excellent," but the car is mostly useable "as is."

3 — Very Good:
Complete operable original or older restoration. Also, a very good amateur restoration, all presentable and serviceable inside and out. Plus, a combination of well-done restoration and good operable components or a partially restored car with all parts necessary to compete and/or valuable NOS parts.

2 — Fine:
Well-restored or a combination of superior restoration and excellent original parts. Also, extremely well-maintained original vehicle showing minimal wear.

1 — Excellent:
Restored to current maximum professional standards of quality in every area, or perfect original with components operating and apearing as new. A 95-plus point show car that is not driven.

1967 Camaro, V-8

	6	5	4	3	2	1
2d IPC	1,640	4,920	8,200	18,450	28,700	41,000
2d Cpe	1,040	3,120	5,200	11,700	18,200	26,000
2d Conv	1,280	3,840	6,400	14,400	22,400	32,000
2d Z28 Cpe	1,920	5,760	9,600	21,600	33,600	48,000

NOTE: Deduct 5 percent for Six, (when available). Add 15 percent for Rally Sport Package, (when available; except incl. w/Indy Pace Car). Add 25 percent for SS-350 (when available; except Indy).

1968 Camaro, V-8

	6	5	4	3	2	1
2d Cpe	980	2,940	4,900	11,030	17,150	24,500
2d Conv	1,140	3,420	5,700	12,830	19,950	28,500
2d Z28	1,700	5,100	8,500	19,130	29,750	42,500

NOTE: Deduct 5 percent for Six (when available). Add 10 percent for A/C. Add 15 percent for Rally Sport Package (when available). Add 25 percent for SS package. Add 15 percent for SS-350 (when available).

1969 Camaro, V-8

	6	5	4	3	2	1
2d Spt Cpe	1,040	3,120	5,200	11,700	18,200	26,000
2d Conv	1,240	3,720	6,200	13,950	21,700	31,000
2d Z28	2,040	6,120	10,200	22,950	35,700	51,000
2d IPC	2,200	6,600	11,000	24,750	38,500	55,000
2d ZL-1*	5,200	15,600	26,000	58,500	91,000	130,000
2d Yenko	3,200	9,600	16,000	36,000	56,000	80,000

NOTE: Deduct 5 percent for Six, (when available). Add 10 percent for A/C. Add 10 percent for Rally Sport (except incl. w/Indy Pace Car). Add 25 percent for SS- 350 (when available; except Indy).

1970 Camaro, V-8

	6	5	4	3	2	1
2d Cpe	760	2,280	3,800	8,550	13,300	19,000
2d Z28	920	2,760	4,600	10,350	16,100	23,000

NOTE: Deduct 5 percent for Six, (except Z28). Add 35 percent for the 375 hp 396, (L78 option). Add 35 percent for Rally Sport and/or Super Sport options.

1971 Camaro, V-8

	6	5	4	3	2	1
2d Cpe	760	2,280	3,800	8,550	13,300	19,000
2d Z28	920	2,760	4,600	10,350	16,100	23,000

NOTE: Add 35 percent for Rally Sport and/or Super Sport options. Add 25 percent for 402 ("396") engine option.

1972 Camaro, V-8

	6	5	4	3	2	1
2d Cpe	760	2,280	3,800	8,550	13,300	19,000
2d Z28	920	2,760	4,600	10,350	16,100	23,000

NOTE: Add 35 percent for Rally Sport and/or Super Sport options. Add 15 percent for SS option.

1973 Camaro, V-8

	6	5	4	3	2	1
2d Cpe	760	2,280	3,800	8,550	13,300	19,000
2d Z28	920	2,760	4,600	10,350	16,100	23,000

NOTE: Add 35 percent for Rally Sport and/or Super Sport options.

1974 Camaro, V-8

	6	5	4	3	2	1
2d Cpe	740	2,220	3,700	8,330	12,950	18,500
2d LT Cpe	760	2,280	3,800	8,550	13,300	19,000

NOTE: Add 10 percent for Z28 option.

Charger

1966

A big, wide, flat car with a roof that looked like a ramp for a Helldriver's hoop jumper was Dodge's answer to the fastback craze. There was nothing like the '66 Charger. Its "electric shaver" grille was distinctive looking. It was racy and it was sporty. The average American family could fit inside the Charger and there was room under the hood for a Pratt & Whitney Turbofan engine.

For buyers who didn't want a jet engine, Chrysler offered factory options that had no peers. The base engine in the Charger was the Mopar 318-cid small block with a two-barrel carb and a not-so-galloping 230 ponies. The one-step-up 361-cid two-barrel V-8 generated 265 hp. For real muscle you had to move up to the big-block 383 with a four-barrel and 325 hp or the heftier 426-cid/425-hp "Street Hemi."

■ *The 1966 Dodge Charger captured attention in front with hidden headlights in a razor-like grille. And all eyes noted the slanted roofline in back and the sculptured sides of the car.*
Jerry Heasley

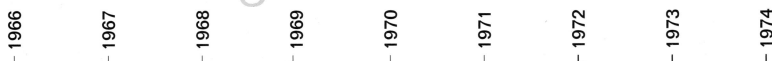

1966 1967 1968 1969 1970 1971 1972 1973 1974

1966: Dodge gets serious about building muscle cars with the introduction of the new fastback Charger. More than 37,000 of the sleek new machines hit the roads.

1966: The lethal 426 Hemi introduced on the new Charger, raising the bar in the already hot American muscle car wars.

1967: 440 Magnum engine option introduced to the Charger lineup. The 375-hp mill was standard on the R/T model.

1968: Major redesign for the Charger, followed by huge increase in sales.

1969: Racing-inspired Charger 500 and Charger Daytona introduced.

1970: New chrome "loop" bumper part of another significant Charger redesign.

1971: Last year for the 426 Hemi.

1971: Another redesign gives the Charger a slightly more curvaceous body.

1972: 440 Six Pack engine becomes the top muscle car power plant option at a modest 330 hp.

1973: Larger quarter windows part of another mild redesign that also included cosmetic changes to the front and rear.

1966 1967 1968 1969 1970 1971 1972 1973 1974

The 383-powered Charger was good for 0 to 60 mph in 7.2 seconds and a 15.6-second quarter-mile at 89 mph. A Hemi could shave two seconds or more off those acceleration times. It included two four-barrel carburetors, extra-wide dual exhausts and all sorts of heavy-duty performance hardware. The Hemi package also included engine call-out badges, a heavy-duty suspension, larger brakes and 7.75 x 14 Blue Streak racing tires. The use of either a four-speed manual gearbox or a TorqueFlite automatic transmission was mandatory. Dodge warned the Hemi's short 12-month or 12,000 miles warranty would be invalidated by "extreme operation" or driveline modifications.

Dodge promoted the '66 Charger as a "Sports Sedan," even though it had two doors and was really a sport coupe. The term "sedan" seemed to widen its sales appeal beyond the teeny-bopper set and made buyers think of family transportation and oodles of luggage space. It must have taken Chrysler a lot of self control to keep from offering a rooftop luggage carrier for the Charger and spinning off a "Traveler" version.

■ *In 1964, a Dodge show car was called the "Charger." The topless Charger show car had a low, sleek line and a definite performance look, but not the fastback roofline of the production model.*

Doug Mitchel

Charger 1966-1974

■ *The first and last Hemi V-8-powered Dodge Chargers are portrayed together in this unique photo. On the left is the 1971 version while the 1966 Charger is alongside on the right.*

Jerry Heasley

As a Coronet spin-off itself, the Charger was every inch a roomy, almost-full-size intermediate car. The interior had the bright, clean look of contemporary Mopars in a super-sized sports car format. Mom and Dad and both kids could fit inside, but Grandma and Grandpa would have to wait at home. With seating for only four on its front and rear bucket seats, the Charger was not really sedan-like in the passenger-carrying department. It had the space, but not the furniture.

The Charger's real appeal was its ability to serve as a sports car for youthful dads with *real* seats for the young 'uns in the back. "Honey, it's almost like a station wagon," the anxious buyer would say. "And we'd better get that Hemi engine so we can safely keep up with the traffic on the freeway."

Soon after the Charger arrived on the scene, almost every car enthusiast magazine rushed to test the car. It was new and exciting. Dodge didn't mind giving out press cars. Having the Charger on lots of magazine covers was a sure way to pump up sales. Total production of 1966 Chargers hit 37,300 cars. Of these, only 468 had Hemis.

NASCAR race drivers thought the Charger's fastback roof would give it good aerodynamics for Grand National stock car competition, but the fastback actually tended to lift at the rear. Racecar builders solved the problem by adding a small rear deck lid spoiler. After that, the Chargers took 18 checkered flags.

■ *Inside, the 1966 Dodge Charger featured bucket seats, a floor-mounted shifter and console as well as round gauges. Dodge called it a "Sports Sedan" and it was spacious as well as sporty.*

Jerry Heasley

■ *Rear seat passengers in the 1966 Dodge Charger also enjoyed the advantages of bucket seats and a console. There was a lot of visibility and room to stretch. The seats folded for plenty of cargo.*

Jerry Heasley

■ *The back of the 1966 Dodge Charger was unforgettable with its slanted roofline intersecting with the sculptured, Coronet-based sides of the car. This one is extra special, a Hemi Charger.*

Jerry Heasley

■ *While every Charger had style, only 468 had Hemi V-8s under the hood. The "Street Hemi" displaced 426 cubic inches, produced 425 horses and came with performance extras.*

Jerry Heasley

■ *The use of either this four-speed manual gear box or a TorqueFlite automatic transmission was mandatory in Hemi Chargers. By the time the dashboard odometer read 12,000 miles, the warranty on the Hemi was used up.*

Jerry Heasley

■ *The Hemi package also included a heavy-duty suspension, larger brakes and 7.75 x 14 Blue Streak racing tires. Styled road wheels with a tri-bar-spinner look added to the Charger's hot image.*

Jerry Heasley

■ *The Charger was based on the Coronet, but had a more streamlined look and richer interior appointments and trimmings. With its low and wide roof line, the Charger showcased a drastic interpretation of fastback styling.*

Jerry Heasley

Charger 1966-1974

1967

A '67 Charger is much rarer than a '66—only 15,788 were built. Product changes were few. Front fender turn signal indicators were added, along with a few more pieces of chrome trim. Standard equipment again included four bucket seats, but the console running between them was now an extra-cost item. In its place, you could order a center cushion with folding armrest that allowed three-place seating. If you opted for a console, you got a shorter type that stopped just behind the front seats. The shorter console allowed rear passengers to move across the car. A folding rear center armrest was standard. The Charger also included an oil pressure gauge and tachometer and a 60-lb. The lighter 318-cid/230-hp V-8 could motivate the car from 0 to 60 mph in 10.9 seconds and through the quarter-mile in 18.6 seconds at 76 mph.

There were a number of optional V-8s, each with added performance. The first step up was a 383-cid/326-hp big-block V-8 that took the Charger from 0 to 60 mph in 8.9 seconds and down the quarter-mile in 16.5 seconds at 86.4 mph. There was also a new 440-cid/375-hp "wedge" engine good for 0 to 60 in 8

■ *The Hemi Chargers, equipped with powerful racing versions of the fabled V-8, were popular choices in NASCAR racing, especially with the sloped roofline. This is a NASCAR replica.* Doug Mitchel

seconds and a 15.5-second quarter-mile at 93 mph. But the top dog was the 426-cid/425-hp Hemi. With this engine, the Charger blasted off like an elephant on a rocket sled—0 to 60 mph in 6.4 seconds and 14.2 seconds at 101 mph for the quarter-mile.

When equipped with either the 440 or the Hemi, the three-speed TorqueFlite automatic transmission came with a high-upshift speed governor. If you ordered a four-speed manual transmission, the Sure-Grip no-slip rear axle was mandatory. A good idea for the Hemi Charger was 11-inch front disc brakes, which could slow the car down from 60 mph in an amazing 133 feet.

With Richard Petty's Plymouth dominating NASCAR racing in 1967, Chargers took only five checkered flags in that league, but things were different over in USAC territory, where a Charger piloted by Don White took nine races and the championship title.

■ *The 1968 Chargers received a new look that definitely was inspired by racing. Its smooth, flowing lines and clean edges made a performance statement in motion or standing still.*

Doug Mitchel

"Mopar muscle car expert Anthony Young called this machine "A splendid performance styling statement—one of the best-looking muscle cars of the '60s."

1968

One of the most memorable 1968 Chargers is the black one that Steve McQueen chased with his GT-390 Mustang in *Bullitt*. The image of that black beast jumping over the top of a San Francisco hill with all four wheels off the ground kind of sums up the new semi-fastback Dodge. Mopar muscle car expert Anthony Young called this machine "A splendid performance styling statement—one of the best-looking muscle cars of the '60s."

Dodge design chief Bill Brownlie said he wanted "Something extremely masculine that looked like it had just come off the track at Daytona." Stylist Richard Sias gave him a long, narrow car with bulging fender lines that swept together in a racy blend of curvaceous lines and succulent air vents. The rear body kick-up (an almost mandatory styling gimmick at this time) started below the front vent windows and ran a "football field's" length to the smoothly lipped rear end.

The Charger R/T was the name of the new high-performance version of the sporty Dodge. *Motor Trend* magazine summed up the look of the R/T model as "a Charger with a set of mag wheels, wide oval tires and a bumblebee stripe around its rear end." Appropriate name badges, heavy-duty underpinnings and a 440-cid/375-hp Magnum V-8 put extra emphasis on the car's split personality. The wedge engine had a 4.32 x 3.75-inch bore and stroke, a 10.1:1 compression ratio and a single four-barrel carburetor.

Like the base model, the R/T (short for Road/Track) had a full-width grille with black-out finish and hidden headlights. Standard features included TorqueFlite automatic transmission, a heavy-duty suspension, dual exhausts with chrome tips, heavy-duty brakes, racing stripes and fat F-70 x 14 tires. Neat styling details of the R/T version included an integral rear deck lid spoiler and a competition-type gas filler cap. Chargers retained a 117-inch wheelbase, but for '68 the rear track was widened from 58.5 inches to 59.2 inches.

The '60s was a time when youthful car enthusiasts drove their car to work at the grocery store five days a week just to earn enough to pay the loan they took out to by a muscle car. Then, on Saturday, they took their supercar to the drag strip for some "track time." The Charger R/T was pushed as a machine that was well suited for both purposes. The standard 440-powered R/T could move from 0 to 60 mph in 6.5 seconds and zip down a drag strip in 15 seconds at 93 mph.

The R/T was also the only Charger model that you could get a Hemi in during 1968. Only 475 were built. Of the total, 211 had the four-speed manual gearbox—a no-cost option.

Although it ruled the streets, the '68 Charger didn't follow suit on the high-banked superspeedways, even though it was faster (184 mph top speed) than the earlier versions. Stepped-up competition from Ford and Mercury and a rule requiring carburetor restrictor plates on the Hemi kept the Dodges to a handful of wins this year—and inspired a couple of new-for-'69 models.

■ *The R/T version of the Charger was new in 1968. It was easily identified by the black bands in back. Just 475 1968 Chargers were Hemi-powered and all of them were Charger R/T versions.*

Doug Mitchel

■ *The fender blisters found on the 1969 Dodge Charger Daytona were practical additions. Engineers found they were the best ways to vent the brakes, especially in NASCAR racing.*

Tom Glatch

■ *In 1969, there was no question racing was influencing styling and performance in the Dodge Division. The dramatic Dodge Charger Daytona was designed to dominate NASCAR ovals.*

Jerry Heasley

1969

The new-for-'68 Charger was a hit. Sales climbed from the 15,000 range to nearly 100,000! To capitalize on this, Dodge expanded the line to include a new S/E series and also brought out a pair of unique models that tied into the Charger's racecar image. The Charger 500 and the Charger Daytona were both very special automobiles and both have great appeal to today's hobbyists and Mopar collectors.

The '69 Charger didn't change much. As *Motor Trend* put it, "That brute Charger styling, that symbol of masculine virility, was still intact." (Those were the good old days when you could get away with saying things like that.) The grille was divided into two sections and the tail lights changed from small and round to big and rectangular. Side-marker lights were added to the sides of the sleek body. For the first time, you could get the big fastback with a six, but only about 500 of those were made. The balance of the cars carried some type of V-8—and very often a muscular version.

Inside the Charger, the interior treatment, including the well-designed instrument panel, also had a few changes. New bucket seats were used and you could add a Custom-Comfort seat with over 100 possible adjustments. There was a large-faced tachometer and the instrument panel gauges were done in white on black to make them stand out very distinctly. For looks, you could add new 15-inch cast-aluminum road wheels.

■ *The 1969 Dodge Charger Daytona had a profile that had never been seen before in a North American production vehicle. It was designed to knife through the wind at high speeds.*

Jerry Heasley

"The Charger 500 and the Charger Daytona were very special automobiles and both have great appeal to today's hobbyists and Mopar collectors."

Charger 1966-1971

■ *Chrysler Corporation tested a number of rear wings and fiberglass noses at a Wichita State University wind tunnel before the Dodge Charger Daytona was introduced. The arched wing held the cars to the ground at high speeds and earned them the nickname "Winged Warriors" in competition.*

Jerry Heasley

■ *In 1969, Dodge Charger buyers could order the 440 Magnum V-8. Somewhat overshadowed by its heftier cousins, it was no slouch, producing 375 horsepower ad 480 lbs.-ft. of torque.*
Jerry Heasley

■ *The rear wing looked unusual, but was designed to keep the 1969 Dodge Charger Daytona firmly planted on NASCAR ovals at high speeds. It was adjustable to promote its down force.*

Jerry Heasley

If you favored the multiple-personality approach, you could order up the high-performance Charger R/T and take it to Shop Rite or the Summernationals. It included a 440-cid Magnum V-8, a four-barrel carb and a three-speed TorqueFlite automatic transmission. Also included as part of the R/T package were low-restriction dual exhausts with chrome tips, heavy-duty manual brakes, F70-14 Red Line tires, an R/T heavy-duty handling package and bumblebee stripes.

Performance was in the same bracket as the year before. With a 3.55:1 rear end, the 440-powered Charger (it came with a column-mounted gearshifter by the way) would do the quarter-mile in 13.9 seconds at 101.4 mph. For $648, you could add the hemi. A new model was the SE (Special Edition) Charger. It included hood-mounted turn signals, a leather bucket seat interior, lots of extra lights and wood-grained trim pieces. Though merchandised like a model, the SE features were more of an option package and could also be added to the R/T model as such. How cool!

"If you favored the multiple personality approach, you could order up the high-peformance Charger R/T and take it to the Shop Rite or the Summernationals."

■ *Aircraft-style air intakes, recessed headlights, a dramatic nose cone, and the ever-visible rear wing attracted the attention of anyone who saw the 1969 Dodge Charger Daytona.*
Jerry Heasley

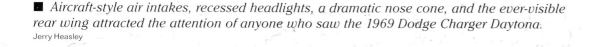

Charger 1966-1974

■ *Once again in 1969, the R/T version of the Dodge Charger could be purchased with the Hemi engine. This one wears "dog dish" hubcaps and striped tires that match its dramatic red paint.*

■ *The famed "Street Hemi" was available again on the 1969 Dodge Charger R/T edition. The Hemis produced 425 very healthy horses and 490 lbs.-ft. of torque in their cast-iron blocks.*

The '69 Charger 500 was issued as a special limited-production model based on a prototype made in 1968. Wind-tunnel testing had revealed that the good-looking Charger's recessed grille and tunneled-in rear window created wind turbulence on NASCAR superspeedways. Dodge engineers found out that a flush grille and flush-mounted rear glass could reduce wind resistance and add 5 mph. A 1968 Dodge Coronet grille was flush-mounted at the front of the Charger 500 and the rear window, roof pillars and trunk lid were redesigned so flush-fitting glass could be used

The Charger 500 was released to the public on September 1, 1968 as a 1969 model. Dodge Division literature said it was offered specifically for high-performance racing tracks and available only to qualified race drivers. Pretty soon, muscle car freaks were banging on the door to place their orders. Chances are good that, if they didn't get one, they at least drove away in Charger, Charger R/T or Charger SE.

"Pretty soon, muscle car freaks were banging on the door to place their orders."

■ *Competition influenced styling changes that made the Dodge Charger 500 unique. The flush-mounted window and sloped roofline were different from other production Chargers.*

Jerry Heasley

■ *The R/T logo meant a 1970 Dodge Charger was a performance-equipped car. R/T exterior clues included reverse-facing side scoops, exterior striping and dual hood scoops.*
Jerry Heasley

The Charger 500's handcrafted body modifications reflected the workmanship of a company called Creative Industries, which was an aftermarket firm in Detroit, Michigan. A minimum of 500 such cars had to be sold to the public to authorize the changes and make the car legal for racing under NASCAR rules. The Charger 500 model designation was based on the number of cars that were scheduled to be made.

Some sources say the Hemi was standard in the Charger 500, but research indicates that only about 9 percent of the cars had a Hemi. The model also included heavy-duty suspension, a four-speed manual or TorqueFlite automatic transmission, a bumblebee stripe, "500" model badges and a custom rear window package shelf.

Shortly after the Dodge Charger 500 bowed, Ford introduced the Torino Talladega and Mercury Cyclone Spoiler. Both models shared a wind-cheating fastback body that helped them outrun the slippery Charger 500s and capture the NASCAR title. As a reaction, Dodge launched the '69 Charger Daytona to get NASCAR's top award back.

Creative Industries received the contract to build 500 Daytonas. That magic number would legalize the 200-mph body modifications for stock car competition. The rear window was flush. The front end was lengthened and lowered. Reinforced-plastic parts were used on the front-end extension and hood parts. A set of concealed headlights popped up like frog's eyes. The hood featured a fresh air intake similar to the NASA inlets employed on aircraft. The hood and fenders had cooling vents. At the rear was a tall wing-type spoiler that enhanced the aerodynamics. Dodge press releases noted the modifications had been submitted to NASCAR for approval.

Dodge was determined to win the race that bore the Ford model name "Talladega." Held at Alabama International Motor Speedway, a track built to rival Daytona, the inaugural Talladega 500 race was controversial. Due to concerns over the new track, the drivers formed an association that confronted NASCAR boss Bill France. In the end, a number of replacement drivers and cars were used to keep the event on schedule.

Dodge engineers brought a test car, No. 88, that was a Ray Nichels entry. Charlie Glotzbach qualified at 199.466 mph, but he skipped the race. The Nichels team wanted the Chrysler contract and kept driver Richard Brickhouse's No. 99, car in the race. With a shortage of entries, NASCAR allowed Camaros and Mustangs to race. Brickhouse (average speed 153.778 mph) won and Dodges took the first four places, but it was far from a clean victory.

Daytonas and Superbirds eventually won 14 races on the big tracks in '69-'70. Buddy Baker's Daytona was the first car to officially hit the 200-mph closed-course mark at Talladega, in March 1970. The winged cars won so much that NASCAR outlawed the Hemi and wedge engines with piston displacements over 305 cubic inches.

"It'd be hard for race fans today to understand just how well the Charger stuck to the ground with that big wing on it," Buddy Baker once said about his *Winged Warrior*. "Even without the wing, the old Dodge with the Hemi ran well over 200 mph at Daytona and Talladega. It was a time in the sport when you looked at the car and knew you wanted one of 'em. They were fast. When it cranked up, everybody looked. The car had a certain mystique about it that

■ *In 1970, it didn't get much better for those who wanted a Dodge Charger than the R/T version with the SE option package. It was high performance with a healthy dash of comfort and style.*
Jerry Heasley

■ *This Panther Pink 1970 Dodge Charger R/T was probably a terror of "Wild Rose Country" in Alberta. Car lovers in Canada enjoyed the styling and performance of the Chargers as well.*

Jerry Heasley

people still remember. When you say Charger, you think racing. Names stick out for certain manufacturers, and I think it would be hard to improve on Charger for Dodge. What else is there to say? Charge!"

Of course, it would be just plain wrong to leave the '69 Charger story without mentioning a rascally Rebel named General Lee. Actually, a whole fleet of Hemi Orange Chargers decorated with the Confederate flag were used to play the role of The General in the "Dukes of Hazzard" television series. On the screen, the off-roading, puddle-jumping, foot-stompin' '69 Charger kept the Duke Boys one step ahead of the dimwitted antics of small-town Sheriff Roscoe P. Coltrane without suffering a dent or scratch. In real life, 14 or more Chargers of all varieties were beaten and battered until the production company had its own semi-fastback salvage yard.

1970

A splash of weird colors (shared with the Challenger) was the main change for the '70 Charger. In addition to the 13 conventional colors, you could order it in Plum Crazy (purple), Sublime ("day-glow" green), Go Mango (a bright yellow-green blend), Hemi Orange (an orange lover's orange) and Banana ("day-glow" yellow). Warning: such colors are not recommended for cars owned by introverts—or even normal, well-adjusted people. However, if you wanted to make a splash, they were available.

The Charger still had the cool-looking '68-style semi-fastback body with its sexy, long, hunched-up rear end. Very minor trim changes set it apart from earlier models. The standard version again came with a six or a V-8. There were two additional models this season. The Charger 500 name was now applied to a mid-range series. It was even available with the six-cylinder engine. This new type of 500 included all base Charger features plus vinyl bucket seats—yes

■ *Another engine choice for the 1970 Dodge Chargers was the 440 "Six Pack." It didn't refer to a beverage but rather the triple two-barrel Holly carbs that helped coax 390 horses from the V-8.*

Jerry Heasley

■ *The old saying "pretty in pink" certainly applies to this 1970 Dodge Charger R/T. It was decked in Panther Pink, one of many wild colors available in the psychedelic era.*
Jerry Heasley

Virginia, once upon a time vinyl seats were really popular—an electric clock and wheel lip moldings. Unfortunately, it no longer had the flush made-for-racing grille and flush rear window or a hemi V-8. There were nice-looking 500 badges for the grille and tail light surrounds, but it was more of a Grand Touring car than a Grand National machine.

Most of the '70 Charger 500s were sold with at least a 318-cid V-8. The 383-cid engine came in both two- and four-barrel versions. The four-barrel V-8 was offered in 330-hp and 335-hp options and the latter was significantly different than the former. The more powerful version used the 375-hp/440-cid engine's Plymouth Commando/Dodge Magnum camshaft and freer-flowing heads. It had a new cast-iron intake manifold that carried a Holley four-barrel carburetor, rather than a Carter AVS carburetor. Writing about a 383-powered version in the December 1970 issue of *Motor Trend*, A.B. Shuman noted, "The engine is flexible; the transmission is easy to work. Shuman said he could sense that this "383" Charger was an outstanding drive-it-daily muscle car that combined above-average street performance with a fairly affordable window sticker and decent road manners. The 440 wedge and 426 hemi were not regular options for the '70 500.

A new interior for the Charger 500 and Charger R/T included real bucket seats that came in vinyl in five sold colors and one two-tone combo or in a single black

■ *The restyled 1971s would be the last Dodge Charger R/Ts to have the Hemi engine under the hood. This rare Charger R/T is one of just 63 that came Hemi-equipped in 1971.* Jerry Heasley

vinyl-and-cloth choice. Dodge continued to keep a center console and a center armrest seat cushion available on the options list, but you couldn't fit both. The SE option package was available for 500 and R/T models. Four-speed cars got a new pistol-grip shifter. A brand new extra was an electric sunroof, which required the buyer to order a vinyl roof.

The R/T (Road/Track) edition played the same high-performance role it had always filled. It had a new grille with a horizontal blade across its center, a new loop-style front bumper, two hood scoops (one near each outside edge of the hood), big bolt-on reverse-facing side scoops with R/T badges on the doors and a choice of longitudinal or bumblebee racing stripes on the rear.

The 440-cid Magnum V-8 was standard R/T equipment, along with Mopar's sturdy TorqueFlite automatic transmission. Other Charger R/T features included a heavy-duty 70-amp/hour battery, heavy-duty automatic-adjusting drum brakes, heavy-duty front and rear shock absorbers, an extra-heavy-duty suspension, three-speed windshield wipers, all-vinyl front bucket seats, carpeting, a cigar lighter, F70-14 fiberglass-belted white sidewall tires (or black sidewall raised-white-letter tires), blacked-out escutcheon panels and large bumblebee stripes running across the trunk lid and down the rear fender sides. R/T model designations were also carried on the center of the rear escutcheon panel, directly below the Dodge name.

For a big car, the Charger R/T packed a big wallop when it came to high-speed performance. *Car Life* reported, "They keep making the Charger go like stink and handle better than a lot of so-called sportsters." *Motor Trend* did a comparison test between a 440-powered Charger R/T, a Mercury Cyclone GT and an Oldsmobile Cutlass SX in its April 1970 issue. The Charger test car had the standard equipment V-8, which produced 375 hp at 4600 rpm and 480 lbs.-ft. of torque at 3200 rpm. It also had a 3.55:1 rear axle. The car did 0 to 60 mph in 6.4 seconds and covered the quarter-mile in 14.9 seconds at 98 mph. It also averaged 14.9 to 15.7 mpg, which was much better fuel mileage than the two other cars. The magazine liked the Charger R/T's image and its race-bred heritage.

"For a big car, the Charger R/T packed a big wallop when it came to high-speed performance."

1971

The '71 Dodge Charger was completely restyled. It had a semi-fastback roofline with a flush rear window and an integral rear deck lid spoiler. The company decided that it was time to split the Charger off from the Coronet and give its own identity. "It was evident after the initial success of the '68-'70 Chargers, the Dodge stylists would have to burn some midnight oil to create a fresh approach that would again make the Charger something unique in an industry where very little is unique," said *Motor Trend* in December 1970. "As far as the *Motor Trend* staff is concerned, they succeeded."

The 115-inch-wheelbase two-door hardtops became the Chargers. The Coronet name was used only on 118-inch-wheelbase four-door sedans. The re-sized Charger looked big, but wasn't. It was had a 2-inch-shorter stance and a 3-inch-shorter overall length than the '70 model. The new design gave it 3 additional inches of front overhang. It was also 3 1/2 inches wider.

There were two distinct Charger body types: semi-fastback coupe and two-door hardtop. Both models featured new rear quarter window styling that swept up from the fender to meet the sloping upper rear window frame. A full-

■ *Many chose the vinyl roof option in 1971 for their Dodge Charger R/Ts. This white over blue combination offers high style and takes nothing away from the performance stance of the car.* Jerry Heasley

■ *The sporty interior shows features the Charger, like this 1971 model, helped make popular including bucket seats and a console-mounted automatic transmission gear selector.*
Jerry Heasley

■ *The 1971 Dodge "Magnum" engine displaced 440 cubic inches, offered a 9.70 to 1 compression ratio and produced 370 horsepower. Many remember its unique air cleaner cover.*
Jerry Heasley

width bumper and grille combination was seen up front. It was split in half by a large vertical divider and the rear end was set off with a small "lip" on the trunk lid that formed a short air spoiler. The high-haunches "Coke-bottle" shape was retained to give the rear quarters an aggressive look.

Both of the base Charger models were offered with the 225-cid slant six, but most buyers preferred at least the 318-cid small-block V-8. The hotter Charger 500 series included three models: the 500, the Super Bee and the SE.

The Super Bee was formerly a two-door Coronet, but became a Charger for just this one year. Featuring the newly restyled body, it was aimed at the same market niche as the Coronet Super Bee and represented a value-priced serious high-performance package like the Plymouth Road Runner and GTO Judge. The Super Bee included a 383-cid/300-hp Magnum V-8 with a four-barrel carb and floor-shifted three-speed manual transmission. Above the motor was a "power bulge" hood with flat black finish.

The Charger Super Bee had tape stripes and bumblebee decals. The interior was similar to that of the Charger 500, but substituted a standard bench seat for bucket seats. Dodge's Rallye suspension was used. It included heavy-duty front torsion bars, heavy-duty rear springs, a front anti-sway bar, heavy-duty shock

■ *"Down Under," Chrysler-Australia's Hemi was a six-cylinder truck engine. The popular Hemi 265 produced 248 horsepower using triple Weber carbs. There also was a 280-hp racing engine.*
Jerry Heasley

■ *Make way mate! It's the front of the 1971 Valiant Charger, produced by Chrysler-Australia with styling cues from its North American Dodge Charger cousins. Today, it's very collectible.*
Jerry Heasley

absorbers all around and heavy-duty brakes (11 x 3 inches up front and 11 x 2.5 inches in the rear). The standard tires were fat F70-14 RWLs. The optional equipment list was fat, too.

Optional engines included the 440 Wedge with "Six Pack" carburetion or the 426-cid Street Hemi. Unlike the 8.7:1 compression base engine, these muscle car mills had high-test hardware and continued to offer 390 or 425 hp. Other neat extras were a first-for-the-Charger functional Ramcharger hood scoop, color-keyed bumpers, a Super Trak-Pack performance axle (with up to 4.10:1 gearing), a four-speed gearbox with Hurst "pistol grip" shifter, a dual-point distributor, heavy-duty cooling aids and bucket seats.

Dodge's third offering was the SE notchback. The Charger SE came standard with a 383-cid "big-block" V-8.

For high-performance buffs, there was also a one-car Charger R/T series. The R/T included a 70-amp-hour battery, heavy-duty front and rear brakes, heavy-duty shock absorbers at all four corners, a pedal dress-up kit, an extra-heavy-duty Rallye suspension and TorqueFlite automatic transmission. A four-speed manual gearbox could be substituted for the automatic with no change in price. The R/T also included a 440-cid Magnum V-8 as standard equipment, plus specific R/T identification pieces.

The 440 had the same 3.75-inch stroke as the 426-cid Hemi, but a larger 4.32-inch bore size. The base version, with a single four-barrel carburetor, produced 370 hp at 4600 rpm and 480 lbs.-ft. of torque at 3200 rpm. It had a 9.1:1 compression ratio. In a four-Charger test in December 1970, *Motor Trend* drove a 370-hp 1971 Charger SE with automatic transmission and a 3.23:1 rear axle. It did 0 to 60 mph in a flat 7 seconds and covered the quarter-mile in 14.93 seconds at 96.4 mph.

Also featured in the same test was a 1971 Charger Super Bee with the 440 "Six Pack" engine. This version added three two-barrel carburetors and a 10.3:1 compression ratio. The Six-Pack V-8 developed 385 hp at 4700 rpm and 490 lbs.-ft. of torque at 3200 rpm. The car it was in also had an automatic transmission, but it was hooked to a 4.10:1 rear axle. This cut the 0-to-60 time to 6.9 seconds. The quarter-mile required 14.74 seconds with a terminal speed of 97.3 mph.

■ *In 1971, Chrysler-Australia offered a Hemi 6-Pack in a smaller car, also called the Charger. The wildly popular Chargers became racing legends in both Australia and New Zealand.*

Jerry Heasley

"With a Hemi stuffed under its hood, the Charger quickly deveoped a bad attitude, especially when GM and FoMoCo muscle cars rolled by."

■ *With its own identity in place in 1971, the Dodge Charger offered some memorable styling cues including the split grille, rectangular turn signals and flowing body stripe accents.*
Jerry Heasley

The 426-cid Hemi V-8 was also available in Charger R/Ts for $707 extra and in Charger Super Bees for an additional $837. The "Street Hemi" had a 4.25 x 3.75-inch bore and stroke, a 10.25:1 compression ratio and twin Carter AFB four-barrel carburetors. It produced 425 hp at 5600 rpm! According to Mopar authority Galen V. Govier, Hemi Charger production was extremely low. The big engine was bolted into 22 of the 1971 Charger Super Bees and 63 Charger R/Ts.

With a Hemi stuffed under its hood, the Charger quickly developed a bad attitude, especially when GM and FoMoCo muscle cars rolled by. In December 1970, *Motor Trend* road tested a Hemi Super Bee with automatic transmission and a 4.10:1 ratio rear axle. The car did 0 to 60 mph in 5.7 seconds. The quarter-mile was covered in an elapsed time of 13.73 seconds at 104 mph.

In *Motor Trend*, A. B. Shuman wrote, "If the Super Bee SE was interesting, the Hemi car was remarkable. It was a Hemi and you knew it!"

■ *This 1971 Magnum 440 engine used dual air intake passages on its air cleaner cover. With the hood open, there was plenty of room to work on the cast-iron V-8 in the Charger's engine bay.*

Jerry Heasley

■ *Never shy about graphics in the late '60s and early '70s, this Dodge Charger let everyone know it was an R/T with reversed lettering matching the body color surrounding its blackened hood top.*

Jerry Heasley

■ *This more basic 1971 Charger R/T interior shows bucket seats, but a column-mounted shift lever rather than the floor/console-mounted version. Note the round gauges in the instrument panel.*

Jerry Heasley

■ *In the 1972 model year, the Super Bee and R/T editions were eliminated yet the Charger still offered a combination of sleek styling and powerful stance that brought a loyal following.* Doug Mitchel

1972

It was cut, cut, cut and cut some more in Chargerland in 1972. Three models replaced the six offered in 1971, with the R/T and Super Bee both putting on disappearing acts, as did the Hemi. The 440 Six Pack engine was initially promoted as the top option. Some sources indicate this engine never made it into a production car, but those in the know say a handful of Chargers with a new Rallye option package left the factory with it. The remaining mills were designed to cut smog rather than to burn tires—they all had reduced compression ratios.

The sole high-performance offering was the Rallye option. It was available for the coupe and hardtop. Charger Rallyes included a power-bulge hood with black-out paint, sway bars and both ends, F70 x 14 whitewalls, a new front seat with a divided backrest and black-out tail lights with louvers over them. They looked hot, but engine selections started with a mild 150-hp 318 running a two-barrel carb. You could also get the 340 with 240 hp. In the big-block range, a 400 with 255 hp replaced the 383. The 440 four-barrel produced 280 hp and the Six Pack version was rated at 330 net horsepower.

More in step with the times was the fancier Charger SE (Special Edition). The SE featured a new, formal-looking roofline (with vinyl covering of course) and hidden headlights. It came only with V-8s and the 318 was standard equipment.

On NASCAR racetracks, the Charger gave "King" Richard Petty the title in Winston Cup racing this year. In fact, Petty won three (1972, 1974 and 1975) of his seven titles driving Chargers and earned 37 victories behind the wheel of one.

1973

By 1973, the muscle car era was officially over. Changes in the product line were like the Dodge Boys swapping their Refrigerator White cowboy hat for an Eggshell White one—in other words, primarily cosmetic. Modest updating was done to the grille, but the most obvious revision was a new quarter window treatment. Model offerings were the same. Engines included the 318, the 400, the 340 and the 440 "Magnum" V-8s, as well as the base six in standard Chargers. Thanks to Richard Petty (who took six checkered flags in his Charger) the nameplate retained its hi-po reputation, though you had to add quite a few options to make a street version modestly muscular.

This year the top-of-the-line SE was the top seller, too. That raised divisional profits. The optional Rallye package returned with a new paint treatment that allowed the body color to peek through the flat-black finish on the power-bulge hood. This gave it kind of a "Hot Wheels" look. Hood-locking pins were a new piece of standard content. Gradated tape stripes and raised-white-letter tires were included. The 440-powered Charger took 7.4 seconds to hit 60 mph from a standing start. Quarter-mile times were north of 15 seconds—way out of the *real* muscle car bracket.

1974

This was the last year for the beautiful Charger body that debuted in '71. Starting in '75, the Charger would become a luxury variant of an all-new Coronet, which was derived from Riccardo Montalban's favorite Chrysler, the Cordova (rich Corinthian leather not included on the Dodge as far as I know). The grille and tail lights were updated a bit and advertised horsepower ratings headed further south. With 275 hp, the 440 was tops. New, except in California, was a 360-cid V-8 with 245 hp. Models and their images were the same as in '74. There was a big decline in production.

In NASCAR, the '74 Charger driven by Richard Petty proved to be a far cry from the ones that sat in Dodge showrooms. Petty's car had more wins than any other. "The King" took his fifth driving championship by winning 10 contests in a 30-race schedule and finishing in the top 10 cars 23 times. The car

■ *There were no questions about the engine that lurked under the hood of this 1969 Dodge Daytona. The badge told everyone this car was powered by the legendary "Street Hemi" V-8.*

Tom Glatch

■ *With the passage of time and the memories of record NASCAR performances, the once ugly duckling 1969 Dodge Charger Daytona has become of the classic swan among car collectors.*

Jerry Heasley

was so dominant that Petty decided to run it the following year, too, when he won 13 of 30 races and finished in the top five 21 times. Naturally, he took his sixth championship. Today, the car is owned by the Talledega Motorsport Hall of Fame.

"The 1974 Dodge Charger was probably the best overall car we ever had," Petty says. "Sure, we had it about five or six years and had a lot of time to work on it. Back then we didn't have specialty cars. The car was just good on everything. It didn't matter if it was a short track, superspeedway or road course. It was just a good overall car. This was a real universal car."

CHARGER YEAR-BY-YEAR SPEC'S

1966

Engine	Bore/Str.	Comp. Ratio	CID	BHP	WT.	W.B.	O.L.	Width	HT
V-8*	3.91 x 3.31	09.00	318	230 @4400	3,504	117.0	203.6	75.3	54.5
V-8 **	4.12 x 3.38	09.00	361	265 @4400	3,504	117.0	203.6	75.3	54.5
V-8 **	4.25 x 3.38	10.00	383	325 @4800	3,504	117.0	203.6	75.3	54.5
V-8 **	4.25 x 3.75	10.25	426	425 @5000	3,504	117.0	203.6	75.3	54.5

* Base engine
** Optional

1967

Engine	Bore/Str.	Comp. Ratio	CID	BHP	WT.	W.B.	O.L.	Width	HT
V-8 *	3.91 x 3.31	09.00	318	230 @4400	3,475	117.0	203.6	75.3	54.5
V-8	4.25 x 3.38	09.20	383	270 @4400	3,475	117.0	203.6	75.3	54.5
V-8	4.25 x 3.38	10.00	383	325 @4800	3,475	117.0	203.6	75.3	54.5
V-8	4.32 x 3.75	10.10	440	375 @4600	3,475	117.0	203.6	75.3	54.5
V-8	4.25 x 3.75	10.25	426	425 @5000	3,475	117.0	203.6	75.3	54.5

* Base engine
** Optional

1968

Engine	Bore/Str.	Comp. Ratio	CID	BHP	WT.	W.B.	O.L.	Width	HT
I6 *	3.40 x 4.13	08.40	225	145 @4000	3,100	117.0	208.0	76.6	53.2
V-8 **	3.91 x 3.31	09.20	318	230 @4400	3,100	117.0	208.0	76.6	53.2
V-8	4.25 x 3.38	09.20	383	290 @4400	3,100	117.0	208.0	76.6	53.2
V-8	4.25 x 3.38	10.00	383	330 @5000	3,100	117.0	208.0	76.6	53.2
V-8 ***	4.32 x 3.75	10.10	440	375 @4600	3,100	117.0	208.0	76.6	53.2
V-8	4.25 x 3.75	10.25	426	425 @5000	3,100	117.0	208.0	76.6	53.2

* Base six-cylinder
** Base V-8 (except R/T)
*** Base V-8 Charger R/T

1969

Engine	Bore/Str.	Comp. Ratio	CID	BHP	WT.	W.B.	O.L.	Width	HT
I6 *	3.40 x 4.13	08.40	225	145 @4000	3103	117.0	206.6	76.7	52.3
V-8 **	3.91 x 3.31	09.20	318	230 @4400	3103	117.0	206.6	76.7	52.3
V-8 ****	4.25 x 3.38	10.00	383	330 @5000	3103	117.0	206.6	76.7	52.3
V-8 ***	4.32 x 3.75	10.10	440	375 @4600	3103	117.0	206.6	76.7	52.3
V-8 ****	4.25 x 3.75	10.25	426	425 @5000	3103	117.0	206.6	76.7	52.3

* Base six-cylinder
** Base V-8 (except R/T)
*** Base V-8 Charger R/T
**** Optional

1970

Engine	Bore/Str.	Comp. Ratio	CID	BHP	WT.	W.B.	O.L.	Width	HT
I6 *	3.40 x 4.13	08.40	225	145 @4000	3,228	117.0	208.0	76.6	53.0
V-8 **	3.91 x 3.31	09.20	318	230 @4400	3,228	117.0	208.0	76.6	53.0
V-8 ****	4.25 x 3.38	09.20	383	290 @4400	3,228	117.0	208.0	76.6	53.0
V-8 ****	4.25 x 3.38	10.00	383	330 @5000	3,228	117.0	208.0	76.6	53.0
V-8 ****	4.25 x 3.38	10.00	383	335 @5000	3,228	117.0	208.0	76.6	53.0
V-8 ***	4.32 x 3.75	10.10	440	375 @4600	3,228	117.0	208.0	76.6	53.0
V-8 *****	4.32 x 3.75	10.50	440	390 @4700	3,228	117.0	208.0	76.6	53.0
V-8 ****	4.25 x 3.75	10.25	426	425 @5000	3,228	117.0	208.0	76.6	53.0

* Base six-cylinder
** Base V-8 (except R/T)
*** Base V-8 Charger R/T
**** Optional
***** Optional Charger R/T

1971

Engine	Bore/Str.	Comp. Ratio	CID	BHP	WT.	W.B.	O.L.	Width	HT
I6 *	3.40 x 4.13	08.40	225	145 @4000	3,228	115.0	206.0	77.0	53.0
V-8 **	3.91 x 3.31	08.60	318	230 @4400	3,228	115.0	206.0	77.0	53.0
V-8 ****	4.25 x 3.38	08.50	383	275 @4400	3,228	115.0	206.0	77.0	53.0
V-8 ****	4.25 x 3.38	08.50	383	300 @5000	3,228	115.0	206.0	77.0	53.0
V-8 ***	4.32 x 3.75	09.50	440	370 @4600	3,228	115.0	206.0	77.0	53.0
V-8 *****	4.32 x 3.75	10.30	440	365 @4700	3,228	115.0	206.0	77.0	53.0
V-8 ****	4.25 x 3.75	10.20	426	425 @5000	3,228	115.0	206.0	77.0	53.0

* Base six-cylinder
** Base V-8 (except R/T)
*** Base V-8 Charger R/T
**** Optional
***** Optional Charger R/T

1972

Engine	Bore/Str.	Comp. Ratio	CID	BHP	WT.	W.B.	O.L.	Width	HT
I6 **	3.40 x 4.13	08.40	225	110 @4000	3,245	115.0	206.0	77.0	53.0
V-8 ***	3.91 x 3.31	08.60	318	150 @4000	3,318	115.0	206.0	77.0	53.0
V-8 ****	4.04 x 3.31	08.20	340	240 @4800	3,318	115.0	206.0	77.0	53.0
V-8 *****	4.34 x 3.38	08.20	400	190 @4400	3,318	115.0	206.0	77.0	53.0
V-8 ******	4.34 x 3.38	08.20	400	225 @4800	3,318	115.0	206.0	77.0	53.0
V-8 *******	4.32 x 3.75	08.20	440	280 @4800	3,228	115.0	206.0	77.0	53.0
V-8 *******	4.32 x 3.75	10.30	440	330 @4800	3,228	115.0	206.0	77.0	53.0

* All ratings are net horsepower
** Base six-cylinner
*** Base V-8 in Rallye V-8
**** Optional
***** Optional (two-barrel)
****** Optional (four-barrel)
******* Optional (four-barrel; TorqueFlight standard)
******* The 440 Six-Pack (330 hp) was listed as an optional engine in the '72 sales brochure, but dropped in initial production.

1973

Engine	Bore/Str.	Comp. Ratio	CID	BHP	WT.	W.B.	O.L.	Width	HT
I6 **	3.40 x 4.13	08.40	225	110 @4000	3,395	115.0	213.0	77.0	53.0
V-8 ***	3.91 x 3.31	08.60	318	150 @4000	3,460	115.0	213.0	77.0	53.0
V-8 ****	4.04 x 3.31	08.20	340	240 @4800	3,318	115.0	213.0	77.0	53.0
V-8 *****	4.34 x 3.38	08.20	400	175 @3600	3,318	115.0	213.0	77.0	53.0
V-8 ******	4.34 x 3.38	08.20	400	260 @4800	3,318	115.0	213.0	77.0	53.0
V-8 *******	4.32 x 3.75	08.20	440	280 @4800	3,228	115.0	213.0	77.0	53.0

* All ratings are net horsepower
** Base six-cylinder
*** Base V-8 in Rallye V-8
**** Optional
***** Optional (two-barrel)
****** Optional (four-barrel)
******* Optional (four-barrel; TorqueFlight standard)

1974

Engine	Bore/Str.	Comp. Ratio	CID	BHP	WT.	W.B.	O.L.	Width	HT
I6 **	3.40 x 4.13	08.40	225	110 @4000	3,470	116.0	214.0	77.0	53.0
V-8 ***	3.91 x 3.31	08.60	318	150 @4000	3,550	116.0	214.0	77.0	53.0
V-8 ****	4.00 x 3.58	08.40	360	180 @4000	3,550	116.0	214.0	77.0	53.0
V-8 ****	4.00 x 3.58	08.40	360	200 @4000	3,550	116.0	214.0	77.0	53.0
V-8 ****	4.00 x 3.58	08.40	360	245 @4000	3,550	116.0	214.0	77.0	53.0
V-8 ****	4.34 x 3.38	08.20	400	205 @4400	3,550	116.0	214.0	77.0	53.0
V-8 ****	4.34 x 3.38	08.20	400	250 @4400	3,550	116.0	214.0	77.0	53.0
V-8 ****	4.32 x 3.75	08.20	440	275 @4800	3,550	116.0	214.0	77.0	53.0

* All ratings are Net Horsepower
** Base six-cylinder
*** Base V-8 in Rallye V-8
**** Optional

Note: Compiled from a variety of contemporary sources. Minor differences in measurements are due to the way the car was measured, rather than changes in the car itself or related to the fact that different body styles were used as the basis for factory specifications tables. Weight is for lightest model.

"The 1974 Charger was probably the best overall car we ever had."

— Richard Petty

■ *In 1970, those opting for a Dodge Charger R/T and the SE package could also look up and see the sky! An electric sunroof offered open-top motoring. A vinyl top was mandatory with the sunroof.*

Jerry Heasley

PRODUCTION STATISTICS AND BREAKOUTS

1966 CHARGER

Year	Body Code	Body Type	Engine Type	MSP Price	Model Yr. Prod.
66	29	2HT	V-8	$3,146	37,344
ALL CHARGER TOTAL					**37,344**

1967 CHARGER

Year	Body Code	Body Type	Engine Type	MSP Price	Model Yr. Prod.
67	29	2HT	V-8	$3,128	15,788
ALL CHARGER TOTAL					**15,788**

1968 CHARGER

Year	Body Code	Body Type	Engine Type	MSP Price	Model Yr. Prod.
CHARGER 6					
68	29	2HT	I6	$2,934	908
CHARGER V-8					
68	29	2HT	V-8	$,040	76,893
CHARGER R/T V-8					
68	29	2HT	V-8	$3,506	18,307
ALL CHARGER TOTAL					**96,108**

1969 CHARGER-DAYTONA

Year	Body Code	Body Type	Engine Type	MSP (Price	Model Yr. Prod. (1)
BASE CHARGER 6					
69	29	2HT	I6	$3,020	500
BASE CHARGER V-8					
69	29	2HT	V-8	$3,126	Note 2
CHARGER R/T					
69	29	2HT	V-8	$3,592	20,100
CHARGER 500					
69	29	2HT	V-8	$3,860	Note 2
CHARGER DAYTONA					
69	29	2HT	V-8	$4,298	503

Note 1: All production totals except Charger Daytona are rounded-off numbers
Note 2: 48,000 combined

ALL CHARGER TOTAL					**69,100**

1970 CHARGER

Year	Body Code	Body Type	Engine Type	MSP Price	Model Yr. Prod.
BASE CHARGER 6-CYL					
70	29	2HT	I6	$3,001	Note 1
BASE CHARGER V-8					
70	29	2HT	V-8	$3,108	Note 1
CHARGER 500 6-CYL					
70	29	2HT	I6	$3,139	Note 1
CHARGER 500					
70	29	2HT	V-8	$3,246	Note 1
CHARGER R/T					
70	29	2HT	V-8	$3,711	10,337

Note 1: Combined production was 39,431
Note 2: About 300 six-cylinder Chargers were made.

ALL CHARGER TOTAL					**49,768**

1971 CHARGER

Year	Body Code	Body Type	Engine Type	MSP Price	Model Yr. Prod.
BASE CHARGER 6-CYL					
71	21	2CPE	I6	$2,707	Note 1
71	23	2HT	I6	$2,975	Note 1
BASE CHARGER V-8					
71	21	2CPE	V-8	$2,802	Note 1
71	23	2HT	V-8	3,070	Note 1
CHARGER 500					
71	23	2HT	V-8	$3,223	11,948
CHARGER 500 SUPERBEE					
71	23	2HT	V-8	$3,271	5,054
CHARGER 500 SE					
71	29	2HT	V-8	$3,422	15,811
CHARGER R/T					
71	23	2HT	V-8	$3,777	3,118

Note 1: Combined production was 46,183

ALL CHARGER TOTAL					**82,114**

1972 CHARGER

Year	Body Code	Body Type	Engine Type	MSP Price	Model Yr. Prod.
BASE CHARGER 6-CYL					
72	21	2CPE	I6	$2,652	Note 1
72	23	2HT	I6	$2,913	Note 2
BASE CHARGER V-8					
72	21	2CPE	V-8	$2,759	Note 1
72	23	2HT	V-8	$3,020	Note 2
CHARGER SE					
72	29	2HT	V-8	$3,249	22,430

Note 1: Combined production was 7,803
Note 2: Combined production was 45,361

ALL CHARGER TOTAL					**75,594**

1973 CHARGER

Year	Body Code	Body Type	Engine Type	MSP Price	Model Yr. Prod.
BASE CHARGER 6-CYL					
73	21	2CPE	I6	$2,810	Note 1
73	23	2HT	I6	$3,060	Note 2
BASE CHARGER V-8					
73	21	2CPE	V-8	$2,922	Note 1
73	23	2HT	V-8	$3,171	Note 2
CHARGER SE					
73	29	2HT	V-8	$3,540	61,908

Note 1: Combined production was 11,995
Note 2: Combined production was 45,415

ALL CHARGER TOTAL					**119,318**

1974 CHARGER

Year	Body Code	Body Type	Engine Type	MSP Price	Model Yr. Prod.
BASE CHARGER 6-CYL					
74	21	2CPE	I6	$3,212	Note 1
74	23	2HT	I6	$3,412	Note 2
BASE CHARGER V-8					
74	21	2CPE	V-8	$3,327	Note 1
74	23	2HT	V-8	$3,526	Note 2
CHARGER SE					
74	29	2HT	V-8	$3,742	35,624
ALL CHARGER TOTAL					**57,410**

Note 1: Combined coupe production was 11,995
Note 2: Combined hardtop production was 45,415

■ *At first, the winged Dodge Charger Daytona and the similar Plymouth Road Runner Superbird, were slow sellers. Their popularity and value has increased greatly through the years.*

Phil Kunz

PRICE GUIDE

Vehicle Condition Scale

6 — Parts car:
May or may not be running, but is weathered, wrecked and/or stripped to the point of being useful primarily for parts.

5 — Restorable:
Needs complete restoration of body, chassis and interior. May or may not be running, but isn't weathered, wrecked or stripped to the point of being useful only for parts.

4 — Good:
A driveable vehicle needing no or only minor work to be functional. Also, a deteriorated restoration or a very poor amateur restoration. All components may need restoration to be "excellent," but the car is mostly useable "as is."

3 — Very Good:
Complete operable original or older restoration. Also, a very good amateur restoration, all presentable and serviceable inside and out. Plus, a combination of well-done restoration and good operable components or a partially restored car with all parts necessary to compete and/or valuable NOS parts.

2 — Fine:
Well-restored or a combination of superior restoration and excellent original parts. Also, extremely well-maintained original vehicle showing minimal wear.

1 — Excellent:
Restored to current maximum professional standards of quality in every area, or perfect original with components operating and apearing as new. A 95-plus point show car that is not driven.

1966 Charger

	6	5	4	3	2	1
2d HT	1,040	3,120	5,200	11,700	18,200	26,000

NOTE: Autos equipped with 426 Hemi, value inestimable.

1967 Charger

	6	5	4	3	2	1
2d HT	1,080	3,240	5,400	12,150	18,900	27,000

NOTE: Autos equipped with 426 Hemi, value inestimable.

1968 Charger

	6	5	4	3	2	1
2d HT	1,480	4,440	7,400	16,650	25,900	37,000

NOTE: Autos equipped with 426 Hemi, value inestimable.

1968 Charger R/T

	6	5	4	3	2	1
2d HT	1,640	4,920	8,200	18,450	28,700	41,000

NOTE: Autos equipped with 426 Hemi, value inestimable.

1969 Charger

	6	5	4	3	2	1
2d HT	1,520	4,560	7,600	17,100	26,600	38,000

NOTE: Autos equipped with 426 Hemi, value inestimable.

1969 Charger SE

	6	5	4	3	2	1
2d HT	1,560	4,680	7,800	17,550	27,300	39,000

NOTE: Autos equipped with 426 Hemi, value inestimable.

1969 Charger 500

	6	5	4	3	2	1
2d HT	1,920	5,760	9,600	21,600	33,600	48,000

NOTE: Autos equipped with 426 Hemi, value inestimable.

1969 Charger R/T

	6	5	4	3	2	1
2d HT	2,080	6,240	10,400	23,400	36,400	52,000

NOTE: Autos equipped with 426 Hemi, value inestimable.

1969 Charger Daytona

	6	5	4	3	2	1
2d HT	3,000	9,000	15,000	33,750	52,500	75,000

NOTE: Autos equipped with 426 Hemi, value inestimable.

1970 Charger

	6	5	4	3	2	1
2d HT	1,360	4,080	6,800	15,300	23,800	34,000
2d HT 500	1,520	4,560	7,600	17,100	26,600	38,000
2d HT R/T	1,680	5,040	8,400	18,900	29,400	42,000

NOTE: Autos equipped with 426 Hemi, value inestimable.

1971 Charger

	6	5	4	3	2	1
2d HT 500	1,160	3,480	5,800	13,050	20,300	29,000
2d HT	1,080	3,240	5,400	12,150	18,900	27,000
2d Super Bee HT	1,200	3,600	6,000	13,500	21,000	30,000
2d HT R/T	1,280	3,840	6,400	14,400	22,400	32,000
2d HT SE	1,240	3,720	6,200	13,950	21,700	31,000

NOTE: Autos equipped with 426 Hemi, value inestimable.

1972 Charger

	6	5	4	3	2	1
2d Sed	680	2,040	3,400	7,650	11,900	17,000
2d HT	688	2,064	3,440	7,740	12,040	17,200
2d HT SE	760	2,280	3,800	8,550	13,300	19,000

NOTE: Add 20 percent for Rallye.

1973 Charger

	6	5	4	3	2	1
2d Cpe	620	1,860	3,100	6,980	10,850	15,500
2d HT	640	1,920	3,200	7,200	11,200	16,000
2d "SE" HT	648	1,944	3,240	7,290	11,340	16,200
2d Rallye	660	1,980	3,300	7,430	11,550	16,500

1974 Charger

	6	5	4	3	2	1
2d Cpe	344	1,032	1,720	3,870	6,020	8,600
2d HT	380	1,140	1,900	4,280	6,650	9,500
2d "SE" HT	400	1,200	2,000	4,500	7,000	10,000

Charger 1966-1974

Chevelle

1964 Chevelle Malibu SS

The mid-'60s would bring sweeping changes to the U.S. automobile market. Before the year 1964 ended, cars like the Ford Mustang, the Pontiac GTO and the Olds 4-4-2 would bow. But the only all-new car introduced at the start of the model year was a box-like Chevrolet product called the Chevelle. Smaller than a "real Chevy" and larger than a Corvair or Chevy II, the Chevelle was once described as a "car that fits between parking meters."

This mid-sized car came in all kinds of variations, from taxicab plain to "sports-car" sporty. Since the supercar era hadn't started, you couldn't call the original top-powered 283-cube Chevelle a "muscle car." With the SS equipment package it looked sporty, and with 220 hp it was kind of snappy, but 0 to 60 was still going to take 9.7 seconds, according to Bob McVay of *Motor Trend*. The top speed was 109 mph.

■ *The Chevelle featured minor enhancements to the squared shape introduced in 1964. In 1965, the grille and tail lights were among changes. This is the Z-16 version of the Malibu SS.*
Jerry Heasley

Chevelle Timeline

1964 — 1965 — 1966 — 1967 — 1968 — 1969 — 1970 — 1971

1964: Chevrolet introduces the Chevelle as an all-new car available in 22 different engine and body-style combinations. The SS 327 is the muscle car of the lineup.

1965: The power-packed Z-16 option goes in 201 Chevelles. The 396-cid engines were rated at 375 hp.

1966: The 396, with 325 hp becomes standard in the SS. The stronger L34 396 was also available, with the L84 396 showing up later in the year.

1966: Chevelle SS renamed SS 396.

1967: Disc brakes, better tires and 14-inch wheels help the Chevelle drive and handle better.

1968: Major redesign features a longer hood, shorter deck and shorter wheelbase.

1969: SS 396 package available on all Chevelles.

1970: 454 LS5 and LS6 engine packages are the biggest ever offered on a Chevelle and so-equipped cars eventually achieve cult status.

1971: LS6 killed as part of GM's attempt to meet emissions standards, but LS5 remained with 365-hp rating.

1964 — 1965 — 1966 — 1967 — 1968 — 1969 — 1970 — 1971

What Chevy called the "swashbuckling" Chevelle Malibu SS package included extra chrome moldings, vinyl upholstery, carpets, front bucket seats, a shifter console, special Super Sport wheel covers, SS badges and other creature amenities. A special yellow color was also offered, along with 14 regular Chevelle choices. The SS package was available on hardtops and convertibles with a choice of two six-cylinder engines and (initially) and equal number of V-8s. But this was soon to change.

When Pontiac shoved its big 389-cid/325-hp V-8 into GTO-optioned Tempests in mid-'64, the pressure was suddenly put on Chevrolet to keep up with "Poncho." When Olds answered quickly with a 330-cid/310-hp "police" option for its F-85, the first 4-4-2 evolved and Chevy felt an even greater challenge. The bow-tie brand was not about to bow out of the running.

In *Car Life* magazine's March 1964 comparison road test of an El Camino and two Chevelles the writer said, "As *Car Life* testers began work, Chevrolet announced that the 327-cid Corvette engine would be available in three bhp ratings, increasing the power options (to 17) (See chart on p. 112)."

■ *In an era when size often was popular, the Chevelle was a smaller, mid-size Chevrolet offering. In SS trim at sunset, this Malibu two-door hardtop shows the classic beauty of its clean lines.*
Jerry Heasley

■ *The new Chevrolet Chevelle eventually included a well-dressed 327-cid Corvette V-8 under the hood 250-, 300- and 365-hp versions. This one has a dual-air passage chrome air cleaner cover.*

Jerry Heasley

CHEVELLE POWER OPTIONS

Engines	Transmissions			
Cu. In./bhp	3-speed	H/D clutch	4-speed	PG
194/120	X	X		X
230/155	X			X
283/195	X		X	X
283/220	X		X	X
327/250	X		X	X
327/300			X	X

With the release of these awesome small-block 327 V-8s, the Chevelle was well on its way to becoming a hot car on the streets. "Somehow, we couldn't help feeling we'd driven the Chevelle before, about eight years ago," said *Motor Trend* in its March 1964 road test. "It's basically similar to the popular 1955 Chevrolet—a shade shorter in overall length and height. But with the same basic engine/chassis combination."

■ *In 1965, the Chevelle was raised a few performance-minded notches with the Z-16 model, named after its production package order code, RPO Z16. Included was a 375-hp, 396-cid V-8.*

Jerry Heasley

1965 Chevelle SS 396 (Z16)

Chevrolet produced nearly 340,000 Chevelles in 1964, registering a smashing success in the new mid-size car market niche. The '65 model was mildly updated, particularly with a front radiator grille that gave it a more aggressive look. There were different trim placements, some redesigned body badges and other modest changes. But big things would start happening under the hood by the end of the year after the SS 396 option arrived. This package included more than just a big motor. It was a comprehensive assortment of high-performance equipment sold to only a few enthusiasts.

■ *By 1965, Chevelle buyers had learned the clean, cursive Malibu name combined with the SS letters in a circle meant a pleasing package of style and performance with a dash of luxury.*

Jerry Heasley

Car Life called the SS 396 the "First of the Red-Hot Malibus." When *Motor Trend* technical editor John Ethridge road tested the 375-hp SS 396 Chevelle in July of 1965, he tagged it the "Almighty Malibu." His article pointed out that the name Chevelle 396 was selected to get the idea across in very few words. Eventually, the package (RPO Z16) became better known as simply "SS 396." Those two letters and three numbers said it all. Its displacement was bigger than the 389 of the GTO, the 330 of the 4-4-2 and the 390 used in many Fords. More important, the SS 396 was not just an engine swap.

You could not order the SS 396 engine and simply add it to any Chevelle. In fact, you couldn't add it to just any Malibu—only a Malibu SS hardtop or convertible. And the package included more than a monster engine. You got it only with a beefed-up Malibu convertible frame (for both body styles), fat dual exhausts, a large, thick radiator, a staggered five-blade fan, heavy-duty wheels, big 11-inch brakes, anti-roll bars, stiffer springs and shocks, special 7.75 x 14 Goodyear gold-stripe tires and styled wheels that looked like real mag rims.

Like the car that it rode in, the 396 Chevy engine was a hardware store on wheels. Its "inventory" included impact-extruded pistons, chrome-moly rings, special alloy connecting rods, four-bolt mains, a special high-lift hydraulic cam, a big Holley 4150 carburetor and heavy-duty valve train components. This

motor required a four-speed manual gearbox. Its advertised horsepower was 375 at 5600 rpm and it red lined at 5800 rpm. It produced a whopping 420 lbs.-ft. of torque at 3600 rpm.

At $2,647, the bone-stock SS 396 was probably one of the greatest high-performance bargains in the world, but a few options could easily boost the price up to $4,500 or more. This was still not bad for a car that did 0 to 60 mph in 6.7 seconds and topped 135 mph flat out. The quarter-mile took just 15.3 seconds.

Despite its low price and high-performance capabilities, the SS 396 was rare. Only 201 were built—200 coupes and a convertible used by Chevrolet general mananger E. M. "Pete" Estes. These were what Chevy called "brass hat" or

■ *In 1966, the Chevelle SS 396 was more than an option package. It was a new model with new styling shared by all Chevelles. This black two-door hardtop stands out in a country setting.* Jerry Heasley

■ *In 1966, the flared five-spoke wheels continued to be popular among the SS 396 buying crowd. It was also a fashion trend among performance car buyer to have thin, red-striped tires in this era.* Jerry Heasley

image cars and were made available mostly to writers and VIPs (and Pete Estes, of course). According to a story in *Car Life*, the general public couldn't buy an SS 396 convertible in '65, but Chevy let it be known that a '66 version was coming and would be available in showrooms across America. After all the stories appearing in the buff books, it's likely that customers were lining up early.

1966 Chevelle SS 396

The '66 Chevelle SS 396 was quite a different car from the mid-'65 limited-edition version. It had the name, the look and the engine, but many things about the car had changed. First, it was a model, rather than an option package. Second, it was a Chevelle, rather than a Malibu. Third, it had an all-new body—not just a face-lifted grille and rear end. Fourth, it lacked the same hardware; the convertible-type frame was not used and the brakes and suspension parts were standard Chevelle items. There was no rear stabilizer bar. Red- or white-stripe tires replaced the gold-stripe version.

Below the hood, instead of 375 hp, Chevy offered a standard 325-hp version of the 396 and an optional 360-hp job. A water-cooled Powerglide automatic transmission was new, too. Now, you could get a Chevelle SS 396, even if you didn't know how to "drive stick."

Though watered down a bit from the "brass hat" cars, the production-type SS 396 did have its pluses. The springs were some 30 percent stiffer than conventional Chevelle springs, the shocks used heavy-duty valving and the differential carrier was beefed up and had a bigger ring gear. Eric Dahlquist of *Hot Rod* liked such features and gave the car a good review, but other road testers weren't as soft on it. They didn't like the horsepower reductions and the '66's handling and the "grocery-hauler" brakes. *Road Test* magazine put it bluntly, saying, "As enthusiasts, people who have spent years in competition and driving for fun, we would like to see some good chassis engineering brought to bear on the Chevelle SS 396, Pontiac GTO, Buick Skylark GS and Olds 442, instead of the perpetration of a snow job on the public through advertising and propaganda while continuing to fob off 1936-type cars with unlimited-displacement engines."

Such criticisms stung and Chevy couldn't afford to justify claims of a watered-down muscle car when the market was taking off like a rocket. In June 1966, *Motor Trend* announced a new L78 engine that was "about the equivalent to last year's Z16 except for a solid-lifter cam and new exhaust manifolds to more conveniently fit the Chevelle chassis." This motor was rated for 375 hp at 5600 rpm. It seems that the '66 L78 never got into test driver hands or reported on.

The 360-hp engine, coded the L34, was the one used in most SS 396s built in 1966 according to reliable sources. This one was also tested by most car magazines and *Motor Trend* wasn't its only fan. In March 1966 *Car and Driver* did a six-car comparison test and said the SS 396 "scored very high with us because of its intrinsic balance." *Car Life* nailed down a 0-to-60 time of 7.9 seconds and a 15.5-seconds quarter-mile at 89 mph. John Lawler, of *Motorcade* magazine, was also critical of the '66 model, but to be fair pointed out that it cost $1,324 less than the built-for-racing '65 Malibu SS 396.

In real-life terms, for the money it cost, the '66 SS 396 was a hell of a car with the potential to be even better in the future. And the public seemed to agree largely with this contention as it plunked down the money necessary to take 72,272 copies home. Most of the cars—66,843 to be exact—were two-door hardtops; the other 5,429 were convertibles.

"The bone-stock SS 396 was probably one of the greatest high-performance bargains in the world."

■ *Chevrolet-built cars looked great in these styled wheels. Chevelles, the new Camaros, full-size Chevys and Corvettes all wore them beginning in this model year, often with red striped tires.*
Jerry Heasley

■ *Inside the SS 396 was a bench seat in this case. The steering wheel badge reminded drivers about the car they were piloting. The floor-mounted four-speed shifter was angled conveniently.*
Jerry Heasley

1967 Chevelle SS 396

The '67 Chevelle SS 396 continued to use the one-year-old cigar-shaped body, but the forward thrust of front fenders was toned down slightly. The black-out radiator grille insert sat behind four more prominent horizontal bars. Details like the design of the bumper slot and body emblems were changed, too. "Super Sport" appeared in script on the rear fenders. The tail lights were notched into the rear fender tips so you could see them from the side view. Flat black paint covered the rear body panel for a *stealthy* look.

Chevelle SS 396s again had twin simulated hood air intakes, but of a new design with longer chrome ribs. Also retained as part of the contents were ribbed color-accented sill and rear fender lower moldings and specific SS 'bottle cap' wheel covers. The '67 bottle caps had a bright metal center and dark bow tie—the reverse of the '66 treatment. A bench seat with vinyl upholstery was standard equipment.

■ *A new front grille was one change for the 1967 Chevelles. This SS 396 two-door hardtop continued to be offered with several engine, transmission and component choices.*
Jerry Heasley

■ *The SS 396 shared the clean lines of all 1967 Chevelles. The black strip below the trunk line and dual exhausts was probably seen by many drivers who tried to keep up with this super Chevy.*
Jerry Heasley

The 325-hp 396 was carried over as the base engine in 1967. The L34 was also offered again, but its official horsepower rating dropped to 350 to stay within tighter new corporate guidelines. The L78 was *not* listed on Chevy specifications sheets to avoid giving the brass an excuse to lower the guillotine, but it was possible to purchase the components needed to "build"

this option at your Chevy dealer's parts counter. The total cost of everything needed to upgrade a 350-hp engine to a 375-hp job was $475.80.

SS 396 buyers could initially get the 325-hp engine with a standard heavy-duty three-speed manual transmission, a four-speed manual gearbox or Powerglide automatic. Later in the year, the "big-car" Turbo-Hydra-Matic was made available. THM was much better suited to handle the 396's torque.

There was a choice of nine axle ratios from 3.07:1 to 4.10:1, but specific options depended upon transmission choice. The 350-hp engine came with the heavy-duty three-speed manual, wide- or close-ratio four speeds or Powerglide. There were eight rear axle ratios from 3.07:1 to 4.88:1, but you could not get all of them with every engine and transmission setup.

This year a car with the L78 engine was tested, even though it wasn't a regular offering in the sales catalog. The 375-hp sport coupe did 0 to 60 mph in 6.5 seconds and the quarter-mile in 14.9 seconds. Comparative numbers for the 325-hp version were 7.5 seconds and 15.9 seconds. Annual production of SS 396s fell a bit, with 63,006 being made, including 59,685 sport coupes and 3,321 convertibles. Only 612 of the cars had the L78 option.

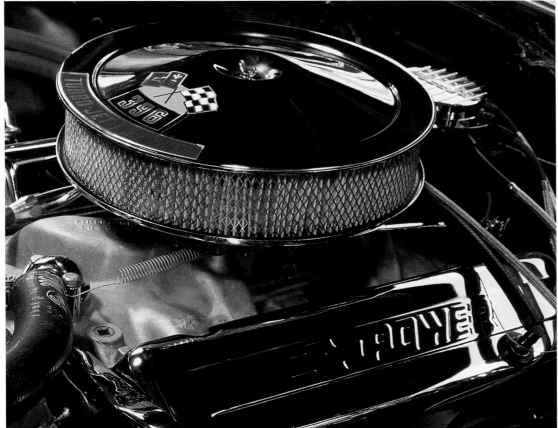

■ The 1967 Chevelle SS 396 two-door hardtop is in a natural setting—a straight country road tempting the driver to extend the car to its limits. Some reached 60 mph in just 6.5 seconds.

Jerry Heasley

■ The 1967 Chevelle SS 396 engine with a pair of aftermarket chrome valve covers but still wearing the familiar air cleaner with chrome sandwiching the white paper filter.

Jerry Heasley

1968 Chevelle SS 396

"To say Chevelle is all-new is an understatement," boasted the 1968 sales catalog for Chevy's hot mid-sized model. "It is brilliantly original for '68! Out-of-the-ordinary roof lines, front fenders and tail light arrangements. The latest look in long-hood/short deck styling. Two wheelbases: 112 in. for coupes and convertibles, 116 in. for sedans and wagons. An expansive grille to emphasize wider tread."

The new '68 Chevelle body had a "wrap-over" front end to give it a distinctive character. It also had the long-in-front-short-in-back styling that was all the rage in this era. As with other '68 GM intermediates, the use of two wheelbases allowed for sportier-looking Chevelle coupes and ragtops.

The high-performance SS 396 was a separate series in 1968. It included a sport coupe base-priced at $2,899 and a convertible priced at $3,102. Both had the shorter wheelbase, of course. Overall length, at 197.1 inches, was just a tad longer than in 1967, even though the wheelbase was down sized by 3 inches. Front and rear tread widths were also up an inch to 59 inches. The new Chevelle was also nearly an inch taller at 52.7 inches.

■ *Even the dash carried 396 badging on the 1968 SS.* Zone Five Photo

■ *The heavily restyled 1968 Chevelles had a more rounded fastback profile.*
Zone Five Photo

The SS 396 models were made even more distinctive by the use of matte black finish around the full lower perimeter of the bodies, except when the cars were finished in a dark color. Other SS features included F70 x 14 wide-oval red-stripe tires, body accent stripes, a special twin-domed hood with simulated air intakes, "SS" badges, vinyl upholstery and a heavy-duty three-speed transmission with floor-mounted shifter.

The standard engine was the RPO L35 version of the 396-cid V-8, which had an advertised 325 hp. The RPO L34 version with 350 hp was $105 extra and was the only option early in the year. That situation didn't last long, as competitors like the 375-hp Dodge Charger R/T and 350-hp Olds 4-4-2 were soon stealing sales away from Chevrolet based on horsepower alone.

At midyear, Chevy re-released the RPO L78 version of the 396 with 375 hp. This option cost $237 more than a base V-8. A '68 SS 396 with this engine and the close-ratio four-speed manual gearbox was road tested from 0 to 60 mph in 6.6 seconds and did the quarter-mile in 14.8 seconds at 98.8 mph.

As in the past, Chevrolet continued to offer the SS 396 with a wide range of transmission and rear axle options. Also standard were finned front brake drums and new bonded brake linings all around. About 57,600 Chevelle SS 396s were made and this total included 4,751 with the L78 engine and 4,082 with the L34 option.

■ Yenko Chevrolet took the Central Office Production Order (COPO) option even further producing limited editions, including this 1969 Chevelle Yenko two-door hardtop. Phil Kunz

■ By 1969, some pollution control equipment was coming into view, but the unmistakable 396-cid V-8 was still center stage in many Chevelle engine bays, delighting performance drivers.

Jerry Heasley

1969 Chevelle SS 396

The '69 Chevelle SS 396 was merchandised in a new way. There was no separate SS 396 series this year. The Super Sport equipment package became the Z25 option. It was available on sport coupe and convertible models in two series—Chevelle 300 Deluxe and Malibu. That added up to four distinct SS 396 options.

Product-wise, Chevy made no basic change in the design or configuration of its mid-size muscle car. In other words, when a buyer checked off the Z25 package, he got a car with about the same characteristics and content as before (perhaps a bit less tinsel if it wasn't a Malibu).

■ *The rare 1969 Yenko Chevelles received the firm's performance treatment as well as distinct hood and side striping, hood graphics and even graphics in the seat backs.*

Jerry Heasley

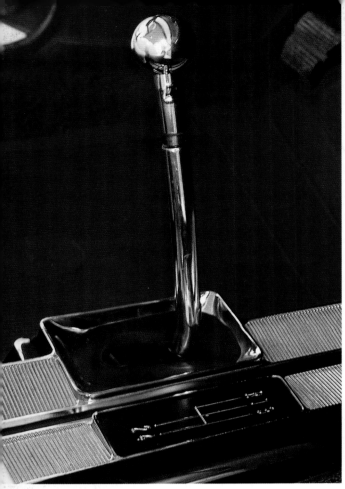

■ *From the beginning, fun and Chevelles went together. Introduced for the 1964 model year, the Chevelle Malibu SS included a floor-mounted console with a four-speed transmission option.* Jerry Heasley

■ *The specially prepared Yenko Chevelles circumvented the GM rule that mid-size cars should be produced with engines under 400 cubic inches. Yenko used the 427-cid V-8 in its Chevelles.* Jerry Heasley

■ *In the late 1960s, seeing the SS 396 badge on the front or back of a Chevelle meant the viewer was experiencing a special car from Chevrolet. Thousands of people were proud to own them.* Jerry Heasley

The Z25 package included the 396-cid/325-hp engine, dual exhausts with oval tailpipes and bright tips, a black-painted grille, bright wheel opening and roof drip moldings, a black-painted rear cove panel, Malibu-style rear quarter end caps, Malibu tail lights and tail light bezels, a twin power dome hood, special "SS 396" emblems on the grille (as well as front fenders and rear deck lid) and 14 x 7-inch Super Sport wheels with F70 x 14 white-letter tires.

The interior featured a black steering wheel and column, a steering wheel shroud with a black-accented center area and horn-blowing tab, an "SS" steering wheel emblem, an SS 396 nameplate on the instrument panel, a black-accented instrument panel and SS 396 emblems on the door sidewalls.

There were three 396 options. The mildest was the L34 with 350 hp, then came the 375-hp L78. A new possibility was the L78/L89, which was advertised at 375 hp, but actually produced more. It had special features like high-performance aluminum cylinder heads. A road test of the 1969 SS 396-375 showed a 0-to-60 time of 7.6 seconds and a 15.4-second quarter-mile.

Muscle Car

■ *The front of the 1969 Chevelle was artfully modified in 1969 with squared headlight housings, a one-bar trim piece in the grille and a blackened grille. It was good looking on this SS 396 model.*
Jerry Heasley

Since these were the wild and wooly days of musclecardom, there were car dealers throughout the country that specialized in selling muscle cars. Some had mechanics with a knack for making things go fast and some had clout with the factory. Fred Gibb in Illinois, Nickey Chevrolet in Chicago, Yenko Sports Cars in Canonsburg, Pennsylvania and Motion Performance in Baldwin, N.Y. were among the most famous high-performance dealers.

General Motors had a corporate rule that limited its mid-sized cars to engines with less than 400 cubic inches. Since they built most of their cars for weekend drag racers or professional drivers, the hot-car hawkers had a lot of demand for big-block engine swaps. This was expensive and inefficient. Some of these dealerships also sold a lot of regular cars and had clout with the factory.

Working in conjunction with Vince Piggins, Chevy's performance products manager, the dealers started ordering batches of cars with special equipment by utilizing GM's Central Office Production Order system. The COPO system was set up for special-order fleet vehicles like police cars and taxicabs. Fred Gibbs

■ *Many Chevelles wore a new mag-type wheel in 1969, a style that enhanced the beauty of these popular mid-sized Chevys, especially when paired with the period-popular red striped tires.*
Jerry Heasley

99

A memorable Chevelle SS look came in 1970 with refined styling, split horizontal grille and centered SS badge. Long black strips on the hood enhanced the performance look.
Jerry Heasley

was one of the first dealers to use the system to get special muscle cars built for drag racer Dickie Harrell.

The COPO cars were made in batches and there were equipment distinctions for each batch. For example, the cars built under COPO order number 9562AA would have a four-speed manual gearbox, while those produced under COPO order number 9562BA would have the M40 three-speed automatic.

Some of the COPO Chevelles were further modified by the specialty dealers. Others were not. As you can imagine, few of these cars were sold with exactly the same equipment. Most were one-of-a-kind items. They were very plain looking with little chrome and bottle cab hubcaps. They did not have SS identification features. Typical performance figures were under-14-seconds for the quarter-mile (at 101 mph). Experts say that production was somewhere north of 320 cars, with about 100 being Yenkos. The cars were made only in '69; the 400-cube rule was lifted in 1970.

1970 Chevelle SS 396/SS 454

For '70, Chevelles had a "meatier and mightier" look and new power plants to back up the image. Ads showed a hardtop moored down like a boat prepared to ride out a hurricane, but in truth the shackles were off, as "The General" dropped its 400-cube limit and stuffed a 454-cid/450-hp V-8 into the hottest SS model. *Super Stock* magazine said that driving it was "like being the guy in charge of triggering the atomic bomb tests."

The new body was more sculptured than ever before. A horizontally split grille with "blended" dual headlights carried an "SS" emblem smack dab in its center. Like the front, the rear was blunter. The overall styling theme was unchanged, but details like the tail lights, bumper and black-finished back panel were all completely restyled.

Although the 454 starred as "King Kong," the SS 396 played a supporting role as "Mighty Joe Young." Shortly after the assembly lines got it in gear, the bore size of this engine was increased from 4.094-inches to 4.125 inches. It doesn't take a genius to guess it was no longer a "396." Specifically, the upgrade increased displacement to 402 cubic inches. But, in spite of this change, Chevrolet continued to identify the engine as the "Turbo-Jet 396."

"'The General' droped its 400-cube limit and stuffed a 454-cid/450-hp V-8 V-8 into the hottest SS model."

—Super Stock Magazine

■ *The 1970 Chevelle SS 396 looked good at the lake or posed with just about any scenery, for that matter. Buyers could choose several versions of the SS 396, including 350- and 375-hp versions.* Phil Kunz

In addition to a base 350-hp engine (L34), the SS 396 package included chrome engine parts, power front disc brakes, fat dual exhausts with bright tips, a black-accented grille, wheel lip moldings, a black resilient rear bumper panel, a special domed hood, a heavy-duty suspension, special chassis features, SS emblems on the grille, fenders, rear bumper, steering wheel and door trim, 17 x 7-inch Rally rims and fat F70 x 14 raised-white-letter tires.

A 375-hp L78 version of the 396 was optional. It was installed in 2,144 cars. An L78/L89 V-8 with large-valve aluminum heads was also advertised at 375 hp, although that number was only used to placate insurance companies. Its real output was higher. This solid-lifter engine was only offered very early in the model year. Only 18 buyers ordered it. The L89 adds a lot to a car's value.

The '70 SS 396 was a snappy performer, but muscular newcomers with bigger V-8s were "eating its lunch" on the streets and drag strips. To keep the Chevelle in the race, Chevy product planners came up with a new big-block 454 V-8 for Chevelles. The SS 454 was the hottest of the red hot Super Sports.

The 454 was available in two formats. The 360-hp LS5 featured a 10.25:1 compression ratio and a 750-cfm Rochester Quadrajet carb. For a little bit extra, you could get the awesome 450-hp LS6 with its 11.25:1 compression ratio and a 780-cfm Holley four-barrel. The LS6 was a super-high-performance engine

■ *Just one look at this 1970 Chevelle SS convertible with the LS 6 option tells you it was ready to perform. This one looks even more menacing in black ragtop over black body paint.*
Jerry Heasley

featuring four-bolt mains, nodular iron bearing caps, heavy-duty con rods, big-diameter exhaust valves and a solid-lifter cam. An LS6 test car did 0 to 60 mph in 5.4 seconds and the standing-start quarter-mile in 13.81 seconds at 103.8 mph. Those numbers were racked up with a Turbo-Hydra-Matic transmission and a 3.77:1 rear axle. Three four-speed sticks were optional. Only 3,773 cars had a 454, and only a handful were LS6s.

■ *For Chevy lovers interested in ultimate performance, the LS6 option was offered for 1970 Chevelles with the SS 454 option. The \$263 package added a version of the big V-8 that was conservatively rated at 450 hp.* Jerry Heasley

1971 Chevelle SS 454

"There's still an SS 454," said Chevy's '71 sales brochure. "Any car that was named the best of its kind in *Car and Driver's* reader's choice (the 1970 Chevelle SS 454) is sure to stay around." While the name may have been the same, the car was starting to change—and not just in terms of cosmetics.

Now, buyers could order Super Sport equipment on any Malibu Sport Coupe or convertible as long as it had a 350-, 400- or 454-cid V-8. The $357 package included power front-disc/rear-drum brakes, a black grille, a hefty suspension, a power dome, hood lock pins, SS I.D., a remote-control sports mirror, the gray-finished Sport wheels, F60 x 14 white-letter tires, a black-accented steering column and a steering wheel with the SS nameplate.

■ *Despite pressures from insurance companies and pollution control laws, Chevrolet brought back the 454-cid V-8-powered Chevelle choice in 1971 with new styling from every angle.*   Jerry Heasley

Styling-wise, the '71 Chevelle had Monte Carlo-like single headlights and Camaro-style 15-inch Camaro Sport wheels. A new twin-level grille was divided by a bright horizontal bar. The front parking lights were moved from the bumper into the fender tips. This season, the SS badges on the body sides did not carry engine call-outs—unless the 454 V-8 (LS5) was ordered. Then, they said "SS 454." The rear no longer had a black insert panel. Instead of boxy tail lights, the '71 had two round tail lights on either side of the license plate indent. The rear SS badge was centered on the bumper above this indent.

To get an SS 454, you could order one of the two big-block engines listed in the catalog as an add-on option. However, it seems that only one of the engines was ever put in a production car. You can find magazine road tests of

■ *Here is a 1971 version of the 454 V-8 and labeled with 365 horsepower. The engine filled the Chevelle engine bay and used dual air intake passages. It was called the LS5 package.* Jerry Heasley

■ *The big power bulge of this 1971 Chevelle SS might mean a mild-mannered engine underneath, but the hood tie downs mean it's something powerful. In this case it's a 454 V-8.*   Jerry Heasley

the '71 Chevelle with a 325-nhp LS6 V-8, but all 14 cars fitted with the LS6 were pre-production or special units. The 285-nhp LS5 was the only 454 sold to the public. It came with either a four-speed manual gearbox or three-speed THM.

Chevrolet put together an estimated 80,000 cars that carried the 1971 SS option. Of those units, 19,292—nearly 25 percent—had the 454 V-8s. After testing the '71 and racing up a 13.77-second quarter-mile, *Car Craft* called the LS5 a "personal performance car." In movie terms, that meant that it was "Smokey and the Bandit" fast, but no "Bullit" catcher.

1972 Chevelle SS 454

By 1972, the end of the muscle car market was in sight. There were only a handful of big-block high-performance V-8s available in American iron and Chevy's 454-cid LS5 engine was the king.

There were very few differences between '72 Chevelles and the previous models. What stood out most were the single-unit front turn signals and side markers. In 1971, there had been multiple lenses "stacked" on one another, but this year there was a one-piece lens with horizontal lines molded on it. The headlights were now housed within the grille, instead of being separate from it. Another small change was the substitution of a body-colored Sport-style rearview mirror in place of a plated one.

The Super Sport package could be ordered for any Malibu sport coupe or convertible with a V-8, even the base 307. Since convertibles were V-8-only models, they didn't cost much more than an SS 307 sport coupe, in which a V-8 was an extra-cost item. Now, don't you wish you had coughed up the roughly $250 extra for a ragtop? It's rarer and would be worth a lot more today.

■ *The SS 454 Chevelle returned in 1972 with minor styling changes.* Phil Kunz

The RPO Z15 Super Sport package included power front disc–rear drum brakes, a black-finished grille, a special domed hood with locking pins, the left-hand remote-control Sport-style rearview mirror, "SS" emblems, a sport suspension, 15 x 7-inch wheels with bright lug nuts, special wheel center caps, wheel trim rings and F60-15 white-lettered tires. The package required a V-8 engine and an optional transmission. Transmission applications varied according to which engine the car had.

All 1972 engine outputs were expressed in net horsepower. Other engines available in '72 Chevelle Super Sports included 165- and 175-nhp versions of the 350-cid V-8, a 240-nhp version of the 400-cid big-block (not to be confused with the 400-cid small-block of course) and the LS5 with 270 nhp. The big engine cost $272 extra and came only in SS models. A heavy-duty battery ($15 extra) was required. Standard transmission with the 454 was a special four-on-the-floor manual. Turbo Hydra-Matic was optional.

■ *The SS 454 Chevelle returned in 1972 and carried a price tag of $3,809.* Jerry Heasley

Due to tightening emissions standards, California buyers could not order the 307, the 400 or the 454. The two 350s were the sole engines used on the West Coast. For the other 49 states, Chevrolet built 5,333 cars with the SS 454 setup.

As far as performance, the LS5 with automatic did the quarter-mile in 15.1 seconds at 93 mph, while the four-speed version ran the quarter in 14.76 seconds at 97.6 mph.

Those with hot shoes could tell the muscle car era was just about over, but the SS 454 was about as good as it got in '72.

1973 Chevelle SS 454

By 1973, the muscle car had its spinach taken away. The new model year brought the end of the line for the Chevelle Super Sport model. The Chevelle would remain available for a few more years—and even a 454 would be offered—but it was no longer a true high-performance engine and the car it went in was no longer a real muscle car. In fact, the SS package was now available for the Malibu station wagon, as well as for the "Colonnade Coupe." It was the first and only time that you could factory-order a station wagon with SS badges.

Completely redesigned, the '73 Chevelle featured General Motors' new Colonnade styling. Developed to satisfy new and more stringent federal rollover standards, this new type of construction featured a body with inner and outer shells, guard beams inside the doors and better-isolated fuel tanks. The windows and roof pillars had deep-cut, limousine-like character. The styling looked best on two-door hardtops. A variety of quarter window treatments were available, including opera windows and louvered vents.

General styling highlights of Chevrolet's new Chevelle included a cross-hatched grille with a "flat" look that continued beneath the single headlights. The tail lamps were circular units recessed into a back panel that was "veed" horizontally along its center line.

The Chevelle Malibu SS package was a $243 option this year. It included SS emblems for the grille, fenders and area above the rear bumper, accent striping on the lower body, color-keyed wheel cutouts and dual sport mirrors. Super Sports also featured heavy-duty front and rear stabilizers and a special instrument panel.

"Those with hot shoes could tell the muscle car era was just about over, but the SS 454 was about as good as it got in '72."

There was no way to produce a ragtop version of the Colonnade body, so the convertible model was dropped for '73. In reality, there was also no true hardtop or sport coupe. The Colonnade Coupe was a pillared coupe, but when the opera windows were ordered, it had a hardtop look. The Colonnade SS coupe listed for about $3,253, not including the big-block V-8. The price on the Chevelle SS station wagon, also without the 454, was about $3,318.

If you wanted an SS 454, you got a de-tuned version of the LS5 engine. It cost $235 extra. The 1972 version of the 454 continued with the 8.5:1 compression ratio and with a single Rochester 4MV carburetor. It was rated for 245 SAE nhp at 4000 rpm and 375 lbs.-ft. of torque at 2800 rpm. Standard transmission with the 454 was a close-ratio four-speed manual gearbox with floor-mounted gear shifter. Turbo Hydra-Matic was optional at $210 extra.

Chevrolet built 2,500 cars with the SS 454 setup for 1973. While they were not the hottest examples of the big-block Chevelle, they were different and rare and relatively few are seen today—especially the station wagons.

CHEVELLE YEAR-BY-YEAR SPEC'S

1964

Engine	Bore/Str.	Comp. Ratio	CID	BHP	WT.	W.B.	O.L.	Width	HT
Six	3.562 x 3.25	08.50	194	120 @ 4400	2,875	115.0	196.6	74.6	52.9
Six	3.875 x 3.25	08.50	230	150 @ 4400	—	115.0	196.6	74.6	52.9
V-8	3.875 x 3.00	09.25	283	195 @ 4800	3,020	115.0	196.6	74.6	52.9
V-8	3.875 x 3.00	09.25	283	220 @ 4800	—	115.0	196.6	74.6	52.9
V-8	4.00 x 3.25	10.50	327	250 @ 4400	—	115.0	196.6	74.6	52.9
V-8	4.00 x 3.25	10.50	327	300 @ 5000	—	115.0	196.6	74.6	52.9

1965

Engine	Bore/Str.	Comp. Ratio	CID	BHP	WT.	W.B.	O.L.	Width	HT
Six	3.562 x 3.25	08.50	194	120 @ 4400	2,980	115.0	196.6	74.6	52.8
Six	3.875 x 3.25	08.50	230	140 @ 4400	—	115.0	196.6	74.6	52.8
V-8	3.875 x 3.00	09.25	283	195 @ 4800	3,115	115.0	196.6	74.6	52.8
V-8	3.875 x 3.00	09.25	283	220 @ 4800	—	115.0	196.6	74.6	52.8
V-8	4.00 x 3.25	10.50	327	250 @ 4800	—	115.0	196.6	74.6	52.8
V-8	4.00 x 3.25	10.50	327	300 @ 5000	—	115.0	196.6	74.6	52.8
V-8	4.00 x 3.25	11.00	327	350 @ 6000	—	115.0	196.6	74.6	52.8
V-8	4.09 x 3.76	11.00	396	375 @ 5600	—	115.0	196.6	74.6	52.8

1966

Engine	Bore/Str.	Comp. Ratio	CID	BHP	WT.	W.B.	O.L.	Width	HT
V-8	4.09 x 3.76	10.25	396	325 @ 4800	3,375	115.0	197.0	75.0	52.9
V-8	4.09 x 3.76	10.25	396	360 @ 5200	—	115.0	197.0	75.0	52.9
V-8	4.09 x 3.76	11.00	396	375 @ 5600	—	115.0	197.0	75.0	52.9

1967

Engine	Bore/Str.	Comp. Ratio	CID	BHP	WT.	W.B.	O.L.	Width	HT
V-8	4.09 x 3.76	10.25	396	325 @ 4800	3,415	115.0	197.0	75.0	52.9
V-8	4.09 x 3.76	10.25	396	350 @ 5200	—	115.0	197.0	75.0	52.9
V-8	4.09 x 3.76	11.00	396	375 @ 5600	—	115.0	197.0	75.0	52.9

1968

Engine	Bore/Str.	Comp. Ratio	CID	BHP	WT.	W.B.	O.L.	Width	HT
V-8	4.09 x 3.76	10.25	396	325 @ 4800	3,475	112.0	197.1	75.7	52.7
V-8	4.09 x 3.76	10.25	396	350 @ 5200	—	112.0	197.1	75.7	52.7
V-8	4.09 x 3.76	11.00	396	375 @ 5600	—	112.0	197.1	75.7	52.7
V-8	4.09 x 3.76 (L89)	11.00	396	375 @ 5600	—	112.0	197.1	75.7	52.7

1969

Engine	Bore/Str.	Comp. Ratio	CID	BHP	WT.	W.B.	O.L.	Width	HT
SS 396									
V-8	4.09 x 3.76	10.25	396	325 @ 4800	3,475	112.0	197.0	75.7	52.7
V-8	4.09 x 3.76	10.25	396	350 @ 5200	—	112.0	197.0	75.7	52.7
V-8	4.09 x 3.76	11.00	396	375 @ 5600	—	112.0	197.0	75.7	52.7
V-8	4.09 x 3.76 (L89)	11.00	396	375 @ 5600	—	112.0	197.0	75.7	52.7
SS 427 (COPO)									
V-8 (*)	4.25 x 3.76 (L72)	10.25	427	390 @ 4800	—	112.0	197.0	75.7	52.7

(*) Drag racing engine only.

1970

Engine	Bore/Str.	Comp. Ratio	CID	BHP	WT.	W.B.	O.L.	Width	HT
SS 396									
V-8	4.13 x 3.76	10.25	396 (402)	350 @ 5200	—	112.0	197.2	75.4	52.6
V-8	4.13 x 3.76	11.00	396 (402)	375 @ 5600	—	112.0	197.2	75.4	52.6
V-8	4.13 x 3.76 (L78/L89)	11.00	396 (402)	375 @ 5600	—	112.0	197.2	75.4	52.6
SS 454									
V-8	4.25 x 4.00	10.25	454	360 @ 4400	—	112.0	197.2	75.4	52.6
V-8	4.25 x 4.00	11.25	454	450 @ 5600	—	112.0	197.2	75.4	52.6

Note: The increase to 402 cid occurred late in 1969, but the SS 396 designation continued to be used.

1971

Engine	Bore/Str.	Comp. Ratio	CID	BHP	WT.	W.B.	O.L.	Width	HT
SS									
V-8	3.88 x 3.25	08.50	307	140 @ 4400	—	112.0	197.5	75.4	52.7
V-8	4.00 x 3.48	08.50	350	245 @ 4800	—	112.0	197.5	75.4	52.7
V-8	4.00 x 3.48	08.50	350	270 @ 4800	—	112.0	197.5	75.4	52.7
V-8	4.13 x 3.76	08.50	402	260 @ 4400	—	112.0	197.5	75.4	52.7
SS 454									
V-8	4.25 x 4.00	08.50	454	365 @ 4800	—	112.0	197.5	75.4	52.7
V-8	4.25 x 4.00	09.00	454	425 @ 5600	—	112.0	197.5	75.4	52.7

1972

Engine	Bore/Str.	Comp. Ratio	CID	BHP	WT.	W.B.	O.L.	Width	HT
SS									
V-8	3.88 x 3.25	08.50	307	130 @ 4000	3,407	112.0	197.5	75.4	52.7
V-8	4.00 x 3.48	08.50	350	165 @ 4000	—	112.0	197.5	75.4	52.7
V-8	4.00 x 3.48	08.50	350	175 @ 4000	—	112.0	197.5	75.4	52.7
V-8	4.13 x 3.76	08.50	402	240 @ 4400	—	112.0	197.5	75.4	52.7
SS 454									
V-8	4.25 x 4.00	08.50	454	270 @ 4000	—	112.0	197.5	75.4	52.7

Note: Net horsepower ratings.

1973

Engine	Bore/Str.	Comp. Ratio	CID	BHP	WT.	W.B.	O.L.	Width	HT
SS									
V-8	3.88 x 3.25	08.50	307	115 @ 4000	—	112.0	202.9	76.6	53.1
V-8	4.00 x 3.48	08.50	350	145 @ 4000	—	112.0	202.9	76.6	53.1
V-8	4.00 x 3.48	08.50	350	175 @ 4000	—	112.0	202.9	76.6	53.1
SS 454									
V-8	4.25 x 4.00	08.50	454	245 @ 4000	—	112.0	202.9	76.6	53.1

Note: Net horsepower ratings.

■ *There was another choice when the 1967 Chevelle SS 396 was considered. Sun lovers liked all the advantages plus the fun of top-down driving. It's an inviting picture on a sunny day.*   Jerry Heasley

PRODUCTION STATISTICS AND BREAKOUTS

1964 CHEVELLE MALIBU SS

Year	Body Code	Body Type	Engine Type	MSP Price	Model Yr. Prod.
SIX-CYLINDER					
64	SS37	2HT	I6	$2,538	8,224
64	SS67	2CV	I6	$2,749	1,551
V-8					
64	SS37	2HT	V-8	$2,646	57,445
64	SS67	2CV	V-8	$2,857	9,640
TOTAL					**76,860**

1965 CHEVELLE SS 396 (Z16)

Year	Body Code	Body Type	Engine Type	MSP Price	Model Yr. Prod.
396-CID V-8					
65	SS37	2HT	V-8	$2,647	200
65	SS67	2CV	V-8	—	1
TOTAL					**201**

1966 CHEVELLE SS 396

Year	Body Code	Body Type	Engine Type	MSP Price	Model Yr. Prod.
396-CID V-8					
66	SS17	2HT	V-8	$2,776	66,843
66	SS67	2CV	V-8	$2,984	5,429
TOTAL					**72,272**

1967 CHEVELLE SS 396

Year	Body Code	Body Type	Engine Type	MSP Price	Model Yr. Prod.
396-CID V-8					
67	SS17	2HT	V-8	$2,825	59,685
67	SS67	2CV	V-8	$3,033	3,321
TOTAL					**63,006**

1968 CHEVELLE SS 396

Year	Body Code	Body Type	Engine Type	MSP Price	Model Yr. Prod.
396-CID V-8					
68	SS37	2HT	V-8	$2,899	55,309
68	SS67	2CV	V-8	$3,102	2,286
TOTAL					**57,595**

1969 CHEVELLE SS 396

Year	Body Code	Body Type	Engine Type	MSP Price	Model Yr. Prod.
CHEVELLE DELUXE (WITH Z25)					
69	SS37	2HT	V-8	$2,743	—
69	SS11	2CP	V-8	$2,680	—
CHEVELLE MALIBU (WITH Z25)					
69	SS37	2HT	V-8	$2,822	—
69	SS67	2CV	V-8	$3,021	—
TOTAL					**86,307**

1970 CHEVELLE SS 396/SS454

Year	Body Code	Body Type	Engine Type	MSP Price	Model Yr. Prod.
CHEVELLE MALIBU (WITH Z25) SS 396					
70	SS37	2HT	V-8	$3,439	—
70	SS67	2CV	V-8	$3,639	—
TOTAL					**49,826**
CHEVELLE MALIBU (WITH Z15) SS 454					
70	SS37	2HT	V-8	$3,497	—
70	SS67	2CV	V-8	$3,697	—
TOTAL					**3,773**

1971 CHEVELLE SS454

Year	Body Code	Body Type	Engine Type	MSP Price	Model Yr. Prod.
MALIBU SS (WITH Z15) SS 454					
71	SS37	2HT	V-8	$3,443	—
71	SS67	2CV	V-8	$3,645	—
TOTAL					**19,992**

1972 CHEVELLE SS454

Year	Body Code	Body Type	Engine Type	MSP Price	Model Yr. Prod.
MALIBU SS (WITH Z15) SS 454					
72	SS37	2HT	V-8	$3,545	—
72	SS67	2CV	V-8	$3,809	—
TOTAL					**5,333**

1973 CHEVELLE SS

Year	Body Code	Body Type	Engine Type	MSP Price	Model Yr. Prod.
MALIBU SS (WITH Z15) SS 454					
73	SS37	2CC	V-8	$3,103	—
73	SS35	2WG	V-8	$3,533	—
TOTAL					**28,647**

Note: In 1973 the 454-cid V-8 was a $273 option.

PRICE GUIDE

Vehicle Condition Scale

6 — Parts car:
May or may not be running, but is weathered, wrecked and/or stripped to the point of being useful primarily for parts.

5 — Restorable:
Needs complete restoration of body, chassis and interior. May or may not be running, but isn't weathered, wrecked or stripped to the point of being useful only for parts.

4 — Good:
A driveable vehicle needing no or only minor work to be functional. Also, a deteriorated restoration or a very poor amateur restoration. All components may need restoration to be "excellent," but the car is mostly useable "as is."

3 — Very Good:
Complete operable original or older restoration. Also, a very good amateur restoration, all presentable and serviceable inside and out. Plus, a combination of well-done restoration and good operable components or a partially restored car with all parts necessary to compete and/or valuable NOS parts.

2 — Fine:
Well-restored or a combination of superior restoration and excellent original parts. Also, extremely well-maintained original vehicle showing minimal wear.

1 — Excellent:
Restored to current maximum professional standards of quality in every area, or perfect original with components operating and apearing as new. A 95-plus point show car that is not driven.

1964 Chevelle

	6	5	4	3	2	1
2d Sed	504	1,512	2,520	5,670	8,820	12,600
4d Sed	500	1,500	2,500	5,630	8,750	12,500
2d Sta Wag	656	1,968	3,280	7,380	11,480	16,400
4d Sta Wag	648	1,944	3,240	7,290	11,340	16,200

1965 Chevelle

	6	5	4	3	2	1
2d Sed	500	1,500	2,500	5,630	8,750	12,500
4d Sed	496	1,488	2,480	5,580	8,680	12,400
2d Sta Wag	660	1,980	3,300	7,430	11,550	16,500
4d Sta Wag	660	1,980	3,300	7,430	11,550	16,500

1966 Chevelle

	6	5	4	3	2	1
2d Sed	500	1,500	2,500	5,630	8,750	12,500
4d Sed	496	1,488	2,480	5,580	8,680	12,400
4d Sta Wag	508	1,524	2,540	5,720	8,890	12,700

1967 Chevelle Super Sport 396

	6	5	4	3	2	1
2d HT	1,480	4,440	7,400	16,650	25,900	37,000
2d Conv	1,800	5,400	9,000	20,250	31,500	45,000

NOTE: Add 20 percent for 396 cid, 350 hp. Add 30 percent for 396 cid, 375 hp.

1968 Chevelle SS 396

	6	5	4	3	2	1
2d HT	1,280	3,840	6,400	14,400	22,400	32,000
2d Conv	1,560	4,680	7,800	17,550	27,300	39,000

1969 Chevelle Malibu SS 396

	6	5	4	3	2	1
2d Cpe	1,000	3,000	5,000	10,000	17,500	25,000
2d Conv	1,250	3,700	6,200	12,400	21,700	31,000

NOTE: Add 60 percent for Yenko hardtop.

1970 Chevelle Malibu SS 396

	6	5	4	3	2	1
2d HT	1,200	3,600	6,000	13,500	21,000	30,000
2d Conv	1,400	4,200	7,000	15,750	24,500	35,000

1970 Chevelle Malibu SS 454

	6	5	4	3	2	1
2d HT	1,400	4,200	7,000	15,750	24,500	35,000
2d Conv	1,600	4,800	8,000	18,000	28,000	40,000

NOTE: Add 35 percent for 396 cid, 375 hp. Add 100 percent for LS6 engine option.

1971 Chevelle Malibu SS

	6	5	4	3	2	1
2d HT	1,000	3,000	5,000	11,250	17,500	25,000
2d Conv	1,200	3,600	6,000	13,500	21,000	30,000

1971 Chevelle Malibu SS-454

	6	5	4	3	2	1
2d HT	1,200	3,600	6,000	13,500	21,000	30,000
2d Conv	1,400	4,200	7,000	15,750	24,500	35,000

1972 Chevelle Malibu SS

	6	5	4	3	2	1
2d HT	1,000	3,000	5,000	11,250	17,500	25,000
2d Conv	1,200	3,600	6,000	13,500	21,000	30,000

1972 Chevelle Malibu SS-454

	6	5	4	3	2	1
2d HT	1,200	3,600	6,000	13,500	21,000	30,000
2d Conv	1,400	4,200	7,000	15,750	24,500	35,000

1973 Chevelle Malibu V8

	6	5	4	3	2	1
2d Cpe	344	1,032	1,720	3,870	6,020	8,600
4d Sed	340	1,020	1,700	3,830	5,950	8,500

Chevelle 1964-1973

Fairlane

1962

The Fairlane—named after Henry Ford's Michigan estate—was introduced as a top-of-the-line full-sized Ford in 1955. The model name was used by Ford Motor Company from 1955 through 1970. In 1968, some fancy or sporty editions of the Fairlane were called Fairlane Torinos or Fairlane Torino GTs. The following year the same cars were plain Torinos or Torino GTs—the Fairlane name no longer being used for these models. In 1970, Ford limited use of the Fairlane name to the three-car Fairlane 500 series at the lower end of the pricing spectrum. All other mid-sized Ford were then called Torinos.

The fancier '70 Torinos were Broughams; the sportier versions were Torino GTs. The name Cobra was used on the muscle cars, which were officially neither Fairlanes or Torinos, although they all shared the same platform. Torino was used until 1976, but muscular versions were long gone by that time—probably with the last Sportsroof model of 1973.

■ *The 1964 Ford Thunderbolt was lightened with fiberglass fenders and modified to accept the 427-cid Ford V-8. A straight-ahead screamer, it put Ford out front in drag racing competition.* Phil Kunz

Fairlane Timeline

1962 1963 1964 1966 1968 1969 1970 1971 1972

1962: The all-new Fairlane is introduced with Ford's first small-block V-8 under the hood.

1963: The 289-cid V-8 is introduced. It is a bored-out version of the 260 with 271 hp.

1964: Fairlane "Thunderbolt" drag racing cars are unveiled. The 111 no-frills cars feature 427-cid motors and soon become dominant racers.

1966: Redesign gives Fairlane new body lines and slightly longer, lower appearance.

1966: GT and GTA packages added to Fairlane lineup, along with a convertible.

1968: The Fairlane is redesigned again and becomes closer in looks and size to a full-size car.

1968: The sporty and sleek Torino is born.

1968: GT series becomes part of the Torino line.

1969: Torino Cobra and Talladega arrive.

1970: Redesign adds one inch to the wheelbase and six inches to the overall length of the Fairlane.

1971: Fairlane nameplate disappears, but Torino series continues.

1972: The final Torino is an even bigger, heavier car. The Cobra and convertible versions are discontinued.

1962 1963 1964 1966 1968 1969 1970 1971 1972

Early Fairlanes filled a range of purposes from family car to a kind of sports-personal car with a retractable steel convertible top. Early Fairlane engine options spanned the gamut from a 223-cid six up to the hot 352-cid "Thunderbird V-8 with 300 hp. Other V-8s used in Fairlanes included the 292 and the 332. Performance could be snappy or even "blistering' in a few cases, although these cars did not have the small-body/big-engine "muscle car" thing going for them. The hot ones were built for the highway, not the drag strip.

Starting in 1960, Fairlanes began to shrink a bit. A modest restyling was done in 1961, but the '62 edition was an all-new car and became the Big Three's first "mid-size" car. Rambler had a model of about the same size, but GM and Chrysler did not. Sporty new Fairlane body styles also arrived in '62, along with one of Ford's first small-block V-8s—the 221. Promoted as "the world's first economy eight," the 221 became the 260. Still later, the 260 evolved into the 289, which gained fame in Shelby Cobras and Ford Mustangs.

The new Fairlane filled a gap in the market between the compact Falcon and the full-sized Galaxie. The downsized Fairlane proved to be one of Ford's "Better Ideas" and sold 297,116 units in its first year. Some 20 percent of all '62 Fords were Fairlanes.

Like the Falcon that it was based on, the Fairlane was a unit-body car with no ladder frame under it. The front suspension was mounted on top of the upper control arms and limited space in the engine compartment. Big-block V-8s couldn't be shoehorned into the cars without major revisions to front suspension geometry.

"For '63, the hot number was a pre-Mustang 'K-Code' hi-po version of the Z89 with a four-barrel carb."

1963

The '63 Fairlane got a "facial." A new Galaxie-style grille required the reworking of the front-end sheet metal. No parts interchanged between '62 and '63 models, though you could swap complete noses if you wanted to. New trim pieces were used at the rear end, but nothing changed drastically there.

Under the hood, Ford stuffed in more ponies. You could still get a six, a 221-cid/145-hp V-8 and a 260-cid/164-hp V-8. The hot number was a pre-Mustang "K-Code" high-performance version of the 289 with a four-barrel carburetor. It ran a 10.5:1 compression ratio and generated 271 hp at 6000 rpm.

■ *The 1964 Fairlane 500 sport coupe was a wolf dressed in Ford finery. Underneath, it was a rugged performer worthy of the "64HIPO" license. It was all "high performance."* Jerry Heasley

1964

Ford shaved the fins off the '64 Fairlane's butt end and did a bunch of sheet metal tailoring to give it a "Big Ford" look. Both the front and rear suspensions were reworked to provide a "more silky ride" and enlarge the underhood room. Fordomatic and Cruise-O-Matic could be ordered, along with a four-speed manual gearbox with a floor-mounted "stirrer." Leather-like vinyl interiors added to the sporty image of some models.

Along with new styling, the factory-edition '64 Ford Fairlane again offered the K-code 289. This hi-po small-block V-8 was aimed at muscle car afficiandos. As in late-'63 you got a 10.5:1 compression ratio and 271 ponies at 6000 rpm with a single Holley four-barrel carb.

With an active factory-sponsored drag racing program bringing Ford headlines and notoriety, the new '64 Fairlane body was used to build "Thunderbolt" drag cars. FoMoCo stuffed its 427 high-riser V-8 into the mid-size Fairlane to create these just-for-racing models. Only 54 of the rare birds were produced. They have become legendary in racing history. In May 1964, *Car Life*

■ *The 1964 Fairlane 500 was powered by the High Performance Challenger 289 engine. It produced 271 horsepower with four-barrel carburetion. Many just called it the "Hi-Po V-8."* Jerry Heasley

■ *Inside the 1964 Fairlane 500 was a state-of-the-art interior for the times with round gauges, a floor-mounted four-speed shifter, console and bucket seats. The tach was an add-on.* Jerry Heasley

magazine's Allen Hunt said of the T-Bolt, "Obviously it's a racing car … and one calculated to put Ford right back in the front row on the drag strips this summer."

The Thunderbolts had fiberglass fenders, teardrop-shaped hood blisters, Plexiglas windows, lightweight bucket seats, a cold-air induction system, 8000 rpm Rotunda tachometers, modified front suspensions (to accommodate a 427), a long list of equipment deletions and many special competition equipment features. The "425-hp" big-block V-8 actually cranked about 500 hp. It was linked to a beefed-up Lincoln automatic or a Borg-Warner T-10 four-speed manual transmission.

The 1964 Fairlane Special Performance drag vehicles soon adopted their T-Bird-like name and were often called "T-Bolts." Demand was strong enough to prompt the ordering of a second batch of 54 all-white cars. Racing driver Gas Ronda dominated the National Hot Rod Association's 1964 World Championships. He racked up 190 points by running his T-Bolt through the quarter-mile in 11.6 seconds at 124 mph.

Ford records show that the first 11 T-Bolts left the factory painted maroon

■ *The 1966 GTA two-door hardtop version of the Fairlane had faux rocker moldings on the hood, but real power inside with a 335-hp/390-cid V-8. It covered the 0-to-60 sprint in just 6.8 seconds.*
Jerry Heasley

■ *There was plenty of chrome under the hood of the 1966 Fairlane GTA, including the rocker covers, oil filler, air cleaner and more. Even the dipstick sparkled with its chrome coat.*
Jerry Heasley

and 10 of them had four-speed transmissions. One hundred additional cars were produced and painted white. Eighty-nine of them had four-speed gearboxes. At least one 1965 Thunderbolt-style car was raced by Darrell Droke.

The Mustang soon took over as Ford's best offering for drag-car enthusiasts and the T-Bolt's brief existence ended at that point.

1965

1965 was the last year for the first-generation Fairlane. Things up front were revised again, but the changes were not enough to make an old design look new. The car gained a half inch of wheelbase and was a bit longer, too. A 200-cid "Big Six" became the base engine. The Challenger 289-cid V-8 was offered in three states of tune with 200-, 225- and 271-hp options.

Standard equipment featured low-profile tires. As the automotive safety crusade got into first gear, Ford introduced Safety-Yoke door latches and made front seat belts standard equipment.

1966

To be a youth-market car, the Fairlane had to look young, so a new body bowed in '66. Though not as big as full-size Fords of the era, the Fairlane was larger than its '62-'65 Gen I counterparts. Most importantly, it had room under the hood to accommodate big-block V-8 engines. New, GTO-like dual stacked

■ *Those who wanted to drop the top in good weather could choose the convertible version of the 1966 Fairlane GTA. Its great looks were enhanced by sporty chrome wheels.* Jerry Heasley

headlights caught on with buyers as soon as the cars hit the showrooms. A long list of options and performance goodies included dual-quad carburetion, four-speeds, bucket seats, a center console and much more.

A ragtop rejoined the Fairlane series. GT, GTA, 500XL and 500 trim levels were offered. The Fairlane GT came with a standard 390-cid/315-hp V-8, "GT" badges, a special hood, stripes, engine dress-up parts, a heavy-duty suspension, front disc brakes, bucket seats, a center console and a sport steering wheel. The four-barrel 390 featured a hot cam and special manifolds.

"GTA" designated a GT with an automatic transmission. It included a 335-hp version of the 390-cid V-8, chrome-plated parts (rocker covers, oil filter cap, radiator cap, air cleaner cover and dip stick), a high-lift cam, a bigger carb and the shift-like-a-stick SportShift automatic.

The GT/GTA models were the first production Fairlanes able to fit big-block V-8s. They served as Ford's factory hot rods and competed head to head with the GTO. One Fairlane advertisement was titled "How to cook a tiger!" The GTA two-door hardtop with the 390-cid/335-hp V-8 carried only about 10.5 lbs. per horsepower. It could move from 0 to 60 mph in 6.8 seconds and did the quarter-mile in 15.2 seconds.

A limited number of Fairlanes were sold with "side-oiler" 427-cid wedge engines. The 427 Fairlane was the product of corporate thinking—an attempt to salvage some commercial benefit from the 1963 Thunderbolt drag-racing program. While the T-Bolts had been built for racing only, the later big-block

■ *In 1967, some might have looked past this understated Fairlane 500, until the light turned green and its 427-cid V-8 kicked out 410 horsepower. A 425-hp version also was available.* Phil Kunz

Fairlanes were meant to excite buyers seeking the ultimate in street performance machines. Some of these cars even hit the NASCAR ovals. The 427-powered Fairlanes were characterized by a big air scoop that gulped cold air at the front of the hood. Only about 60 Fairlanes with 427s were produced.

Hot Rod's Eric Dahlquist pointed out that Charlie Gray of Ford's Performance Division and Bill Hollbrook of the company's Performance & Economy Section had helped to develop the 427 Fairlane as part of the company's "Total Performance" program. The cars also featured NASCAR-style hood locking pins, chrome engine parts, 11.2-inch diameter disc brakes, a 2 1/4-inch diameter exhaust system, a heavy-duty suspension and a tachometer.

Hot Rod did not do a full road test of the 1966 Fairlane 427, but reported some figures quoted by "some of the mechanics on the project" that indicated quarter-mile runs in 14.5 to 14.6 seconds at 100 mph. Later, on drag strips with some tuning and racing slicks, the cars were found capable of doing the distance in just under 13 seconds at nearly 114 mph.

In drag racing, the Fairlane 427s were so dominant that the rules were soon changed and they wound up in F/SX class, even though they were technically factory production models. In stock car racing, the medium-riser 427s were deemed legal and gave Ford a winning advantage over single four-barrel Mopars. (Dual quad Hemis were not sanctioned to compete.)

"In drag racing, the Fairlane 427s were so dominant that the rules were soon changed ..."

1967

Why change a good thing? That was Ford's philosophy in 1967. The Fairlane got revised body side trim, new emblems and new interior patterns. The blacked-out GT grille was a single aluminum stamping with an aggressive-looking, deeply-recessed design. Vertically-stacked dual headlights made a return appearance.

The hot GTs now wore side stripes just above the rocker panels that varied in width from a narrow to wide to narrow. Power front disc brakes became standard on GTs and optional on other models. Other equipment features included wide-striped wide-oval tires and a dual "power dome" hood (the hood "blisters" were non-functional in terms of air induction, but incorporated integral turn signals). Deluxe full wheel covers, a left-hand remote-control rearview mirror and deluxe seat belts were other GT items.

■ *The 428 logo was a new addition to Ford Fairlane fenders in the 1969 model year. Ford called it the Cobra-Jet and it came in 335-hp and 360-hp versions* Mike Mueller

Standard engine in GTs was the 289. A couple of 390s were optional To get the 320-hp version with a single four-barrel carburetor you were required to order an extra-cost transmission (heavy-duty three-speed manual, four-speed manual or Sport Shift Cruise-O-Matic). When you ordered the automatic, the car was a GTA. A heavy-duty suspension was standard in cars with the 390-cid V-8.

A 289-equipped Fairlane hardtop could go from 0 to 60 mph in 10.6 seconds and do the quarter-mile in 18 seconds at 79 mph. The 390-cid/320-hp version required 8.4 seconds to reach 60 mph and did the quarter-mile in 16.2 seconds at 89 mph.

If you wanted your Fairlane to go even faster, your FoMoCo dealer had the hardware you need to build an awesome street racer or "weekend warrior." Ford ads showed a Fairlane racing car and said, "The 427 Fairlane is also available without numbers."

Amazingly, the fire-snorting 427-cid "side-oiler" was on the factory options list for $975.09. And the milder (yes, "milder") 410-hp single-four-barrel-carburetor version of the 427 was not the sole selection. Also offered was the hairier 425-hp version that carried two four-barrel Holley carburetors.

Both 427s included a transistorized ignition system, a heavy-duty battery, a heavy-duty suspension, Ford's extra-cooling package and a four-speed manual stirrer. Also mandatory (at extra cost) were a minimum of 8.15 x 15 four-ply-rated black nylon tires.

Race versions of the 427 were offered with a dual-quad carburetor setup that gave an extra 30 hp. A tunnel-port kit came as an over-the-counter Ford dealer option. You got a tunnel-port intake on and special cylinder heads.

The 427-powered Fairlanes dominated early-in-the-year NASCAR races before Chrysler complained. The sanctioning rules were then changed to handicap Fairlanes. The National Hot Rod Association placed Fairlane 427s in SS/B class to keep them from sweeping the field in drag racing. These cars were one of the purest expressions of the term "factory hot rod."

1968

The 1968 Fairlanes featured a completely new body style. Some fancy or sporty editions of the Fairlane were called Fairlane Torinos or Fairlane Torino GTs. Fairlane Torinos included six-cylinder and V-8 coupes, four-door sedans and station wagons. Fairlane Torino GTs were V-8 only hardtops and convertibles. The hardtop models came in formal and fastback styles. The fastback was the true "image car" for the muscle car set. Dubbed the "SportsRoof" by Ford, this car had lots of buyer appeal in its era.

Fairlane standard equipment included the basic safety equipment, a 200-cid six or a 302-cid V-8 and 7.35-14 tires. The standard Fairlane Torino models (coupe, sedan or wagon) added wheel covers and an electric clock. The sporty Fairlane Torino GT included all this plus a vinyl bench seat, a GT handling suspension, argent silver styled wheels with chrome trim rings, F70 x 14 wide oval tires, GT body stripes, a gray GT grille, GT nameplates and a 302-cid/210-hp V-8. Power brakes were required if the 390 V-8 was added.

Real muscle car lovers were probably more interested in getting a Torino GT with a 427-cid/390-hp V-8, which was a $623 option for all Fairlane two-door

■ *This 1968 Fairlane Torino GT ragtop has a 390-cid V-8 as its power choice. It was an optional engine that could produce 325 horses. All that and stylish steel wheels with raised-letter tires.* Mike Mueller

■ *In 1968, Ford Torino GT buyers could circle the new 428-cid Cobra-Jet engine option as their power source under the hood. It produced 335-hp and replaced the 427-cid V-8.*
Mike Mueller

■ *Headlights on, this 1968 Torino GT two-door hardtop with fastback styling seems ready for a twilight drive. These mid-size Fords continue to turn heads just as they did in 1968.*
Mike Mueller

hardtops. *Motor Trend* (December 1967) tested a 390-powered Fairlane Torino GT SportsRoof and reported 7.2 seconds for 0 to 60 mph and 15.1 seconds at 91 mph for the quarter-mile. "The new breed of super car from Ford is a full step ahead of its '67 counterpart," the magazine concluded.

During the '68 model year, the 427 option was replaced by a new 428 Cobra-Jet engine. This CJ-428 V-8 was basically the 1966 Ford "FE" big block fitted with 427-type cylinder heads. The base Q-code edition with 10.7:1 compression heads and a single Holley four-barrel produced 335 hp at 5600 rpm. The R-code Super Cobra-Jet (SCJ) version had a 10.5:1 compression ratio, a four-barrel with ram-air induction and advertised 360 hp at 5400 rpm.

The factory grossly underrated the power of the Cobra-Jet V-8 in the mid-sized cars to give them an advantage in drag racing classifications. Later, it was revealed that the CJ-428 produced something like 410 hp. No wonder CJ-428 Fairlane Torinos could blast from 0 to 60 mph in just over 6 seconds and do the quarter-mile in 14.5 seconds.

1969

Minor grille and trim changes set '69 Fairlanes and Torinos apart from previous editions. The offerings were about the same, with a few important changes in muscle car models. The ex-"Fairlane Torino" models were now just Torinos. GTs had sexier body styles and a 302-cid V-8 as the base engine. The big news was the new Cobra line and a model-option called Talladega,

"If the Cobra was Ford's Road Runner, then the Torino Talladega was its Superbird."

■ *Midway through the 1969 model year, Ford introduced the Torino Talladega GT, named after the Alabama NASCAR track. Its grille was a race-inspired alteration to enhance slipstreaming.*

Jerry Heasley

Plymouth invented the "value muscle car" with its Road Runner. Pontiac cloned the concept with its '69 GTO Judge. Ford then jumped in with the Torino Cobra. Contrary to what some people think, it wasn't a "cheap" car; it was Ford's priciest intermediate, but you got a bunch of hi-po hardware for the money.

The Torino Cobra came in notchback and fastback styles with the 428-CJ engine standard. Also standard was a four-speed manual gearbox, a heavy-duty suspension and cartoon decals of a coiled-snake Cobra that looked hungry enough to snake bite a magistrate or eat a speeding bird. The 428 simply had more cubes than the engines in the "double-P" competition.

The emphasis was on performance. The base-engined Cobra came with 10.6:1 heads, a four-speed manual gearbox, a competition suspension, wide-oval black sidewall tires and 6-inch-wide wheels with hubcaps. Optional was the 428-CJ "Ram Air" V-8, which also carried a 335-hp rating, but achieved it at a higher 5600 rpm peak. The Ram Air engine featured a functional hood scoop. This setup was $133 on the Cobra, but cost $421 when ordered for other "Fairlane" models, including Torino GTs. You could get a Cobra with a 351-cid/290-hp V-8 if you wanted, but few people ordered this combination.

"Torque gives rubber big bite for fast acceleration," *Motor Trend* said to sum up the Cobra. "Four speed helps and Ford has many hop up parts for the 428." If you did not like shifting, a Select Shift automatic was optional.

■ Some might have overlooked this Ford until they noticed the Cobra symbol snaking its way up the fender and the tell-tale hood blister. This was the 1969 Torino GT Cobra notchback. Jerry Heasley

Motor Trend road tested a Ram-Air Cobra. The magazine charted 0-to-60 performance at 6.3 seconds and the quarter-mile at 14.5 seconds and 100 mph. Ford had many hop-up parts for the 428. They included special cams, special cylinder heads, an aluminum intake, "eight-barrel" induction, flat-top pistons, a cast crankshaft, a dual-point distributor and a heavy-duty oil pump.

If the Cobra was Ford's Road Runner, then the Torino Talladega was its Superbird. These fastbacks evolved from the "aerodynamic wars" that took place on NASCAR superspeedways in 1969 and 1970. To make them "stock" cars legal for racing in '69, the automakers had to build at least 500 for public sale. That minimum production level was raised to one car per dealer for 1970. Ford's hopes for racing victories rode on the sloped-nosed Talladega.

Ford called its fastback Torinos "SportsRoof" models. The Talladega model was one of them. Its name came from a new 2.66-mile NASCAR superspeedway in Alabama. The Talladega had an extended, sloped nose and a flush radiator grille. A revised Torino rear bumper was used in front and the rocker panels were reworked a bit. The Talladega was nearly 6 inches longer and 1 inch lower than a stock Torino SportsRoof. The race teams ran highly modified cars. The showroom versions were look-alike machines.

The production version used the 335-hp CJ-428 V-8, which was pretty potent, but came only with a C-6 Cruise-O-Matic automatic transmission. The racing cars

■ *A straight road in open country probably beckoned many who owned a 1969 Torino GT Cobra. With its hood-mounted scoop swallowing cool air, it could produce 335 healthy horses.*
Mike Mueller

■ *The only way many saw the front end of the 1969 Torino GT Cobra facing them was in the other lane on the highway. It was a car that could get up to 100 mph in just 14.5 seconds.*
Jerry Heasley

■ *The SportsRoof, as Ford called it, gave the Torino GT Cobra a look that couldn't be beat with its combination of elegant beauty and no-nonsense power. It was a great combination in 1969.*
Mike Mueller

■ *The more traditional notchback, or two-door hardtop, version of the 1969 Torino GT was also powerful. The lack of a hood scoop meant the standard 428-CJ engine was under the hood.*
Jerry Heasley

■ *The Ford Cobra Jet V-8 had 428-cubic inches, produced 360 horses at 5,400 rpm, churned 460 lbs.-ft. of torque and ran with a Holley four-barrel carburetor. It came accented in chrome.*
Mike Mueller

Fairlane 1962-1973

ran the 427-cid big-block at the beginning of the season. Beginning in March, they were allowed to use the new 429-cid "semi-hemi" V-8. These engines were not installed in showroom Talladegas however, since Boss 429 Mustang production satisfied the certification requirements for racing.

The idea behind the Talladega was to get the production work over quickly and let the racers create a performance image for the Torino. It worked. David Pearson won his second straight NASCAR Grand National championship driving a Ford for race team owners Holman & Moody. Street cars were not quite as dominant at the drag strip. The Talladega was heavier than other Torinos and racked up mid-14-second quarter-miles. However, it was much better suited to lefthand turns on oval-shaped race tracks.

■ *The competition for NASCAR prizes meant Ford engineers went back to the drawing board to produce the flush-mounted grille and altered front of the 1969 Torino Talladega.* Phil Kunz

■ *A darker paint scheme made the 1969 Torino GT Cobra SportsRoof look just that much more sinister. The hood scoop meant this car carried the Ram Air version of the 428-CJ engine.* Phil Kunz

The 1969 Talladegas proved very adept at stock-car racing. In fact, test drivers found that their 1970 replacements were some 5 mph slower on the big tracks. As a result, Ford's factory-backed teams ran one-year-old 1969 models at many tracks during the 1970 racing season.

Counting prototypes, Talladega production passed the required 500 units and wound up at 754. The cars came in Wimbleton White, Royal Maroon or Presidential Blue. They had black interiors and came only with bench seats.

1970

Ford had redone its mid-size cars every two years, so it was time for change in 1970. The previous Fairlane and Torino models had been real lookers—and racetrack performers— but it's hard to sell something slightly old when the competition is offering the "latest-and-greatest." As a result, the cars were updated. The changes started with a 1-inch-longer wheelbase and 2-inch longer length.

■ *This 1970 Ford Torino had the 370-hp 429-cid Super Cobra Jet V-8 lurking under its blackened hood with raised hood scoop. The Cobra decal gave fair warning to all who would challenge it.*   Doug Mitchel

The new look further emphasized the long-hood/short-deck school of industrial design and the front fender edges, window treatment and fastback roof line were all more "pinched" and angular looking than before. Bold, eye-catching (some might say gaudy) "laser" side stripes decorated the sides of the body. The egg-crate grille texture got blacked-out finish and side-by-side headlights.

The Fairlane 500 was the base series with a two-door hardtop, four-door sedan and conventional wagon. The next-step-up Torino line added a four-door hardtop and a SportsRoof hardtop. All of these cars could be had with six or V-8 power. The formal two-door hardtop, the sedan and the wagon came with fancy Torino Brougham appointments. The Torino GT line included a Sportsroof and a convertible. The most expensive offering was the SportsRoof-style Cobra.

The 428 was gone from the intermediates for the new year. A massive 429 V-8 that produced 360 hp was the "big mama" now. In fact, it was *standard* equipment in the Torino Cobra, which also included Ford's top-loader four-speed manual transmission (capped by a Hurst shifter), a competition

suspension with staggered rear shocks, 7-inch-wide steel wheels, F70-14 wide oval tires, a black hood with locking devices, black-out trim and Cobra badging. Bench seats were standard. Engine options included the 370-hp CJ-429 or the CJ-429 Ram Air V-8 with the same horsepower rating. Traction-Lok and Detroit-Locker rear axles were available.

The '70 Torino Cobra was expected to be a car for NASCAR Grand National racers, but it turned out to be slower than a '69 Talladega. As a result, the racing teams campaigned year-old cars in 1970.

In addition to the Cobra, several other interesting, high-performance mid-size Fords were possibilities in 1970. By selecting the right equipment from the long options list, you could turn a Fairlane 500 with the formal (non-fastback) roofline into a serious muscle car sporting a CJ-429 V-8, a matte black hood treatment, hood-locking pins and fat tires. Coiled cobra decals decorated the body sides when the big V-8 was added and made the plain-Jane Fairlane look downright nasty. It was one of those "sleeper" cars that

"Coiled cobra decals decorated the body sides when the big V-8 was added and made the plain-Jane Fairlane look downright nasty."

■ *Ford changed the styling on the 1970 Torino Cobra with a more streamlined front end. Standard under the hood was a 429-cid, 360-hp V-8 and performance-inspired blackened hood.* Mike Mueller

you can really enjoy stoplight challenges in. ("Whoa! That taxicab just blew my doors off!").

Even weirder was a "Falcon" version of the Torino that came along at midyear. It was offered as a two-door sedan, a four-door sedan or a wagon. The two-door was based priced at $2,460—about $200 less than any other Fairlane or Torino. It was Ford's version of the "Heavy Chevy" or Pontiac GT-37—a true stripper, but still offering buyers big-block boost at extra cost. This was no compact like the original Falcon. It was a de-contented Torino that the factory could beef up, under the hood, if you wanted to go that route. Ford even built 100 copies of the '70 1/2 Falcon with the CJ-429 engine, a four-speed gearbox and a Detroit-Locker 4.33:1 rear axle. In addition to being cheap, the "70-point-five" Falcon was light—and very, very fast.

■ *This Falcon, restyled with Torino skin as a 1970 1/2 model, could be purchased with the 429-CJ engine. It was one Falcon that could really fly with its light weight and solid power.* J erry Heasley

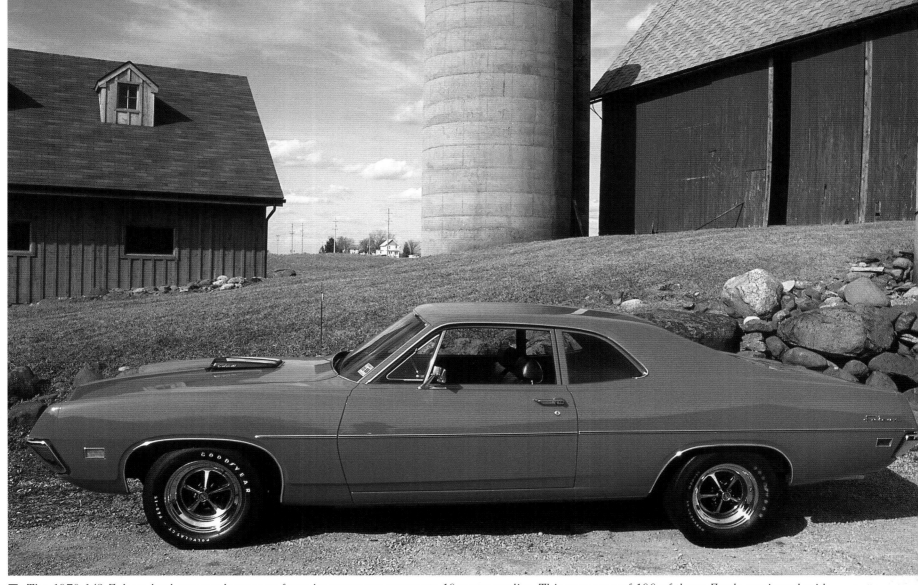

■ *The 1970 1/2 Falcon had come a long way from its economy car roots 10 years earlier. This was one of 100 of these Fords equipped with the hefty 429-CJ V-8 and other performance goodies.*

Jerry Heasley

1971

Motor Trend picked the '71 Torino Cobra as its "Car of the Year," saying "To have had it, 16 years ago, on Main St. in Lockport, N.Y., with all its shuttered-back-lite, fat-tired, shaker-hood, chopped-top magnificence would have equated with having the Bean Bandit's fuel dragster."

Joaquin Arnett and the Bean Bandits were hot rodding legends who had been around since the first drag strip. Their Bean Bandit Mark II— a streamlined, modified roadster/dragster—won the first Southern California Championships at Pomona Raceway with a top speed of 132.35. Later, in 1957, the Bean Bandits campaigned a yellow slingshot dragster that ran the quarter-mile at 154.63 mph in 9.78 seconds.

■ *The convertible version of the 1970 Torino GT had hidden headlights, a two-toned body stripe, mag-style wheels and a hood scoop. Buyers had many Ford engine options to consider.* Jerry Heasley

That bright yellow race car would have attracted a lot of attention in Lockport and so did the '71 Torino Cobra, which looked a lot like the '70, except for its new split grille and integrated hood scoop. The '71 Cobra was really a high-performance Torino Brougham. Standard equipment included all Brougham features, plus a 351 "Cleveland" V-8, a four-speed manual gearbox with Hurst shifter, special Cobra I.D., a heavy-duty suspension, 7-inch-wide argent silver wheels with chrome hub caps, a blacked-out grille and lower escutcheon panel, a black-finished hood with non-reflective paint, polished aluminum wheel well moldings, F70-14 whitewall wide oval tires, a 55-amp heavy-duty battery, a dual exhaust system and pleated vinyl seat trim.

In addition to the 351, the Cobra could be ordered with two versions of Ford's 429-cid V-8. Big-block Cobras had a competition suspension, a "sporty" exhaust noise feature, an 80-amp battery, a 55-amp alternator, dual exhausts, an extra-cooling package, bright engine dress-up parts, cast-aluminum rocker covers and a non-locking rear axle with a 3.25:1 ratio. The 429-cid/370-hp Cobra Jet Ram-Air V-8 included all extras that came with the Copra Jet V-8, plus a "shaker" hood scoop.

The 370-hp Cobra formal hardtop carried about 10.5 lbs per horsepower and could run from 0 to 60 mph in 6 seconds flat. It did the quarter-mile in 14.5 seconds.

■ *This 1970 Torino GT Cobra Sport Roof had the 370-hp CJ-429 V-8 without the Ram Air setup. Note the styled wheels, blackened hood and rear window shade on this classically styled car.* Phil Kunz

1972

Midsized Fords came in three series in 1972. Torino two-door "formal" hardtops and four-door "pillared" hardtops and wagons were offered in six and V-8 lines. There were also Gran Torino versions of the same body styles with the same engine choices. The top-of-the-heap V-8-only Gran Torino Sport series offered formal (notchback) and "sport" (fastback) hardtops, along with a four-door Squire wagon.

The new four-door sedans and wagons had a 1-inch-longer wheelbase than 1971 passenger cars. The two-door models used a smaller 114-inch wheelbase, which was the same used for '71 wagons. Regardless of wheelbase and length, all of the '72 were much heavier in weight.

Styling was completely revamped, especially on the front end, where the headlights were moved closer together and an early version of today's popular Chrysler 300 grille design appeared. The body had a more pronounced "Coke bottle" shape. A massive rear bumper incorporated the tail lights. The fastback model featured an extremely low roofline.

Engine availability included a 250-cid six with 95 nhp, a 302 V-8 with 140 nhp, a pair of 351 V-8s (161 nhp and 248 nhp), a 400 V-8 with 168 nhp and a 205-nhp version of the 429 big-block with a two-barrel carburetor. Clearly, it was the hotter 351 Cleveland engine (made in Ford's engine plant in Ohio) that had the most appeal to the few muscle car fans remaining this year.

1973

In their book *Ford Muscle: Street, Stock, and Strip* authors Bill Holder and Phil Kunz peg 1972 as the last year of mid-sized Ford muscle. From a different perspective, the "Starsky and Hutch" TV Torino kept the image alive through at least 1976. We're going to pick '73 as the end of the line. We base this on the fact that even though you could not get a truly muscular Torino engine that

■ *This 1971 Torino GT Cobra carries SportsRoof fastback styling enhanced by a graceful side stripe and steel wheels. This one has the 429-cid V-8 without the Ram Air version's shaker hood.* Phil Kunz

> "Motor Trend picked the '71 Torino Cobra as its 'Car of the Year'."

FAIRLANE/TORINO YEAR-BY-YEAR SPEC'S

1962

Engine	Bore/Str.	Comp. Ratio	CID	BHP	WT.	W.B.	O.L.	Width	HT
V-8	3.50 x 2.87	08.70	221	145 @4400	2,927	115.5	197.6	71.3	57.8

1963

Engine	Bore/Str.	Comp. Ratio	CID	BHP	WT.	W.B.	O.L.	Width	HT
V-8	3.50 x 2.87	08.70	221	145 @4400	2,996	115.5	197.6	71.3	55.4
V-8	3.80 x 2.87	08.70	260	164 @4400	2,996	115.5	197.6	71.3	55.4

added 1963 1/2

Engine	Bore/Str.	Comp. Ratio	CID	BHP	WT.	W.B.	O.L.	Width	HT
V-8	4.00 x 2.87	09.00	289	195 @4400	2,996	115.5	197.6	71.3	55.4
V-8	4.00 x 2.87	10.50	289	271 @6000	2,996	115.5	197.6	71.3	55.4

1964

Engine	Bore/Str.	Comp. Ratio	CID	BHP	WT.	W.B.	O.L.	Width	HT
V-8	3.80 x 2.87	08.80	260	164 @4400	2,962	115.5	197.6	72.2	55.8
V-8	4.00 x 2.87	09.00	289	195 @4400	2,962	115.5	197.6	72.2	55.8
V-8	4.00 x 3.50	09.30	352	250 @4400	2,962	115.5	197.6	73.8	55.7
V-8	4.05 x 3.78	10.00	390	300 @4400	2,962	115.5	197.6	72.2	55.8
V-8	4.23 x 3.78	11.50	427	410 @5600	2,962	115.5	197.6	72.2	55.8
V-8	4.23 x 3.78	11.50	427	425 @5600	2,962	115.5	199.0	73.8	55.7

1965

Engine	Bore/Str.	Comp. Ratio	CID	BHP	WT.	W.B.	O.L.	Width	HT
V-8	4.00 x 2.87	09.30	289	200 @4400	3,050	115.5	199.0	73.8	55.7
V-8	4.05 x 3.78	10.00	390	300 @4600	3,050	115.5	199.0	73.8	55.7
V-8	4.00 x 3.50	09.30	352	250 @4400	3,050	115.5	197.6	73.8	55.7
V-8	4.23 x 3.78	11.50	427	425 @5600	3,050	115.5	199.0	73.8	55.7

1966

Engine	Bore/Str.	Comp. Ratio	CID	BHP	WT.	W.B.	O.L.	Width	HT
V-8	4.00 x 2.87	09.30	289	200 @4400	2,961	116.0	197.0	74.7	55.0
V-8	4.05 x 3.78	10.50	390	315 @4600	2,961	116.0	197.0	74.7	55.0
V-8	4.05 x 3.78	10.50	390	320 @4600	2,961	116.0	197.0	74.7	55.0
V-8	4.05 x 3.78	11.00	390	335 @4800	2,961	116.0	197.0	74.7	55.0
V-8	4.23 x 3.78	11.50	427	425 @5600	2,961	116.0	197.0	74.7	55.0

1967

Engine	Bore/Str.	Comp. Ratio	CID	BHP	WT.	W.B.	O.L.	Width	HT
V-8	4.00 x 2.87	08.70	289	195 @4600	2,951	116.0	197.0	74.7	55.2
V-8	4.05 x 3.78	10.50	390	315 @4600	2,951	116.0	197.0	74.7	55.2
V-8	4.05 x 3.78	10.50	390	320 @4600	2,951	116.0	197.0	74.7	55.2
V-8	4.23 x 3.78	11.50	427	425 @5600	2,951	116.0	197.0	74.7	55.2

1968

Engine	Bore/Str.	Comp. Ratio	CID	BHP	WT.	W.B.	O.L.	Width	HT
V-8	4.00 x 2.87	09.30	289	200 @4400	3,083	116.0	201.1	74.5	55.0
V-8	4.00 x 3.00	09.00	302	210 @4400	3,083	116.0	201.1	74.5	55.0
V-8	4.00 x 3.00	10.00	302	230 @4800	3,083	116.0	201.1	74.5	55.0
V-8	4.05 x 3.78	09.50	390	265 @4400	3,083	116.0	201.1	74.5	55.0
V-8	4.05 x 3.78	10.50	390	325 @4800	3,083	116.0	201.1	74.5	55.0
V-8	4.23 x 3.78	10.90	427	390 @4600	3,083	116.0	201.1	74.5	55.0
V-8	4.13 x 3.98	10.70	428	335 @5600	3,083	116.0	201.1	74.5	55.0

1969

Engine	Bore/Str.	Comp. Ratio	CID	BHP	WT.	W.B.	O.L.	Width	HT
V-8	4.00 x 3.00	09.00	302	220 @4600	3,120	115.5	201.1	74.8	53.7
V-8	4.00 x 3.50	09.50	351	250 @4600	3,120	115.5	201.1	74.8	53.7
V-8	4.00 x 3.50	10.70	351	290 @4800	3,120	115.5	201.1	74.8	53.7
V-8	4.05 x 3.78	09.50	390	265 @4400	3,120	115.5	201.1	74.8	53.7
V-8	4.05 x 3.78	10.50	390	320 @4600	3,120	115.5	201.1	74.8	53.7
V-8	4.13 x 3.98	10.60	428	335 @5600	3,120	115.5	201.1	74.8	53.7

1970

Engine	Bore/Str.	Comp. Ratio	CID	BHP	WT.	W.B.	O.L.	Width	HT
V-8	4.00 x 3.00	09.50	302	220 @4600	3,115	117.0	207.0	77.0	55.0
V-8	4.00 x 3.50	09.50	351	250 @4600	3,115	117.0	207.0	77.0	55.0
V-8	4.00 x 3.50	11.01	351	300 @5400	3,115	117.0	207.0	77.0	55.0
V-8	4.36 x 3.59	10.50	429	360 @4600	3,115	117.0	207.0	77.0	55.0
V-8	4.13 x 3.98	11.30	429	370 @5400	3,115	117.0	207.0	77.0	55.0
V-8	4.13 x 3.98	11.50	429	375 @5200	3,115	117.0	207.0	77.0	55.0

1971

Engine	Bore/Str.	Comp. Ratio	CID	BHP	WT.	W.B.	O.L.	Width	HT
V-8	4.00 x 3.00	09.00	302	210 @4600	3,225	117.0	207.0	77.0	55.0
V-8	4.00 x 3.50	09.00	351	240 @4600	3,225	117.0	207.0	77.0	55.0
V-8	4.00 x 3.50	10.70	351	285 @5400	3,225	117.0	207.0	77.0	55.0
V-8	4.13 x 3.98	11.30	429	370 @5400	3,225	117.0	207.0	77.0	55.0
V-8	4.13 x 3.98	11.30	429	375 @5600	3,225	117.0	207.0	77.0	55.0

1972

Engine	Bore/Str.	Comp. Ratio	CID	BHP	WT.	W.B.	O.L.	Width	HT
V-8	4.00 x 3.00	08.50	302	140 @4000	3,548	114.0	208.0	80.0	56.0
V-8	4.00 x 3.50	08.30	351	161 @4000	3,548	114.0	208.0	80.0	56.0
V-8	4.00 x 3.50	08.60	351	248 @5400	3,548	114.0	208.0	80.0	56.0
V-8	4.00 x 4.00	08.40	400	168 @4200	3,548	114.0	208.0	80.0	56.0
V-8	4.13 x 3.98	08.50	429	205 @4400	3,548	114.0	208.0	80.0	56.0

NOTE: Net horsepower
NOTE: Wheelbase and length given are for two-door "high-performance" models; height estimated

1973

Engine	Bore/Str.	Comp. Ratio	CID	BHP	WT.	W.B.	O.L.	Width	HT
V-8	4.00 x 3.00	08.00	302	137 @4200	3,683	114.0	208.0	80.0	56.0
V-8	4.00 x 3.50	08.00	351	156 @3800	3,683	114.0	208.0	80.0	56.0
V-8	4.00 x 3.50	08.00	351	159 @5400	3,683	114.0	208.0	80.0	56.0
V-8	4.00 x 3.50	08.00	351	246 @5400	3,683	114.0	208.0	80.0	56.0
V-8	4.00 x 4.00	08.00	400	168 @3800	3,683	114.0	208.0	80.0	56.0
V-8	4.13 x 3.98	08.00	429	197 @4400	3,683	114.0	208.0	80.0	56.0
V-8	4.13 x 3.98	08.00	429	201 @4400	3,683	114.0	208.0	80.0	56.0
V-8	4.36 x 3.85	08.80	460	274 @4400	3,683	114.0	208.0	80.0	56.0

NOTE: Net horsepower; same engine in heavier car like station wagon has different net horsepower rating
NOTE: Wheelbase and length given are for two-door "high-performance" models; height estimated
NOTE: 460P is police interceptor V-8

(Compiled from a variety of contemporary sources. Minor differences in measurements are due to the way the car was measured, rather than changes in the car itself or related to the fact that different body styles were used as the basis for factory specifications tables. Weight is for lightest V-8 model.)

"The Starsky and Hutch TV Torino kept the image alive through at least 1976."

season, Ford did struggle to keep the look of a muscle car alive by offering the Sportsroof body style one final time.

Sporting a totally different and much more conventional frontal appearance, the '73 Torino was again heavier. A new federally mandated crash-proof bumper added significantly to weight (and sluggishness). To make matters worse, the same engines were carried over from 1972, but all of them had a few less horsepower. Enthusiasts who walked into Ford showrooms to buy a fastback Torino with a 351 Cleveland V-8 or a 429 may have thought they were being cool, but the car that they left with was definitely not "your father's muscle car."

PRODUCTION STATISTICS AND BREAKOUTS

1962 FAIRLANE

Year	Body Code	Body Type	Engine Type	MSP Price	Model Yr. Prod.
FAIRLANE SIX					
62	62A	2SD	6	$2,154	23,511
62	54A	4SD	6	$2,216	27,996
TOTAL FAIRLANE SIX					**51,507**
FAIRLANE V-8					
62	62A	2SD	V-8	$2,257	10,753
62	54A	4SD	V-8	$2,319	18,346
TOTAL FAIRLANE V-8					**29,099**
TOTAL FAIRLANE 500 (SIX & V-8)					**80,606**
FAIRLANE 500 SIX					
62	62A	2SD	6	$2,242	26,533
62	54A	4SD	6	$2,304	31,113
TOTAL FAIRLANE 500 SIX					**57,664**
FAIRLANE 500 V-8					
62	62B	2SD	V-8	$2,345	42,091
62	54B	4SD	V-8	$2,407	98,145
TOTAL FAIRLANE 500 V-8					**140,236**
TOTAL FAIRLANE 500 (SIX & V-8)					**197,882**
FAIRLANE 500 SPORT SIX					
62	62C	2SD	6	$2,403	1,659
62	62C	2SD	V-8	$2,506	17,969
TOTAL FAIRLANE 500 SPORT					**19,628**
GRAND TOTAL					**29,8116**

Note: 1962-1968 tables are from recently released General Motors marketing study on competitor's 1955-1968 production data records.

1963 FAIRLANE

Year	Body Code	Body Type	Engine Type	MSP Price	Model Yr. Prod
FAIRLANE SIX					
63	62A	2SD	6	$2,154	20,347
63	54A	4SD	6	$2,216	24,727
63	71A	4W-6	6	$2,525	5,972
63	71A	4W-9	6	$2,575	1,180
TOTAL FAIRLANE SIX					**52,226**
FAIRLANE V-8					
63	62A	2SD	V-8	$2,257	8,637
63	54A	4SD	V-8	$2,319	19,727
63	71A	4W-6	V-8	$2,628	12,691
63	71A	4W-9	V-8	$2,678	4,163
TOTAL FAIRLANE V-8					**45,218**
TOTAL FAIRLANE (SIX & V-8)					**97,444**

FAIRLANE 500 SIX

63	62B	2SD	6	$2,242	11,494
63	54B	4SD	6	$2,304	20,915
63	65B	2HT	6	$2,324	4,610
63	71B	4W-6	6	$2,613	1,313
63	71B	4W-9	6	$2,663	897
TOTAL FAIRLANE 500 SIX					**39,229**
FAIRLANE 500 V-8					
63	62B	2SD	V-8	$2,345	23,270
63	54B	4SD	V-8	$2,407	83,260
63	65B	2HT	V-8	$2,427	37,031
63	71B	4W-6	V-8	$2,716	13,838
63	71B	4W-9	V-8	$2,766	13,564
TOTAL FAIRLANE 500 V-8					**170,963**
TOTAL FAIRLANE 500 (SIX & V-8)					**210,192**
FAIRLANE 500 SPORT SIX					
63	65D	2HT	6	$2,504	1,351
63	71D	4W-6	6	$2,781	197
63	71D	4W-9	6	$2,831	133
TOTAL FAIRLANE 500 SPORT SIX					**1,681**
FAIRLANE 500 SPORT V-8					
63	65E	2HT	V-8	$2,607	26,917
63	71E	4W-6	V-8	$2,884	3,872
63	71E	4W-9	V-8	$2,934	3,781
TOTAL FAIRLANE 500 SPORT V-8					**34,570**
TOTAL FAIRLANE 500 SPORT (SIX & V-8)					**36,251**
GRAND TOTAL					**34,387**

Note: 1962-1968 tables are from recently released General Motors marketing study on competitor's 1955-1968 production data records.

1964 FAIRLANE

Year	Body Code	Body Type	Engine Type	MSP Price	Model Yr. Prod
FAIRLANE SIX					
64	62A	2SD	6	$2,194	14,777
64	54A	4SD	6	$2,235	22,233
64	71D	4W-6	6	$2,531	7,324
TOTAL FAIRLANE SIX					**44,334**
FAIRLANE V-8					
64	62A	2SD	V-8	$2,294	5,644
64	54A	4SD	V-8	$2,335	14,460
64	71D	4W-6	V-8	$2,631	13,656
TOTAL FAIRLANE V-8					**33,760**
TOTAL FAIRLANE (SIX & V-8)					**78,094**

FAIRLANE 500 SIX

64	62B	2SD	6	$2,276	8,760
64	54B	4SD	6	$2,317	18,791
64	65A	2HT	6	$2,341	4,467
64	71B	4W-6	6	$2,612	2,666
TOTAL FAIRLANE 500 SIX					**34,684**
FAIRLANE 500 V-8					
64	62B	2SD	V-8	$2,376	14,687
64	54B	4SD	V-8	$2,417	68,128
64	65A	2HT	V-8	$2,441	38,266
64	71B	4W-6	V-8	$2,712	22,296
TOTAL FAIRLANE 500 V-8					**143,377**
TOTAL FAIRLANE 500 (SIX & V-8)					**178,061**
FAIRLANE 500 SPORT SIX					
64	65B	2HT	6	$2,502	946
TOTAL FAIRLANE 500 SPORT SIX					**946**
64	65B	2HT	V-8	$2,602	20,485
TOTAL FAIRLANE 500 SPORT V-8					**20,485**
TOTAL FAIRLANE 500 SPORT (SIX & V-8)					**21,431**
GRAND TOTAL					**27,758**

Note: 1962-1968 tables are from recently released General Motors marketing study on competitor's 1955-1968 production data records.

1965 FAIRLANE

Year	Body Code	Body Type	Engine Type	MSP Price	Model Yr. Prod
FAIRLANE SIX					
65	62A	2SD	6	$2,183	10,376
65	54A	4SD	6	$2,223	15,886
65	71D	4W-6	6	$2,512	5,953
TOTAL FAIRLANE SIX					**32,215**
FAIRLANE V-8					
65	62A	2SD	V-8	$2,288	3,309
65	54A	4SD	V-8	$2,329	9,492
65	71D	4W-6	V-8	$2,616	7,958
TOTAL FAIRLANE V-8					**20,759**
TOTAL FAIRLANE (SIX & V-8)					**52,974**
FAIRLANE 500 SIX					
65	62B	2SD	6	$2,263	7,053
65	54B	4SD	6	$2,303	19,496
65	65A	2HT	6	$2,327	5,666
65	71B	4W-6	6	$2,592	2,847
TOTAL FAIRLANE 500 SIX					**35,062**

FAIRLANE 500 V-8

Year	Body Code	Body Type	Engine Type	MSP Price	Model Yr. Prod
65	62B	2SD	V-8	$2,369	9,039
65	54B	4SD	V-8	$2,409	58,340
65	65A	2HT	V-8	$2,432	35,739
65	71B	4W-6	V-8	$2,697	17,659
TOTAL FAIRLANE 500 V-8					**120,777**
TOTAL FAIRLANE 500 (SIX & V-8)					**155,839**

FAIRLANE 500 SPORT SIX

Year	Body Code	Body Type	Engine Type	MSP Price	Model Yr. Prod
65	65B	2HT	6	$2,484	875
TOTAL FAIRLANE 500 SPORT SIX					**875**

FAIRLANE 500 SPORT V-8

Year	Body Code	Body Type	Engine Type	MSP Price	Model Yr. Prod
65	65B	2HT	V-8	$2,590	14,266
TOTAL FAIRLANE 500 SPORT V-8					**14,266**
TOTAL FAIRLANE 500 SPORT (SIX & V-8)					**15,141**
GRAND TOTAL					**22,3954**

Note: 1962-1968 tables are from recently released General Motors marketing study on competitor's 1955-1968 production data records.

1966 FAIRLANE

Year	Body Code	Body Type	Engine Type	MSP Price	Model Yr. Prod
FAIRLANE SIX					
66	62A	2SD	6	$2,240	8,440
66	54A	4SD	6	$2,280	11,731
66	71D	4W-6	6	$2,589	3,623
TOTAL FAIRLANE SIX					**23,794**
FAIRLANE V-8					
66	62A	2SD	V-8	$2,345	4,258
66	54A	4SD	V-8	$2,386	11,774
66	71D	4W-6	V-8	$2,694	8,530
TOTAL FAIRLANE V-8					**24,562**
TOTAL FAIRLANE (SIX & V-8)					**48,356**
FAIRLANE 500 SIX					
66	62B	2SD	6	$2,317	4,617
66	54B	4SD	6	$2,357	12,017
66	63B	2HT	6	$2,378	7,300
66	76B	2CV	6	$2,603	1,033
66	71B	4W-6	6	$2,665	1,613
66	71E	4W-SQ	6	$2,796	771
TOTAL FAIRLANE 500 SIX					**27,351**
FAIRLANE 500 V-8					
66	62B	2SD	V-8	$2,423	8,949
66	54B	4SD	V-8	$2,463	53,454
66	63B	2HT	V-8	$2,484	65,343
66	76B	2CV	V-8	$2,709	8,039
66	71B	4W-6	V-8	$2,770	17,904
66	71E	4W-SQ	V-8	$2,901	10,787
TOTAL FAIRLANE 500 V-8					**164,476**
TOTAL FAIRLANE 500 (SIX & V-8)					**191,827**

FAIRLANE 500 XL SIX

Year	Body Code	Body Type	Engine Type	MSP Price	Model Yr. Prod
66	63C	2HT	6	$2,543	629
66	76C	2CV	6	$2,768	155
TOTAL FAIRLANE 500 XL SIX					**784**

FAIRLANE 500 XL V-8

Year	Body Code	Body Type	Engine Type	MSP Price	Model Yr. Prod
66	63C	2HT	V-8	$2,590	21,315
66	76C	2CV	V-8	$2,592	4305
TOTAL FAIRLANE 500 XLV-8					**25,620**
TOTAL FAIRLANE 500 XL (SIX & V-8)					**26,404**

FAIRLANE GT V-8

Year	Body Code	Body Type	Engine Type	MSP Price	Model Yr. Prod
66	63D	2HT	V-8	$2,843	33,015
66	76D	2CV	V-8	$3,068	4,327
TOTAL FAIRLANE GT					**37,342**
GRAND TOTAL					**303,929**

Note: 1962-1968 tables are from recently released General Motors marketing study on competitor's 1955-1968 production data records.

1967 FAIRLANE

Year	Body Code	Body Type	Engine Type	MSP Price	Model Yr. Prod
FAIRLANE SIX					
67	62A	2SD	6	$2,297	6,948
67	54A	4SD	6	$2,339	9,461
67	71D	4W-6	6	$2,643	3,057
TOTAL FAIRLANE SIX					**19,466**
FAIRLANE V-8					
67	62A	2SD	V-8	$2,402	3,680
67	54A	4SD	V-8	$2,445	10,279
67	71D	4W-6	V-8	$2,748	7,824
TOTAL FAIRLANE V-8					**21,783**
TOTAL FAIRLANE (SIX & V-8)					**41,249**
FAIRLANE 500 SIX					
67	62B	2SD	6	$2,377	2,934
67	54B	4SD	6	$2,417	7,149
67	63B	2HT	6	$2,439	4,879
67	76B	2CV	6	$2,664	454
67	71B	4W-6	6	$2,718	1,067
67	71E	4W-SQ	6	$2,902	425
TOTAL FAIRLANE 500 SIX					**16,908**
FAIRLANE 500 V-8					
67	62B	2SD	V-8	$2,482	5,539
67	54B	4SD	V-8	$2,522	44,403
67	63B	2HT	V-8	$2,545	62,256
67	76B	2CV	V-8	$2,770	4,974
67	71B	4W-6	V-8	$2,824	14,835
67	71E	4W-SQ	V-8	$3,007	7,923
TOTAL FAIRLANE 500 V-8					**142,930**
TOTAL FAIRLANE 500 (SIX & V-8)					**159,838**

FAIRLANE 500 XL SIX

Year	Body Code	Body Type	Engine Type	MSP Price	Model Yr. Prod
67	63C	2HT	6	$2,619	330
67	76C	2CV	6	$2,843	49
TOTAL FAIRLANE 500 XL SIX					**379**

FAIRLANE 500 XL V-8

Year	Body Code	Body Type	Engine Type	MSP Price	Model Yr. Prod
67	63C	2HT	V-8	$2,724	14,541
67	76C	2CV	V-8	$3,064	1,894
TOTAL FAIRLANE 500 XLV-8					**16,435**
TOTAL FAIRLANE 500 XL (SIX & V-8)					**16,814**

FAIRLANE GT V-8

Year	Body Code	Body Type	Engine Type	MSP Price	Model Yr. Prod
67	63D	2HT	V-8	$2,839	18,670
67	76D	2CV	V-8	$3,064	2,117
TOTAL FAIRLANE GT					**20,787**
GRAND TOTAL					**238,688**

Note: 1962-1968 tables are from recently released General Motors marketing study on competitor's 1955-1968 production data records.

1968 FAIRLANE

Year	Body Code	Body Type	Engine Type	MSP Price	Model Yr. Prod
FAIRLANE SIX					
68	54A	4SD	6	$2,464	8,828
68	65A	2HT	6	$2,496	15,753
68	71B	4W	6	$2,770	573
TOTAL FAIRLANE SIX					**25154**
FAIRLANE V-8					
68	54A	4SD	V-8	$2,551	9,318
68	65A	2HT	V-8	$2,544	28,930
68	71B	4W	V-8	$2,748	14,227
TOTAL FAIRLANE V-8					**52,475**
TOTAL FAIRLANE (SIX & V-8)					**77,629**
FAIRLANE 500 SIX					
68	54B	4SD	6	$2,543	5,142
68	65B	2HT	6	$2,566	1,269
68	63B	2FB	6	$2,591	2,723
68	76B	2CV	6	$2,822	215
68	71D	4W-6	6	$2,881	2,496
TOTAL FAIRLANE 500 SIX					**11,845**
FAIRLANE 500 V-8					
68	54B	4SD	V-8	$2,611	37,788
68	65B	2HT	V-8	$2,653	27,899
68	63B	2FB	V-8	$2,679	28,738
68	76B	2CV	V-8	$29,10	3,207
68	71D	4W-6	V-8	$29,68	7,694
TOTAL FAIRLANE 500 V-8					**105,326**
TOTAL FAIRLANE 500 (SIX & V-8)					**117,171**
FAIRLANE 500 (BUCKET SEATS) SIX					
68	65E	2HT	6	$2,676	80
68	63E	2FB	6	$2,701	100
68	76E	2CV	6	$2,932	11
TOTAL FAIRLANE 500 (BUCKET SEATS) SIX					**379**

FAIRLANE 500 (BUCKET SEATS) V-8

68	65E	2HT	V-8	$2,763	3,204
68	63E	2FB	V-8	$2,789	1,721
68	76E	2CV	V-8	$2,910	3,207

TOTAL FAIRLANE 500 (BUCKET SEATS) V-8 **8,132**

TOTAL FAIRLANE 500 BUCKET SEATS (SIX & V-8) **8,511**

FAIRLANE TORINO SIX

68	54C	4SD	6	$2,688	502
68	65C	2HT	6	$2,710	773
68	71E	4W	6	$3,032	325

TOTAL FAIRLANE TORINO SIX **1,600**

FAIRLANE TORINO V-8

68	54C	4SD	V-8	$2,776	17,460
68	65C	2HT	V-8	$2,798	35,191
68	71E	4W	V-8	$3,119	14,448

TOTAL FAIRLANE TORINO V-8 **67,099**

TOTAL FAIRLANE TORINO (SIX & V-8) **68,699**

FAIRLANE TORINO GT V-8

68	65D	2HT	V-8	$2,747	23,939
68	63D	2FB	V-8	$2,772	74,135
68	76D	2CV	V-8	$3,001	5,310

TOTAL FAIRLANE TORINO GT **103,384**

GRAND TOTAL **372,327**

Note: 1962-1968 tables are from recently released General Motors marketing study on competitor's 1955-1968 production data records.

1969 FAIRLANE

Year	Body Code	Body Type	Engine Type	MSP Price	Model Yr. Prod
FAIRLANE SIX					
69	54A	4SD	6	$2,488	*
69	65A	2HT	6	$2,499	*
69	71B	4W	6	$2,841	*

* Production was reported by series and body style with no breakout per engine type. See totals below.

FAIRLANE V-8

69	54A	4SD	V-8	$2,578	27,296 **
69	65A	2HT	V-8	$2,589	85,630 **
69	71B	4W	V-8	$2,931	10,882 **

** Combined six-cylinder and V-8 production

TOTAL FAIRLANE (SIX & V-8) **123,808**

FAIRLANE 500 SIX

69	54B	4SD	6	$2,568	*
69	65B	2HT	6	$2,626	*
69	63B	2FB	6	$2,601	*
69	76B	2CV	6	$2,851	*
69	71B	4W-6	6	$2,951	*

* Production was reported by series and body style with no breakout per engine type. See totals below.

FAIRLANE 500 V-8

69	54B	4SD	V-8	$2,658	40,888 **
69	65B	2HT	V-8	$2,716	28,179 **
69	63B	2FB	V-8	$2,691	29,849 **
69	76B	2CV	V-8	$2,941	2,264 **
69	71B	4W-6	V-8	$3,041	12,869 **

** Combined six-cylinder and V-8 production

TOTAL FAIRLANE 500 (SIX & V-8) **114,049**

FAIRLANE TORINO SIX

69	54C	4SD	6	$2,733	*
69	65C	2HT	6	$2,754	*
69	71E	4W	6	$3,107	*

* Production was reported by series and body style with no breakout per engine type. See totals below.

FAIRLANE TORINO V-8

69	54C	4SD	V-8	$2,823	11,971 **
69	65C	2HT	V-8	$2,844	20,789 **
69	71E	4W	V-8	$3,197	14,472 **

** Combined six-cylinder and V-8 production

TOTAL FAIRLANE TORINO (SIX & V-8) **47,232**

FAIRLANE TORINO GT V-8

69	65D	2HT	V-8	$2,747	17,951
69	63D	2FB	V-8	$2,772	61,319
69	76D	2CV	V-8	$3,001	2,552

TOTAL FAIRLANE TORINO GT **81,822**

COBRA V-8

69	65E	2HT	V-8	$2,747	***
69	63E	2FB	V-8	$2,772	***

*** Cobra production appears to be included in Torino GT numbers. Recent undocumented research indicates that slightly over 14,000 Cobras were built and about 11,000 were fastback models.

GRAND TOTAL **36,6911**

1970 FAIRLANE

Year	Body Code	Body Type	Engine Type	MSP Price	Model Yr. Prod
70	54B	4SD	6	$2,627	*
70	65B	2HT	6	$2,660	*
70	71B	4W	6	$2,957	*

* Production was reported by series and body style with no breakout per engine type. See appropriate Fairlane 500 "B" V-8 totals below.

FAIRLANE 500 V-8 ("B")

70	54B	4SD	V-8	$2,716	25,780 **
70	65B	2HT	V-8	$2,750	70,636**
70	71B	4W	V-8	$3,047	13,613**

** Combined six-cylinder and V-8 production

FAIRLANE 500 V-8

70	54A	4SD	V-8	$2,528	30,443
70	62A	2SD	V-8	$2,479	26,071
70	71D	4W	V-8	$2,856	10,539

TOTAL FAIRLANE 500 (SIX & V-8) **177,082**

TORINO SIX

70	54C	4SD	6	$2,689	*
70	57C	4HT	6	$2,795	*
70	65C	2HT	6	$2,722	*
70	63C	2FB	6	$2,801	*
70	71C	4W-6	6	$3,074	*

* Production was reported by series and body style with no breakout per engine type. See totals below.

TORINO V-8

70	54C	4SD	V-8	$2,778	30,117 **
70	57C	4HT	V-8	$2,885	14,312 **
70	65C	2HT	V-8	$2,812	49,826 **
70	63C	2FB	V-8	$2,899	12,490 **
70	71C	4W-6	V-8	$3,164	10,613 **

** Combined six-cylinder and V-8 production

TOTAL TORINO (SIX & V-8) **117,358**

TORINO BROUGHAM V-8

70	57E	4HT	V-8	$3,078	14,543
70	65E	2HT	V-8	$3,006	16,911
70	71E	4W	V-8	$3,379	13,166

TOTAL TORINO BROUGHAM (SIX & V-8) **44,620**

TORINO GT V-8

70	63F	2FB	V-8	$3105	56,819
70	76F	2CV	V-8	$3,212	3,939

TOTAL TORINO GT **60,758**

COBRA V-8

70	63H	2FB	V-8	$3,270	7,675

GRAND TOTAL **407,493**

1971 FAIRLANE

Year	Body Code	Body Type	Engine Type	MSP Price	Model Yr. Prod
TORINO SIX					
71	54B	4SD	6	$2,672	*
71	65B	2HT	6	$2,706	*
71	71B	4W	6	$3,023	*

* Production was reported by series and body style with no breakout per engine type. See appropriate Torino V-8 totals below.

TORINO V-8

71	54A	4SD	V-8	$2,767	29,501 **
71	62A	2SD	V-8	$2,801	37,518 **
71	71D	4W	V-8	$3,118	21,570 **

** Combined six-cylinder and V-8 production

TOTAL TORINO (SIX & V-8) **88,589**

TORINO 500 SIX

71	54C	4SD	6	$2,855	*
71	57C	4HT	6	$2,959	*
71	65C	2HT	6	$2,887	*
71	63C	2FB	6	$2,943	*
71	71C	4W-6	6	$3,170	*

* Production was reported by series and body style with no breakout per engine type. See totals below.

TORINO 500 V-8

Year	Body Code	Body Type	Engine Type	MSP Price	Model Yr. Prod
71	54C	4SD	V-8	$2,950	35,650**
71	57C	4HT	V-8	$3,054	12,724**
71	65C	2HT	V-8	$2,982	89,966**
71	63C	2FB	V-8	$3,038	11,150**
71	71C	4W-6	V-8	$3,265	23,270**

** Combined six-cylinder and V-8 production

TOTAL TORINO 500 (SIX & V-8)   **172,760**

TORINO BROUGHAM V-8

Year	Body Code	Body Type	Engine Type	MSP Price	Model Yr. Prod
71	57E	4HT	V-8	$3,248	4,408
71	65E	2HT	V-8	$3,175	8,593
71	71E	4W	V-8	$3,560	15,805

TOTAL TORINO BROUGHAM (SIX & V-8)   **28,806**

TORINO GT V-8

Year	Body Code	Body Type	Engine Type	MSP Price	Model Yr. Prod
71	63F	2FB	V-8	$3,150	31,641
71	76F	2CV	V-8	$3,408	1,613

TOTAL TORINO GT V-8   **33,254**

COBRA V-8

Year	Body Code	Body Type	Engine Type	MSP Price	Model Yr. Prod
71	63H	2FB	V-8	$3,295	3,054

COBRA V-8 TOTAL   **3,054**

GRAND TOTAL   **326,463**

1972 FAIRLANE

TORINO SIX

Year	Body Code	Body Type	Engine Type	MSP Price	Model Yr. Prod
72	53B	4HT	6	$2,641	*
72	65B	2HT	6	$2,673	*
72	71B	4W	6	$2,955	*

* Production was reported by series and body style with no breakout per engine type. See appropriate Torino V-8 totals below.

TORINO V-8

Year	Body Code	Body Type	Engine Type	MSP Price	Model Yr. Prod
72	53B	4HT	V-8	$2,959	33,486**
72	65B	2HT	V-8	$2,706	33,530**
72	71B	4W	V-8	$3,023	22,204**

** Combined six-cylinder and V-8 production

TOTAL TORINO (SIX & V-8)   **89,220**

GRAN TORINO SIX

Year	Body Code	Body Type	Engine Type	MSP Price	Model Yr. Prod
72	53D	4HT	6	$2,856	*
72	65D	2HT	6	$2,878	*
72	71D	4W-6	6	$3,096	*

* Production was reported by series and body style with no breakout per engine type. See totals below.

GRAN TORINO V-8

Year	Body Code	Body Type	Engine Type	MSP Price	Model Yr. Prod
72	53D	4HT	6	$2,947	102,300**
72	65D	2HT	6	$2,967	132,285**
72	71D	4W-6	6	$3,186	45,212**

** Combined six-cylinder and V-8 production

TOTAL TORINO (SIX & V-8)   **279,797**

GRAN TORINO SPORT V-8

Year	Body Code	Body Type	Engine Type	MSP Price	Model Yr. Prod
72	63R	2FB		$3,094	60,794
72	65R	2HT		$3,094	31,239

TOTAL GRAN TORINO SPORT V-8   **92,033**

GRAN TORINO SQUIRE V-8

Year	Body Code	Body Type	Engine Type	MSP Price	Model Yr. Prod
72	71K	4W-6	V-8	$3,486	35,595

TOTAL GRAN TORINO SQUIRE   **35,595**

GRAND TOTAL   **496,645**

1973 FAIRLANE

TORINO SIX

Year	Body Code	Body Type	Engine Type	MSP Price	Model Yr. Prod
73	53B	4HT	6	$2,701	*
73	65B	2HT	6	$2,732	*

* Production was reported by series and body style with no breakout per engine type. See appropriate Torino V-8 totals below.

TORINO V-8

Year	Body Code	Body Type	Engine Type	MSP Price	Model Yr. Prod
73	53B	4HT	V-8	$2,796	37,524**
73	65B	2HT	V-8	$2,826	28,005**
73	71B	4W	V-8	$3,198	23,982**

** Combined six-cylinder and V-8 production

TOTAL TORINO (SIX & V-8)   **89,511**

GRAN TORINO SIX

Year	Body Code	Body Type	Engine Type	MSP Price	Model Yr. Prod
73	53D	4HT	6	$2,890	*
73	65D	2HT	6	$2,921	*

* Production was reported by series and body style with no breakout per engine type. See totals in next column.

GRAN TORINO V-8

Year	Body Code	Body Type	Engine Type	MSP Price	Model Yr. Prod
73	53D	4HT	6	$2,984	98,404**
73	65D	2HT	6	$3,015	138,962**
73	71D	4W-6	6	$3,559	60,738**

** Combined six-cylinder and V-8 production

TOTAL TORINO (SIX & V-8)   **298,104**

GRAN TORINO BROUGHAM SIX

Year	Body Code	Body Type	Engine Type	MSP Price	Model Yr. Prod
73	53D	4HT	6	$2,890	***
73	65D	2HT	6	$2,921	***

*** No separate production breakout is available for Gran Torino Broughams

GRAN TORINO BROUGHAM V-8

Year	Body Code	Body Type	Engine Type	MSP Price	Model Yr. Prod
73	53D	4HT	6	$2,984	***
73	65D	2HT	6	$3,015	***

*** No separate production breakout is available for Gran Torino Broughams

GRAN TORINO SPORT V-8

Year	Body Code	Body Type	Engine Type	MSP Price	Model Yr. Prod
73	63R	2FB	V-8	$3,664	51,853
73	65R	2HT	V-8	$3,650	17,090

TOTAL GRAN TORINO SPORT V-8   **68,943**

GRAN TORINO SQUIRE V-8

Year	Body Code	Body Type	Engine Type	MSP Price	Model Yr. Prod
73	71K	4W-6	V-8	3559	40023

TOTAL GRAN TORINO SQUIRE   **40,023**

GRAND TOTAL   **496,581**

■ *The race-inspired roofline of the 1968 Torino GT glistens in the sun and left competition in its wake on the NASCAR ovals. It still has a terrific looking stance after all these years.*

Mike Mueller

PRICE GUIDE

Vehicle Condition Scale

6 — Parts car:
May or may not be running, but is weathered, wrecked and/or stripped to the point of being useful primarily for parts.

5 — Restorable:
Needs complete restoration of body, chassis and interior. May or may not be running, but isn't weathered, wrecked or stripped to the point of being useful only for parts.

4 — Good:
A driveable vehicle needing no or only minor work to be functional. Also, a deteriorated restoration or a very poor amateur restoration. All components may need restoration to be "excellent," but the car is mostly useable "as is."

3 — Very Good:
Complete operable original or older restoration. Also, a very good amateur restoration, all presentable and serviceable inside and out. Plus, a combination of well-done restoration and good operable components or a partially restored car with all parts necessary to compete and/or valuable NOS parts.

2 — Fine:
Well-restored or a combination of superior restoration and excellent original parts. Also, extremely well-maintained original vehicle showing minimal wear.

1 — Excellent:
Restored to current maximum professional standards of quality in every area, or perfect original with components operating and apearing as new. A 95-plus point show car that is not driven.

1962 Fairlane, V-8

	6	5	4	3	2	1
4d Sed	332	996	1,660	3,740	5,810	8,300
2d Sed	336	1,008	1,680	3,780	5,880	8,400
2d Spt Cpe	352	1,056	1,760	3,960	6,160	8,800

1963 Fairlane, V-8

	6	5	4	3	2	1
4d Sed	332	996	1,660	3,740	5,810	8,300
2d Sed	336	1,008	1,680	3,780	5,880	8,400
2d HT	420	1,260	2,100	4,730	7,350	10,500
2d Spt Cpe	440	1,320	2,200	4,950	7,700	11,000
4d Sq Wag	580	1,740	2,900	6,530	10,150	14,500
4d Cus Ran	576	1,728	2,880	6,480	10,080	14,400

NOTE: Add 20 percent for 271 hp V-8.

1964 Fairlane, V-8

	6	5	4	3	2	1
4d Sed	324	972	1,620	3,650	5,670	8,100
2d Sed	328	984	1,640	3,690	5,740	8,200
2d HT	660	1,980	3,300	7,430	11,550	16,500
2d Spt HT	700	2,100	3,500	7,880	12,250	17,500
4d Sta Wag	524	1,572	2,620	5,900	9,170	13,100

NOTE: Add 20 percent for 271 hp V-8.

1965 Fairlane, V-8

	6	5	4	3	2	1
4d Sed	328	984	1,640	3,690	5,740	8,200
2d Sed	332	996	1,660	3,740	5,810	8,300
2d HT	480	1,440	2,400	5,400	8,400	12,000
2d Spt HT	660	1,980	3,300	7,430	11,550	16,500
4d Sta Wag	340	1,020	1,700	3,830	5,950	8,500

NOTE: Add 10 percent for 271 hp V-8.

1966 Fairlane, V-8

	6	5	4	3	2	1
4d Sed	320	960	1,600	3,600	5,600	8,000
2d Clb Cpe	324	972	1,620	3,650	5,670	8,100

1966 Fairlane 500

	6	5	4	3	2	1
4d Sed	350	1,060	1,760	3,960	6,160	8,800
2d Cpe	380	1,140	1,900	4,280	6,650	9,500
2d HT	580	1,740	2,900	6,530	10,150	14,500
2d Conv	880	2,640	4,400	9,900	15,400	22,000

1966 Fairlane 500 XL, V-8

	6	5	4	3	2	1
2d HT	660	1,980	3,300	7,430	11,550	16,500
2d Conv	960	2,880	4,800	10,800	16,800	24,000

1966 Fairlane 500 GT, V-8

	6	5	4	3	2	1
2d HT	720	2,160	3,600	8,100	12,600	18,000
2d Conv	1,000	3,000	5,000	11,250	17,500	25,000

1967 Fairlane

	6	5	4	3	2	1
4d Sed	316	948	1,580	3,560	5,530	7,900
2d Cpe	320	960	1,600	3,600	5,600	8,000

1967 Fairlane 500, V-8

	6	5	4	3	2	1
4d Sed	320	960	1,600	3,600	5,600	8,000
2d Cpe	324	972	1,620	3,650	5,670	8,100
2d HT	500	1,500	2,500	5,630	8,750	12,500
2d Conv	700	2,100	3,500	7,880	12,250	17,500
4d Wag	380	1,140	1,900	4,280	6,650	9,500

1967 Fairlane 500 XL, V-8

	6	5	4	3	2	1
2d HT	520	1,560	2,600	5,850	9,100	13,000
2d Conv	800	2,400	4,000	9,000	14,000	20,000
2d HT GT	640	1,920	3,200	7,200	11,200	16,000
2d Conv GT	840	2,520	4,200	9,450	14,700	21,000

1968 Fairlane

	6	5	4	3	2	1
4d Sed	304	912	1,520	3,420	5,320	7,600
2d HT	380	1,140	1,900	4,280	6,650	9,500
4d Sta Wag	352	1,056	1,760	3,960	6,160	8,800

1968 Fairlane 500, V-8

	6	5	4	3	2	1
4d Sed	308	924	1,540	3,470	5,390	7,700
2d HT	440	1,320	2,200	4,950	7,700	11,000
2d FBk	480	1,440	2,400	5,400	8,400	12,000
2d Conv	720	2,160	3,600	8,100	12,600	18,000
4d Sta Wag	356	1,068	1,780	4,010	6,230	8,900

1968 Torino, V-8

	6	5	4	3	2	1
4d Sed	292	876	1,460	3,290	5,110	7,300
2d HT	500	1,500	2,500	5,630	8,750	12,500
4d Wag	360	1,080	1,800	4,050	6,300	9,000

1968 Torino GT, V-8

	6	5	4	3	2	1
2d HT	640	1,920	3,200	7,200	11,200	16,000
2d FBk	720	2,160	3,600	8,100	12,600	18,000
2d Conv	800	2,400	4,000	9,000	14,000	20,000

1969 Fairlane 500, V-8

	6	5	4	3	2	1
4d Sed	264	792	1,320	2,970	4,620	6,600
2d HT	360	1,080	1,800	4,050	6,300	9,000
2d FBk	380	1,140	1,900	4,280	6,650	9,500
2d Conv	640	1,920	3,200	7,200	11,200	16,000

1969 Torino, V-8

	6	5	4	3	2	1
4d Sed	280	840	1,400	3,150	4,900	7,000
2d HT	480	1,440	2,400	5,400	8,400	12,000

1969 Torino GT, V-8

	6	5	4	3	2	1
2d HT	640	1,920	3,200	7,200	11,200	16,000
2d FBk	720	2,160	3,600	8,100	12,600	18,000
2d Conv	840	2,520	4,200	9,450	14,700	21,000

1969 Cobra, V-8

	6	5	4	3	2	1
2d HT	880	2,640	4,400	9,900	15,400	22,000
2d FBk	920	2,760	4,600	10,350	16,100	23,000

1969 Fairlane, 6-cyl.

	6	5	4	3	2	1
4d Wag	364	1,092	1,820	4,100	6,370	9,100
4d 500 Sta Wag	388	1,164	1,940	4,370	6,790	9,700
4d Torino Sta Wag	372	1,116	1,860	4,190	6,510	9,300

NOTE: Add 30 percent for V-8 where available.

1970 Fairlane 500, V-8

	6	5	4	3	2	1
4d Sed	312	936	1,560	3,510	5,460	7,800
2d HT	360	1,080	1,800	4,050	6,300	9,000
4d Sta Wag	348	1,044	1,740	3,920	6,090	8,700

1970 Torino, V-8

	6	5	4	3	2	1
4d Sed	316	948	1,580	3,560	5,530	7,900
4d HT	360	1,080	1,800	4,050	6,300	9,000
2d HT	420	1,260	2,100	4,730	7,350	10,500
2d Sports Roof HT	540	1,620	2,700	6,080	9,450	13,500
4d Sta Wag	360	1,080	1,800	4,050	6,300	9,000

1970 Torino GT, V-8

	6	5	4	3	2	1
2d HT	640	1,920	3,200	7,200	11,200	16,000
2d Conv	760	2,280	3,800	8,550	13,300	19,000

1970 Cobra, V-8

	6	5	4	3	2	1
2d HT	1,040	3,120	5,200	11,700	18,200	26,000

1971 Torino, V-8

	6	5	4	3	2	1
4d Sed	316	948	1,580	3,560	5,530	7,900
2d HT	380	1,140	1,900	4,280	6,650	9,500
4d Sta Wag	356	1,068	1,780	4,010	6,230	8,900

1971 Torino 500, V-8

	6	5	4	3	2	1
4d Sed	320	960	1,600	3,600	5,600	8,000
4d HT	364	1,092	1,820	4,100	6,370	9,100
2d Formal HT	640	1,920	3,200	7,200	11,200	16,000
2d Sports Roof HT	660	1,980	3,300	7,430	11,550	16,500
4d Sta Wag	320	960	1,600	3,600	5,600	8,000
4d HT Brougham	364	1,092	1,820	4,100	6,370	9,100
2d HT Brougham	500	1,500	2,500	5,630	8,750	12,500
4d Sq Sta Wag	404	1,212	2,020	4,550	7,070	10,100
2d HT Cobra	1,040	3,120	5,200	11,700	18,200	26,000
2d HT GT	760	2,280	3,800	8,550	13,300	19,000
2d Conv	860	2,580	4,300	9,680	15,050	21,500

1972 Torino, V-8

	6	5	4	3	2	1
4d Sed	296	888	1,480	3,330	5,180	7,400
2d HT	380	1,140	1,900	4,280	6,650	9,500
4d Sta Wag	348	1,044	1,740	3,920	6,090	8,700

1972 Gran Torino

	6	5	4	3	2	1
4d Pillared HT	300	900	1,500	3,380	5,250	7,500
2d HT	440	1,320	2,200	4,950	7,700	11,000

1972 Gran Torino Sport, V-8

	6	5	4	3	2	1
2d Formal HT	480	1,440	2,400	5,400	8,400	12,000
2d Sports Roof HT	500	1,500	2,500	5,630	8,750	12,500
4d Sta Wag	340	1,020	1,700	3,830	5,950	8,500

1973 Torino, V-8

	6	5	4	3	2	1
4d Sed	216	648	1,080	2,430	3,780	5,400
2d HT	300	900	1,500	3,380	5,250	7,500
4d Sta Wag	224	672	1,120	2,520	3,920	5,600

1973 Gran Torino, V-8

	6	5	4	3	2	1
4d Pillared HT	220	660	1,100	2,480	3,850	5,500
2d HT	320	960	1,600	3,600	5,600	8,000
4d Sta Wag	268	804	1,340	3,020	4,690	6,700

1973 Gran Torino Sport, V-8

	6	5	4	3	2	1
2d Sports Roof HT	460	1,380	2,300	5,180	8,050	11,500
2d Formal HT	480	1,440	2,400	5,400	8,400	12,000
4d Sq Sta Wag	320	960	1,600	3,600	5,600	8,000

1973 Gran Torino Brgm, V-8

	6	5	4	3	2	1
4d Pillared HT	224	672	1,120	2,520	3,920	5,600
2d HT	460	1,380	2,300	5,180	8,050	11,500

■ *This red-coated 1969 Torino GT Cobra stands out, even next to a red caboose, with its Sports Roof styling, hood tie downs, large hood scoop, steel wheels, and raised-letter tires.*

Mike Mueller

Firebird

Personality, staying power
made this bird a big winner

1967-74

1967

G M's first Firebird was a gas-turbine-powered corporate experimental car made in the mid-'50s. When Pontiac brought out its 1967 production-line Firebird, it posed the dream car with the real-world realization of the dream. Personally, I have always been convinced that Pontiac wanted a two-passenger sports car, since its version of the first Corvette—the Bonneville Special—was built for exhibition at the 1954 GM Motorama. I always felt that the Firebird was supposed to be that car, but corporate politics turned it into a four-passenger Camaro spin-off.

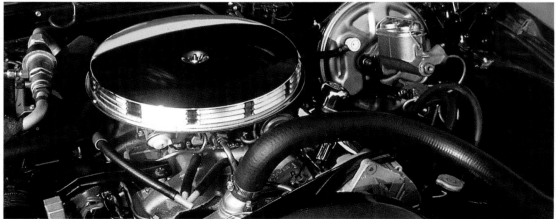

■ *The 1967 Firebird 400 was the top muscle car in the 'bird lineup the first year. It carried a 325-hp version of the same V-8 used in the GTO.*

Jerry Heasley

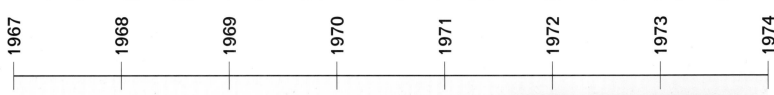

| 1967 | 1968 | 1969 | 1970 | 1971 | 1972 | 1973 | 1974 |

1967: Firebird introduced in February as a late-1967 model based on the Chevy Camaro. A total of 82,560 are sold in a shortened debut year.

1968: Vent windows discontinued.

1968: New 350-cid engine added to options list.

1969: Trans Am introduced March 8 at the Chicago Auto Show. The car was available to the public in April.

1970: Lucerne Blue becomes a color option for the Trans Am. First year for the "shaker" hood scoop.

1971: Honeycomb rims become standard on the Trans Am. High-back bucket seats introduced.

1972: UAW strike crippled Firebird production as the Norwood, Ohio, plant was shut down for 174 days.

1973: The "Screaming Chicken" hood decals and SD-455 models debut.

1974: 455-cid engines are dropped from production at mid-year.

| 1967 | 1968 | 1969 | 1970 | 1971 | 1972 | 1973 | 1974 |

Not wanting to simply produce a Camaro with a split grille and slit tail lights, Pontiac's maverick general manager, John Z. DeLorean, did all he could, within some rigid GM guidelines, to turn the new F-body car into a Pontiac "Corvette." He had PMD engineers beef up the suspension and widen the engine choices, and he rushed the enthusiast-oriented Trans Am model into development.

Pontiac Motor Division did get its two-door sports car when the 1983 Fiero bowed, long after DeLorean was persona non grata at GM. That mid-'80s sporty "world car" with Iron Duke or V-6 motivation was no all-American V-8-powered Corvette. While lovable and fun to drive, the Fiero had nowhere near the Firebird's long-term appeal. It enjoyed a few successful years, then quickly passed from the scene. Like the name "DeLorean," the word "Fiero" was rarely spoken inside GM again.

■ *The red or white line tires were no-cost items on the 1967 400s, but were $31.60 options on the other Firebirds.*
Jerry Heasley

■ *The familiar stacked horizontal tail lights of the early Firebirds were accompanied by 400 badging on the 400 models.*
Jerry Heasley

■ *The Ram Air induction hood gave the Firebird 400 a definite muscle car look in its debut year. This car is wearing aftermarket rims and rubber.*
Jerry Heasley

The Firebird, on the other hand, is a vehicle that inspired passion, built loyalty and survived through thick and thin. During some bleak times in the early '70s, the nameplate nearly vanished, but those who loved it fought like starved wolves to save the car, and it went on to be one of Pontiac's shining successes in the late-'70s and '80s. Word has it that even the post New Millennium disappearance of the Firebird is a temporary break in its history, rather than a permanent burial.

First built in a Lordstown, Ohio factory, starting in early January 1967, the new Firebird was launched at the Chicago Auto Show on February 23, 1967. Perhaps it was fitting to introduce a car with so much wind in its sales in the Windy City. While the Camaro was clearly aimed at the Mustang in a design sense, the Firebird seemed to be taking shots at some marques from "across the pond." Its contorted, undulating, curvy feature lines were more fluid and aggressive-looking than the Camaro's simple and clean-cut appearance. Whereas the Camaro seemed to be smiling, the Firebird had a snarl.

In the engine department, the base 230-cid six and base 326-cid V-8 used in the Firebird matched up in terms of cubic-inch displacement to the Camaro 230 six and 327 V-8, but Pontiac gave you 25 more horsepower with its six and 40 more with its V-8. This was a big selling point if you wanted to be riding the fastest "pony" in Dodge City. Then, too, the Firebird cost about $200 more than the Camaro, model for model, so Pontiac pushed to make the car seem "worth its weight in gold."

The Firebird was offered in coupe and convertible body styles (these were not "models") with Tempest or GTO power trains for motivation. Pontiac had invented the "model-option" when it snuck the GTO package out the door as a stealthy '64 Tempest option. With the Firebird, Pontiac gave fans five model-options to choose from. Each of these option-created-models had specific standard equipment content that gave it a flavor of its own.

The Euro-styled Firebird Sprint featured a 215-hp overhead-cam six-cylinder engine with a four-barrel carburetor, plus a three-speed floor shift and a beefy suspension to make it handle like a European sports car. It had been many

■ *The Trans Am was introduced in 1969 and was designed to be at home on the track—it was inspired by the SCCA sedan racing series.*
Jerry Heasley

■ *Checking the Trans Am option box in 1969 would get you a flashy white car with wide full-body stripes, a 335-hp V-8, heavy-duty shocks and springs, front disc brakes, a deck lid spoiler and other cool stuff.*

Phil Kunz

■ *The redesigned deck lid spoiler was among the many changes on the face-lifted 1970 Trans Am.*

Tom Glatch

decades since an American car was offered with an overhead-cam engine. Like the Corvair's "pancake six," the Pontiac OHC six was different, exciting and exotic. DeLorean loved to pose in pictures with his new "European" power plant and push the selling point that Pontiac had something high-tech that no other American car company offered.

The Firebird Sprint convertible cost $3,019 and the coupe was $2,782. It wasn't a case of the Sprint being the "low-priced six," however, since several of the V-8 model-options were in the same neighborhood as far as window sticker went. Unlike Chevy, Pontiac Motor Division wasn't selling price—it was selling content. You could buy a Firebird set up to race with MGs and Triumphs, or you could buy one set up to drag race a super stock Dodge, but you weren't going to save much money going one way or the other. It was more a question of choosing the style you preferred. Buying extra horsepower was secondary.

Aimed at the average buyer, the Firebird 326 featured a 250-hp two-barrel V-8 for prices only about $20 under a comparable Sprint. It was at this point that you could start paying a little extra to get additional ponies under the hood. The Firebird 326-H.O. used a 285-hp version of the same V-8 with a 10.5:1 compression ratio and a four-barrel carburetor. A column-shift three-speed

manual transmission, dual exhausts, H.O. stripes, a heavy-duty battery and Wide-Oval tires were standard. At this stage of the game, prices were still only about $50 more than those for a Sprint.

The "street performance" version of the early Firebird was the 400. When you had one of these, you were really starting to cook, and adding those extra spices and condiments added to the price tag. The basic Firebird 400 featured a 325-hp version of the 400-cid GTO V-8, a dual-scoop hood, chrome engine parts, a three-speed heavy-duty floor shift and a sport-type suspension. Prices were about $100 higher than a comparable 326 H.O. Ram-Air induction was a $600 extra that gave 325 hp.

If you haven't figured it out yet, the 400 was the model-option that became the Formula 400 and later simply the Formula. Over the years, this offering took on the image of the Firebird with raw power. The two "nostrils" on the hood were the trademark of the 400/Formula for many years.

1968

Since the '67 GM F-bodies arrived later than planned and bowed as midyear additions to the line, the '68 versions of both the Firebird and the Camaro were little changed. Cars of the two years are about as identical as American cars built

with planned obsolescence in mind ever get. In '68, the old "butterfly" style vent windows (which some of us miss immensely) gave way to one-piece side glass. For Firebirds, bias-mounted ("staggered") rear shocks and multi-leaf rear springs were new. Both the '68 coupe and convertible still had under-$3,000 base prices.

The Sprint option had the same European character it had in '67. When you ordered it for $116 extra, Pontiac included a three-speed manual gear stirrer-upper with a floor shifter to grab onto, America's only overhead-cam six engine, Sprint emblems, bright body sill moldings and four fat F70 x 14 tires that made the car look like it could go really fast. The 250-cid overhead-cam six had a single four-barrel carburetor and generated 215 hp.

Pontiac added a 265-hp V-8 to the Firebird when you ordered the 350 package. That may sound like something special today, but in 1968 most cars had V-8s and 265 gross horsepower was not a big eye opener. Don't get me wrong—it was all anyone needed—but the horsepower race was in the stretch in '68 and Detroit was pouring it on. Thus, you had the 350 H.O. option. The "H.O." represented "high output" and meant that you could go motivating over the hill faster than Maybelline. In addition to putting 320 hp on tap, the H.O. content included a three-speed on the tree, throaty dual exhaust pipes, special H.O. side stripes along the lower body, a heavy-duty battery to crank the ponies to life and four F70 x 14 low-profile tires.

The Firebird 400 option kicked prices up another $351-$435 and gave you those slinky-looking dual air scoops to decorate the hood in competition style. Other additions included shiny chrome engine parts, a sport suspension, dual exhausts and snazzy-looking 400 emblems. The 400-cid four-barrel V-8 produced 330 hp and made you an instant hit at the drive-in on Saturday night. If you wanted to hit the drag strip on Sunday, the Ram Air 400 had about the same equipment as the base 400, plus a de-clutching fan and *functional* hood scoops. The Ram Air V-8 produced 335 hp and pushed the car from 0 to 60 in around 7.6 short seconds. Traveling the quarter-mile might take you 15.4 seconds—not bad for a factory hot rod. With a few simple tweaks, you could do even better.

"...The 400 was the model-option that became the Formula 400 and later simply the Formula. Over the years, this offering took on the image of the Firebird with raw power. The two 'nostrils' on the hood were the trademark of the 400/Formula for many years."

■ *The new shaker hood scoop was a prominent feature on the standard 1970 Trans Am's Ram Air 400 engine.*

■ *Only 88 of the 345-hp Ram Air IV motors found their way into 1970 Trans Ams.*

1969

This is the Gen I Firebird that everyone loves. Though not all-new, it got a major re-tailoring that resulted in a squarer body with flatter wheel openings, front fender wind splits, a new roof line and a sculptured lower beltline with a razor-edge crease. Introduced at midyear at the Chicago Auto Show, the new Trans Am was certainly the highlight of the year. With the image of an out-of-the-box sedan-racer, the Trans Am was the most sophisticated Firebird model-option available up to this point. It had a special look and all the bells and whistles needed to put it right up there in the minds of enthusiasts with true sports cars like the Corvette.

All Firebirds had their headlights set into square, body-colored Endura plastic bezels. A boxier split bumper grille was used. With two large rectangles on either side of the center upright, it was a beak that stood right up there with "Buzz" Buzzard's. These design changes gave the front a flatter, taller look. The "Coke bottle" profile was still around, but not quite as pronounced as in '67-'68. The gas filler pipe was relocated behind the rear license plate.

Standard equipment for Firebirds included vinyl front bucket seats, a grained dashboard, floor carpeting, outside rear view mirrors and safety side marker lights. The hardtop and the ragtop were still the basic body styles.

"With the image of an out-of-the-box sedan-racer, the Trans Am was the most sophisticated Firebird model-option available."

■ Side "air extractors" and decaling decorated the front fenders of the 1970 Trans Am.   Tom Glatch

TRANS AM

■ *Plenty of muscle car enthusiasts would argue that the 1970 Trans Am was the coolest car of the crazy-horsepower era. They were truly great-looking cars with lots of horsepower and plenty of "wow" factor.*

Jerry Heasley

Model-options included the Sprint ($121 extra), the Firebird 350 ($111 extra), the Firebird 350 H.O. ($186 extra), the Firebird 400 ($275-$358 extra), the Firebird 400 H.O. ($351-$435 extra) and the Firebird Ram Air 400 ($832 extra)—plus the midyear-and-later Trans Am.

The features of each of the carryover model-options were similar to 1968. The new Trans Am included a heavy-duty three-speed manual gearbox with a floor-mounted gear shifter, a 3.55:1 ratio rear axle, fat glass-belted tires, heavy-duty shock absorbers and springs, a one-inch stabilizer bar, power front disc brakes, variable-ratio power steering, body side scoops that served as engine-air extractors, a rear-deck air foil, a black-textured grille, white finish with dual

longitudinal blue stripes, a leather-covered steering wheel and special "Trans Am" identification decals.

Arriving late in the year, the Trans Am had little trouble generating interest. *Hot Rod* magazine put a solid silver pilot model to the test. When the news got out, Pontiac dealers started feeling demand for the model. Ultimately, the Trans Am hardtop had a production run of just 689 units. In addition, eight copies of a one-year-only Trans Am convertible were built—four with automatic transmission and four with stick.

The Trans Am grew out of the Sports Car Club of America's Trans-American sedan racing series. PMD even had to pay the SCCA a $5 royalty per car to use the name (even though Pontiac spelled it slightly different). The car had the look of a Shelby GT-350H rent-a-racer, but in this case you bought it at the local Pontiac dealership and drove it to the racetrack.

As originally planned, the Trans Am—or "T/A"—was supposed to get a special super-high-performance 303-cid small-block V-8 that would have made it race-eligible under the Trans Am racing formula. About 25 cars were actually fitted with the short-stroke 303-cid tunnel-port V-8s, but these were used exclusively for SCCA Trans-Am competition. None made it to the streets. Production models could have either a 335-hp 400 H.O. (a.k.a. Ram Air III) V-8, or an optional 345-hp Ram Air IV engine. Quarter-miles times for Trans Ams were in the 14- to 14.5- second bracket.

Power outputs for the other model options either stayed the same or rose in a few cases. The overhead-cam six remained at 230 hp and the base 350 stayed at 265 hp. The Firebird 350 H.O. gained five ponies, the base 400 went up to 330 hp and the Ram Air 400 was unchanged from '68. A Ram Air IV package for the Firebird 400 included a 345-hp motor.

1970

Wow, was the '70 1/2 Firebird a different car! It arrived late, but it was sure worth waiting for. Styling changes for started right up front, where there was a new Maserati-inspired Endura front end with a pair of deeply recessed grilles and single headlights. The safety side markers were of a new split-lens design.

"(The 1970 1/2 Firebird) arrived late, but it was worth waiting for."

The fabulous 1970 1/2 Trans Ams (front) had a tough act to follow in the 1969 editions (at top).

Tom Glatch

Pontiac designers gave the car large, open wheel wells, flush door handles and smooth, clean, curvy body panels. The overall effect was to modernize the look and feel of PMD's sports-compact. Firebird lettering and engine badges were placed behind the front wheel openings on most models.

Standard equipment for the basic Firebird included a sourced-from-Chevrolet 250-cid/155-hp *overhead-valve* six, glass-belted tires, front bucket seats, vinyl upholstery, a woodgrained dashboard, carpeting, an outside rearview mirror, manual front disc brakes, wide wheel rims and storage pockets on the interior door panels like a real sports car. Only one body style made the transition to the new design. This sleek two-door hardtop looked more "coupe-like" than ever. It looked for all the world like a European GT coupe that might sell for a much higher price than Pontiac charged for it.

An upscale model-option was introduced along with the new styling. This Esprit edition had chrome "Esprit" signatures on its roof pillars, custom knit-vinyl upholstery, a deluxe steering wheel, dual sport-style outside rearview mirrors, concealed windshield wipers, a concealed radio antenna, a mat for the trunk floor, bright wheel trim rings, chrome decor moldings and a standard 350-cid two-barrel V-8. In reality, this was a Firebird meant for the ladies who wanted to get a little bit sporty without getting crazy.

The performance-oriented Firebird 400 became the Formula 400. This was the "brute-force" performance car made for good ole American boys who carried their cigarettes in the sleeve of their T-shirt. The Formula 400—even the name sounded tough—included fat stabilizer bars to stiffen the suspension, hard-riding high-rate springs, wind-up rear axle controls, bias-belted tires, extra-wide wheel rims, manual front disc brakes, rear drum brakes, carpets, who-cares-if-it's-hot vinyl upholstery, front and rear bucket type seats, dual outside sport rearview mirrors, concealed wipers and antennas and a deluxe steering wheel. Power came from a 400-cid four-barrel V-8 with 10.25:1 compression and 265 hp. It was attached to a sturdy three-speed gearbox with a "hairy" Hurst shifter (on the floor, of course). The Formula 400 had extra-long twin hood scoops and special model nameplates.

"(The Formula 400) was the 'brute-force' performance car made for the good ole American boys who carried their cigarettes in the sleeve of their T-shirt."

Trans Am the II was an all-new car, but it was basically similar in its trademark features to the original 1969 1/2 version. A plethora of aerodynamic enhancements gave the impression that someone had turned left instead of right in the paddocks and wound up driving his sedan-racer out into the street. The Trans Am carried a massive front air dam, a front spoiler and a rear spoiler, a "shaker" hood scoop that literally "rocked" (it stuck through a hole in the hood and actually vibrated), engine air extractors behind the front wheel wells and streamlined racing-style outside mirrors. It had an exotic sports car look.

The Trans Am was no slouch in the performance technology department, either. It had front and rear suspension stabilizers, heavy-duty shock absorbers, heavy-duty springs, a techno-look engine-turned dash insert, a Rally instrument gauge cluster, concealed wipers, front bucket seats, carpets, vinyl upholstery, power brakes, power steering and 11-inch-wide, 15-inch diameter Rally rims with wide F60-15 white-letter tires. Trans Ams came only in white or blue paint colors with contrasting racing stripes in the alternate color.

The standard V-8 in the new Trans Am was a 400-cid/335-hp Ram Air H.O. (Ram Air III) V-8. An improved Ram Air IV with 370 hp was available for $390 extra. A wide-ratio four-speed manual gearbox with Hurst floor shift was standard. The Ram Air III Trans Am did 0 to 60 mph in 6.0 seconds and the quarter-mile in 14.6.

1971

Twenty bonus points anyone who can pick the '71 Trans Am out of a fleet of '70s! Styling updates were absolutely of the minor variety. New high-back seats pirated from the Chevy Vega were used. New wheel covers appeared and all models except the Trans Am added simulated air-intake louvers behind the front wheel cutouts. The standard equipment on the Firebirds was essentially unchanged.

The base engine was a 145-hp/250-cid six. The Espirit (the car for "girly-men") came with a mild 350-cid two-barrel V-8 with 250 hp. The Spartan, but muscular, Formula continued as the "street-performance" version of Pontiac's sporty compact. It could now be ordered three different ways—Formula 350,

■ *In 1971, the Trans Am didn't change much, but it did get the new LS5 335-hp H.O. engine under the hood.* Jerry Heasley

Formula 400 or Formula 455. Each carried a V-8 engine with a cubic-inch count matching the model name and appropriate badging. The engines used were the two-barrel 350-cid V-8, the four-barrel 400-cid V-8 or the four-barrel 455-cid V-8.

Standard equipment for the Trans Am was about the same as in 1970. The "sophisticated performance" version of the Firebird had the new high-back seats and slightly revised grille trim. Styled wheels with a startling (for the time) honeycomb wheel design were a new addition to the options list. A rarely ordered rear console was another option introduced for the year. A chrome engine dress-up kit was no longer standard equipment, though you could spend extra to get it.

■ *Springfield Green paint provided a unique look for this 1972 Firebird.*
Phil Kunz

■ *1972 was the last year of the single wide stripe on the Trans Ams.*
Phil Kunz

A new LS5 455 H.O. engine with four-barrel carburetion and 8.4:1 compression produced 335 hp. In standard configuration, it came hooked to a heavy-duty three-speed manual gearbox with a floor shifter.

Trans Am production dropped very low (2,116) this model year. There was a lot of uncertainty about the future of the muscle car, and this uncertainty was pulling sales of such models down.

As was the case in 1971, the 1972 Trans Am was available in Cameo White or Lucerne Blue with contrasting stripes. A total of 1,286 Trans Ams were built for this model year, making them among the more collectible Firebirds.

Jerry Heasley

■ *This Lucerne Blue 1972 Trans Am was fully restored to showroom condition, right down to the window sticker.*
Tom Glatch

1972

General Motors had plans to banish the Firebird after 1972, so Pontiac wasn't able to make many updates. The overall design of the car was unchanged. New honeycomb pattern inserts filled both halves of the grille. The interior trim selection offered new designs. The hubcaps and wheel covers were restyled.

Standard equipment in the entry-level base Firebird included front bucket seats, bucket style rear seats, all-vinyl upholstery, carpets, an Endura nose, a small full-width front air dam, a Chevy-built six and a "three-on-the-tree" manual transmission. Starting prices were still under $3,000.

The dressy Firebird Esprit had model name scripts on its roof pillars, custom cloth-and-Morrokide upholstery, distinctive door panels, a perforated

headliner and other slightly upscale soft trim that added about $300 to the window sticker. Though not a real enthusiast's car, the Esprit was a great grocery getter and Pontiac sold 11,415 of this model. That was almost as high as the 12,000 base Firebirds sold, so the Espirit was a buggy that beefed-up the bottom line pretty nicely.

The rump-rump-rump Formula retained its muscular street performance car image with a pair of nostril-like up-front air scoops projecting from a special fiberglass hood. A thick front stabilizer and firm shocks gave it a firm ride. Fat tires filling the wheel wells and dual exhausts with chrome tips jutting out the rear added to the attack-dog look. A four-barrel 350-cid V-8 was standard, but 400-cid and 455 H.O. V-8s could also be ordered. With the performance era winding to a close, only one out of six Firebird buyers specified Formula models.

As usual, the Trans Am looked like a racecar that spun off the track and wound up on Main Street. It had a sedan-racer image with a JEGS catalog full of goodies like a Formula steering wheel, an engine-turned instrument panel insert, a rally gauge cluster, a front air dam, flared fender openings and a rear deck lid spoiler. The model option included fast-rate power steering, a king kong suspension, a Safe-T-Track axle and a 300-hp 455 H.O. V-8 with cold-air induction. Stirring the gears was accomplished with a floor-shifted four-speed close-ratio gear box or the no-cost-optional Turbo-Hydra-Matic unit. The '72 was another rare T/A, with a mere 1,286 such cars departing the assembly line.

1973

In terms of high-performance muscle cars, 1973 was the year of the Super-Duty 455 V-8, which Pontiac offered in Firebird Formula and Trans Am models. After its near-death experience in '72, the F-car was now making a comeback of sorts and Pontiac added just a little new sparkle to each model-option. This was also the first year you could get a big "screaming chicken" graphic for the hood of your Trans Am if you wanted to have everyone in the neighborhood talking about your car (and every cop in town laying in wait to write you a "fast driving award.")

All '73 Firebirds came with a new "egg-crate" grille. Styling was not greatly changed, but General Motors technicians were forced to re-engineer the Endura

"After its near-death experience in '72, the F-car was now making a comeback and Pontiac added just a little new sparkle to each model-option."

Firebird 1967-1974

171

■ *The Super-Duty 455 Trans Ams were new to the Firebird lineup in 1973. They were high-performance cars that carried special engine heads and headers. The go-fast updates to the Ram Air IV motors helped propel the cars to 13.5-second quarter-mile times.*

Jerry Heasley

nose piece to make it to meet new federal crash standards. This, of course, added some extra weight. Otherwise, standard equipment was basically similar to 1972. Engine choices, started with the traditional Chevy-built 250-cid inline, overhead-valve six that was down to 100 net hp on paper.

The '73 Firebird Esprit featured a revised custom interior and African crossfire mahogany interior accents. A 150-nhp version of the 350-cid V-8 with a two-barrel carb was standard. This model continued to grow in popularity and model-year production took a nice upward leap to 17,249 units.

Formula Firebirds could again be identified by the special twin-scoop hoods. Other features included a custom cushion steering wheel, a heavy-duty suspension, a black-textured grille, a 175-hp Formula 350 V-8 with dual exhausts and F70-14 tires. Engine options up to 310 nhp were offered.

The popularity of the Formula nearly doubled as people began to realize that it was one of the better bargains in high-performance cars available in 1973. It did not use all of the Trans Am bolt-ons, but it was otherwise a real street machine. In fact, the car magazines of the day were quick to point out that the '73 Formula and Trans Am with the new SD-455 V-8 were noticeably faster than all other American cars that year—including the once king-of-the-hill Corvette.

For the racing-style Trans Am, the most significant alterations made in 1973 were the addition of stylized Firebird graphics for the hood and the release of the Super-Duty 455-cid V-8. Stylist John Schinella created the so-called "chicken" hood decal by taking the legendary Firebird Indian symbol and redoing it in a colorful, stylized rendition. Adding this "artwork" to the hood immediately changed the Trans Am's image from a clean competition coupe look to one of "movie marquee" attention-grabbing flash and brightness. The decaled-hood Trans Am was like the Great White Way on wheels—a rolling flame designed to attract fireflies at every street corner. It still looked "special," but in an entirely

■ *Only 252 of the 4,800 1973 Trans Ams produced featured the SD-455 option (left). The SD-455-equipped cars came only in Brewster Green, Cameo White or Buccaneer Red.* Jerry Heasley

different way. And as things turned out, it was a look that appealed to many car buyers in the late-'70s "Saturday Night Fever" era.

The SD-455 engine was a true engineering marvel in its era. Pontiac's first Super-Duty cars had been early '60s drag machines that relied on cubic inches, high compression ratios and special multi-carb induction systems to produce blazing performance in the quarter-mile. The awesome SD-455 V-8 was different. It evolved from the Trans-Am racing program of the early '70s where the goal was to get power without big cubes. The SD-455 represented a low-compression, extra-horsepower option that could made available, in limited quantities, for street performance applications.

The SD-455 V-8 featured a special cast-iron engine block with reinforced webbing, large forged-steel connecting rods, special aluminum pistons, a heavy-duty oiling system with dry-sump pump provision, a high-lift camshaft, four-bolt main bearing caps, special valve train components, fat dual exhausts and a special intake manifold. The special SD-455 cylinder heads were a variation on Pontiac's Ram Air IV heads. They had 1.77-inch exhaust valves

■ *Buccaneer Red was an eye-catching color for an eye-catching car—the 1973 Super-Duty 455 Trans Am.*

Phil Kunz

and 2.11-inch intake valves with special cupped heads and swirl-polish finish. The SD-455's free-flowing cast-iron round-port exhaust headers were designed for performance, too. The SD-455 Trans Am was capable of 0 to 60 mph in 7.3 seconds. It could run the quarter-mile in 15 seconds flat.

The standard equipment for the '73 Trans Am was the same provided in 1972. For the model year, a total of 4,802 Trans Ams were built. Production of SD-455 Trans Ams totaled 252 (180 with automatic transmission and 72 with manual transmission). Fifty Formula Firebirds also had the SD-455 V-8.

1974

The '74 Trans Am adopted a new, shovel-nosed front end and redesigned horizontal-slot tail lights. The front fender line was lowered a bit and horizontal rectangular inserts with vertical blades filled both grille openings. Some of the new styling motifs were based on a Banshee dream car that made the rounds of auto shows in this era. They didn't greatly improve the Firebird's look, though they did modernize it. Otherwise, very little changed from 1973. Sales of the basic Firebird almost doubled as a resurgence of F-car interest began.

"The awesome SD-455 evolved from the Trans-Am racing program of the early '70s where the goal was to get power without big cubes."

■ *Only 58 of the 1974 Formula Firebirds carried the SD-455 engine. This car is one of the lucky few.*

Phil Kunz

As usual, model badges decorated the Esprit's roof. Standard on this line were the typical trim enhancements and added convenience equipment. The Esprit remained a V-8-only model with a standard 350-cid V-8. This model-option saw another nice increase in sales, though not as much as the base model percentage wise.

For street urchins on wheels, the Formula was back to crawl the highway in search of the next stoplight grand prix. The Formula came with basic hubcaps, but a special dual-scoop fiberglass hood. The grille got the black texture treatment to make the car look "nasty." You could again settle for a Formula 350 or order up Formula 400 and Formula 455 packages. Production went from the 10,000-car range to the 14,500 range—not bad. Overall, the Firebird was on a roll that would continue for a while.

If other Firebirds did well in 1974, the Trans Am did fantastic. Word was getting around the auto industry that the muscle car was dead—except at Pontiac Motor Division, where you could still get the SD-455 V-8 in some models, if you were willing to pay for it. As a result, Pontiac was selling more and more Firebirds to those still interested in driving the fastest car in town.

Trans Am output increased by some 250 percent! The SD-455 V-8 went into 212 Firebirds during the 1974 model year. Most of these cars were Trans Ams, but it was still offered for the Formula Firebird as well.

Standard equipment for '74 Trans Ams included a Formula steering wheel, rally gauges with a clock and tachometer, a swirl-grain dashboard, a full-width rear deck lid spoiler, power steering and front disc brakes, a limited-slip differential, wheel opening flares, front fender air extractors, dual exhausts with chrome extensions, Rally II wheels with trim rings, a special heavy-duty suspension, a four-speed manual transmission or M40 Turbo-Hydra-Matic, dual outside racing mirrors and F60-15 white-lettered tires. Production climbed to 10,255.

When 1974 ended, it was not the end of the Firebird's "muscle car" days— just a temporary break in the trend. The car's performance image got the sales steamroller going and that carried things through the '70s and into the '80s. With so little real change in the product, you can bet your butt that Pontiac made a bundle off the long-lasting second-generation Firebird. In mid-1982, the

■ *Honeycomb wheels, flared fenders, "screaming chicken" graphics and a long, racy profile were established trademarks of the second-generation Trans Ams by 1974.*
Jerry Heasley

Jerry Heasley

FIREBIRD YEAR-BY-YEAR SPEC'S

1967

Engine	Bore/Str.	Comp. Ratio	CID	BHP	WT.	W.B.	O.L.	Width	HT
OHC 6	3.85 x 3.25	07.60	230	155 @ 4400	2,955	108.1	188.8	72.5	51.4
V-8	3.178 x 3.75	09.20	326	250 @ 4600	3,323	108.1	188.8	72.5	51.4
OHC 6	3.85 x 3.25	09.00	230	165 @ 4700	2,955	108.1	188.8	72.5	51.4
OHC 6	3.85 x 3.25	10.50	230	215 @ 5200	2,955	108.1	188.8	72.5	51.4
V-8	3.178 x 3.75	10.50	326	285 @ 5000	3,323	108.1	188.8	72.5	51.4
V-8	4.125 x 3.75	10.75	400	285 @ 5000	3,323	108.1	188.8	72.5	51.4
V-8 RA	4.125 x 3.75	10.75	400	335 @ 5000	3,323	108.1	188.8	72.5	51.4

1968

Engine	Bore/Str.	Comp. Ratio	CID	BHP	WT.	W.B.	O.L.	Width	HT
OHC 6	3.875 x 3.531	09.00	250	175 @ 4800	2,955	108.1	188.8	72.5	51.4
V-8	3.875 x 3.75	09.20	350	265 @ 4600	3,323	108.1	188.8	72.5	51.4
OHC 6	3.875 x 3.531	10.50	250	215 @ 4800	2,955	108.1	188.8	72.5	51.4
V-8	3.875 x 3.75	10.50	350	320 @ 5100	3,323	108.1	188.8	72.5	51.4
V-8	4.125 x 3.75	10.75	400	330 @ 4800	3,323	108.1	188.8	72.5	51.4
V-8 HO	4.125 x 3.75	10.75	400	335 @ 5300	3,323	108.1	188.8	72.5	51.4
V-8 RA IIII	4.125 x 3.75	10.75	400	335 @ 5000	3,323	108.1	188.8	72.5	51.4
V-8 RA IV	4.125 x 3.75	10.75	400	340 @ 5300	3,323	108.1	188.8	72.5	51.4

1969

Engine	Bore/Str.	Comp. Ratio	CID	BHP	WT.	W.B.	O.L.	Width	HT
OHC 6	3.875 x 3.531	09.00	250	175 @ 4800	2,955	108.1	188.8	72.5	51.4
V-8	3.875 x 3.75	09.20	350	265 @ 4600	3,323	108.1	188.8	72.5	51.4
OHC 6	3.875 x 3.531	10.50	250	215 @ 4800	2,955	108.1	188.8	72.5	51.4
V-8	4.12 x 2.83	12.8	303	475 @ 8000	3,323	108.1	188.8	72.5	51.4
V-8	3.875 x 3.75	10.50	350	325 @ 5100	3,323	108.1	188.8	72.5	51.4
V-8	4.125 x 3.75	10.75	400	330 @ 4800	3,323	108.1	188.8	72.5	51.4
V-8 HO	4.125 x 3.75	10.75	400	335 @ 5300	3,323	108.1	188.8	72.5	51.4
V-8 RA IV	4.125 x 3.75	10.75	400	345 @ 5400	3,323	108.1	188.8	72.5	51.4

1970 1/2

Engine	Bore/Str.	Comp. Ratio	CID	BHP	WT.	W.B.	O.L.	Width	HT
OHV 6	3.875 x 3.531	08.50	250	155 @ 4200	2,955	108.1	188.8	72.5	51.4
V-8	3.875 x 3.75	08.80	350	255 @ 4600	3,323	108.1	188.8	72.5	51.4
V-8	4.125 x 3.75	08.80	400	265 @ 4600	3,323	108.1	188.8	72.5	51.4
V-8	4.125 x 3.75	10.25	400	330 @ 4800	3,323	108.1	188.8	72.5	51.4
V-8 RAIII	4.125 x 3.75	10.75	400	335 @ 5000	3,323	108.1	188.8	72.5	51.4
V-8 RA IV	4.125 x 3.75	10.75	400	345 @ 5400	3,323	108.1	188.8	72.5	51.4

1971

Engine	Bore/Str.	Comp. Ratio	CID	BHP	WT.	W.B.	O.L.	Width	HT
OHV 6	3.875 x 3.531	08.50	250	155 @ 4200	2,955	108.1	188.8	72.5	51.4
V-8	3.875 x 3.75	08.20	350	255 @ 4600	3,323	108.1	188.8	72.5	51.4
V-8	4.125 x 3.75	08.20	400	265 @ 4400	3,323	108.1	188.8	72.5	51.4
V-8	4.125 x 3.75	08.20	400	300 @ 4800	3,323	108.1	188.8	72.5	51.4
V-8 RAIII	4.15 x 4.21	08.20	455	325 @ 4400	3,323	108.1	188.8	72.5	51.4
V-8 RA IV	4.15 x 4.21	08.40	455	335 @ 4800	3,323	108.1	188.8	72.5	51.4

1972

Engine	Bore/Str.	Comp. Ratio	CID	BHP	WT.	W.B.	O.L.	Width	HT
OHV 6	3.875 x 3.531	08.50	250	110 @ 4200	2,955	108.1	188.8	72.5	51.4
V-8	3.875 x 3.75	08.00	350	160 @ 4400	3,323	108.1	188.8	72.5	51.4
V-8	3.875 x 3.75	08.00	350	175 @ 4400	3,323	108.1	188.8	72.5	51.4
V-8	4.125 x 3.75	08.20	400	175 @ 4000	3,323	108.1	188.8	72.5	51.4
V-8	4.125 x 3.75	08.20	400	250 @ 4400	3,323	108.1	188.8	72.5	51.4
V-8 HO	4.15 x 4.21	08.40	455	300 @ 4000	3,323	108.1	188.8	72.5	51.4

Net horsepower ratings

1973

Engine	Bore/Str.	Comp. Ratio	CID	BHP	WT.	W.B.	O.L.	Width	HT
OHV 6	3.875 x 3.531	08.50	250	110 @ 4200	2,955	108.1	188.8	72.5	51.4
V-8	3.875 x 3.75	07.60	350	150 @ 4000	3,323	108.1	188.8	72.5	51.4
V-8	3.875 x 3.75	07.60	350	175 @ 4400	3,323	108.1	188.8	72.5	51.4
V-8	4.125 x 3.75	08.00	400	170 @ 3600	3,323	108.1	188.8	72.5	51.4
V-8	4.125 x 3.75	08.00	400	185 @ 4000	3,323	108.1	188.8	72.5	51.4
V-8	4.125 x 3.75	08.00	400	230 @ 4400	3,323	108.1	188.8	72.5	51.4
V-8	4.15 x 4.21	08.00	455	250 @ 4000	3,323	108.1	188.8	72.5	51.4
V-8 SD	4.15 x 4.21	08.00	455	290 @ 4000	3,323	108.1	188.8	72.5	51.4

Net horsepower ratings

1974

Engine	Bore/Str.	Comp. Ratio	CID	BHP	WT.	W.B.	O.L.	Width	HT
OHV 6	3.875 x 3.531	08.50	250	100 @ 3600	2,955	108.1	188.8	72.5	51.4
V-8	3.875 x 3.75	07.60	350	155 @ 3600	3,323	108.1	188.8	72.5	51.4
V-8	3.875 x 3.75	07.60	350	170 @ 4000	3,323	108.1	188.8	72.5	51.4
V-8	4.125 x 3.75	08.00	400	190 @ 3600	3,323	108.1	188.8	72.5	51.4
V-8	4.125 x 3.75	08.00	400	200 @ 4000	3,323	108.1	188.8	72.5	51.4
V-8	4.125 x 3.75	08.00	400	225 @ 4000	3,323	108.1	188.8	72.5	51.4
V-8	4.15 x 4.21	08.00	455	250 @ 4000	3,323	108.1	188.8	72.5	51.4
V-8	4.15 x 4.21	08.00	455	250 @ 4000	3,323	108.1	188.8	72.5	51.4
V-8 SD	4.15 x 4.21	08.00	455	290 @ 4000	3,323	108.1	188.8	72.5	51.4

Net horsepower ratings

third-generation Firebird would debut and offer up a new, high-tech blend of performance that made the F-car a muscle machine in the modern idiom.

From then until the end of production in 2002, the Firebird would carry fourth the muscle car torch in one form or another ranging from a hot Turbo V-6 Indy Pace Car to the all-American-V-8-powered WS6 in "factory" and SLP (Street Legal Performance) versions. Better still, it looks like the Firebird might soon be back to thrill another generation of lead-footed muscle car maniacs.

■ *Pontiac produced about 1,286 Trans Ams for 1972 with a factory price of about $4,200. A survivor carrying a SD-455 motor might fetch 10 times that amount today.*
Jerry Heasley

PRODUCTION STATISTICS AND BREAKOUTS

1967 FIREBIRD PRODUCTION

Year	Body Code	Body Type	Engine Type	MSP Price	Model Yr. Prod.
67	STD37	2HT	6	$2,666	9,374
67	STD67	2CV	6	$2,903	1,483
TOTAL					**10,897**
67	STD37	2HT	8	$2,761	19,119
67	STD67	2CV	8	$2,998	4,406
TOTAL					**23,525**
STANDARD FIREBIRD GRAND TOTAL					**34,382**
67	DLX37	2HT	6	$2,774	5,653
67	DLX67	2CV	6	$3,011	1,161
TOTAL					**6,814**
67	DLX37	2HT	8	$2,869	32,886
67	DLX67	2CV	8	$3,106	8,478
TOTAL					**41,364**
DELUXE FIREBIRD GRAND TOTAL					**48,178**
ALL FIREBIRD TOTAL					**82,560**

Note: 1967-1968 tables are from recently released General Motors 1955-1968 production data records.

1968 FIREBIRD

Year	Body Code	Body Type	Engine Type	MSP Price	Model Yr. Prod.
68	STD37	2HT	6	$2,781	14,000
68	STD67	2CV	6	$2,996	1,969
TOTAL					**15,969**
68	STD37	2HT	8	$2,887	47,302
68	STD67	2CV	8	$3,102	8,580
TOTAL					**55,882**
STANDARD FIREBIRD GRAND TOTAL					**71,851**
68	DLX37	2HT	6	$2,896	2,078
68	DLX67	2CV	6	$3,111	447
TOTAL					**2,525**
68	DLX37	2HT	8	$3,001	26,772
68	DLX67	2CV	8	$3,216	5,964
TOTAL					**32,736**
DELUXE FIREBIRD GRAND TOTAL					**35,261**
ALL FIREBIRD TOTAL					**10,7112**

Note: These are from recently released General Motors 1955-1968 Production data records.

1969 FIREBIRD

Year	Body Code	Body Type	Engine Type	MSP Price	Model Yr. Prod.
BASE FIREBIRD OHC 6					
69	22337	2HT	6	$2,830	74,673 *
69	22367	2CV	6	$3,044	11,641 *
FIREBIRD SPRINT OHC 6					
69	22337	2HT	8	$2,951	*
69	22367	2CV	8	$3,165	*
FIREBIRD 350					
69	22337	2HT	8	$2,941	*
69	22367	2CV	8	$3,155	*
FIREBIRD 350 H.O.					
69	22337	2HT	8	$3,137	*
69	22367	2CV	8	$3,230	*
FIREBIRD 400					
69	22337	2HT	8	$3,262	*
69	22367	2CV	8	$3,460	*
FIREBIRD 400 RAM AIR					
69	22337	2HT	8	$3,388	*
69	22367	2CV	8	$3,602	*
FIREBIRD 400 RAM AIR IV					
69	22337	2HT	8	$3,662	*
69	22367	2CV	8	$3,876	*
TRANS AM					
69	22337	2HT	8	$3,556	689
69	22367	2CV	8	$3,770	8
ALL FIREBIRD TOTAL					**87,011**

Production notes:
* Production figures are recorded by body style. The only breakout available is for the Trans Am models.

1970 1/2 FIREBIRD

Year	Body Code	Body Type	Engine Type	MSP Price	Model Yr. Prod.
BASE FIREBIRD SIX					
70 1/2	22387	2HT	6	$2,875	18,874*
FIREBIRD ESPRIT V-8					
70 1/2	22487	2HT	8	$3,241	18,961
FIREBIRD FORMULA 400 V-8					
70 1/2	22687	2HT	8	$3,370	7,708
TRANS AM V-8					
70 1/2	22887	2HT	8	$4,305	3,196
ALL FIREBIRD TOTAL					**48,739**

Production notes:
* Combined total for six-cylinder and V-8.

1971 FIREBIRD

Year	Body Code	Body Type	Engine Type	MSP Price	Model Yr. Prod.
BASE FIREBIRD SIX					
71	22387	2HT	6	$2,875	23,021*
FIREBIRD ESPRIT V-8					
71	22487	2HT	8	$3,241	20,185
FIREBIRD FORMULA 350 V-8					
71	22687	2HT	8	$3,440	**
FIREBIRD FORMULA 400 V-8					
71	22687	2HT	8	$3,540	**
FIREBIRD FORMULA 455 V-8					
71	22687	2HT	8	$3,625	**
TRANS AM V-8					
71	22887	2HT	8	$4,464	2,116
ALL FIREBIRD TOTAL					**53,124**

Production notes:
* Combined total for six-cylinder and V-8 (2,975 six-cylinder cars were built)
** Combined production for all Formula models was 7,802
Manual transmission used in 2,778 Firebirds; 947 Esprits;1,860 Formula Firebirds and 885 Trans Ams
Automatic transmission used in 20,244 Firebirds; 19,238 Esprits; 5,942 Formula Firebirds and 1,231 Trans Ams

1972 FIREBIRD

Year	Body Code	Body Type	Engine Type	MSP Price	Model Yr. Prod.
BASE FIREBIRD SIX					
72	2S87	2HT	6	$2,838	1,095
BASE FIREBIRD V-8					
72	2S87	2HT	8	$2,956	10,905
FIREBIRD ESPRIT V-8					
72	2T87	2HT	8	$3,194	11,415
FIREBIRD FORMULA 350 V-8					
72	2U87	2HT	8	$3,221	*
FIREBIRD FORMULA 400 V-8					
72	2U87	2HT	8	—	*
FIREBIRD FORMULA 455 V-8					
72	2U87	2HT	8	—	*
TRANS AM V-8					
72	2V87	2HT	8	$4,256	1,286
ALL FIREBIRD TOTAL					**29,951**

Production notes:
* Combined production for all Formula models was 5,250
Manual transmission used in 1,263 Firebirds; 504 Esprits;1,082 Formula Firebirds and 458 Trans Ams
Automatic transmission used in 10,738 Firebirds; 10,911 Esprits; 4,167 Formula Firebirds and 828 Trans Ams

1973 FIREBIRD

Year	Body Code	Body Type	Engine Type	MSP Price	Model Yr. Prod.
BASE FIREBIRD SIX					
73	2FS	2HT	6	$2,895	1,370
BASE FIREBIRD V-8					
73	2FS	2HT	8	$3,013	12,726
FIREBIRD ESPRIT V-8					
73	2FT	2HT	8	$3,249	17,299
FIREBIRD FORMULA 350 V-8					
73	2FU	2HT	8	$3,276	4,771

FIREBIRD FORMULA 400 V-8					
73	2FU	2HT	8	$3,373	4,622

FIREBIRD FORMULA 455 V-8					
73	2FU	2HT	8	$3,430	730

FIREBIRD FORMULA SD-455 V-8					
73	2FU	2HT	8	$3,951	43

TRANS AM V-8					
73	2V87	2HT	8	$4,204	4,550

TRANS AM SD-455 V-8					
73	2V87	2HT	8	$4,256	252

ALL FIREBIRD TOTAL					46,313

1974 FIREBIRD PRODUCTION

Year	Body Code	Body Type	Engine Type	MSP (Price	Model Yr. Prod.
BASE FIREBIRD SIX					
74	2FS	2HT	6	$3,175	7,063
BASE FIREBIRD V-8					
74	2FS	2HT	8	$3,305	18,769
FIREBIRD ESPRIT V-8					
74	2FT	2HT	8	$3,527	22,583
FIREBIRD FORMULA 350 V-8					
74	2FU	2HT	8	$3,614	*

FIREBIRD FORMULA 400 V-8					
74	2FU	2HT	8	$3,711	*

FIREBIRD FORMULA 455 V-8					
74	2FU	2HT	8	$3,768	*

FIREBIRD FORMULA SD-455 V-8					
74	2FU	2HT	8	$4,289	58

TRANS AM 400 V-8					
74	2V87	2HT	8	$4,351	4,664

TRANS AM 455 V-8					
74	2V87	2HT	8	$4,408	4,648

TRANS AM SD-455 V-8					
74	2V87	2HT	8	$4,929	943

ALL FIREBIRD TOTAL					73,729

PRICE GUIDE

Vehicle Condition Scale

6 — Parts car:
May or may not be running, but is weathered, wrecked and/or stripped to the point of being useful primarily for parts.

5 — Restorable:
Needs complete restoration of body, chassis and interior. May or may not be running, but isn't weathered, wrecked or stripped to the point of being useful only for parts.

4 — Good:
A driveable vehicle needing no or only minor work to be functional. Also, a deteriorated restoration or a very poor amateur restoration. All components may need restoration to be "excellent," but the car is mostly useable "as is."

3 — Very Good:
Complete operable original or older restoration. Also, a very good amateur restoration, all presentable and serviceable inside and out. Plus, a combination of well-done restoration and good operable components or a partially restored car with all parts necessary to compete and/or valuable NOS parts.

2 — Fine:
Well-restored or a combination of superior restoration and excellent original parts. Also, extremely well-maintained original vehicle showing minimal wear.

1 — Excellent:
Restored to current maximum professional standards of quality in every area, or perfect original with components operating and apearing as new. A 95-plus point show car that is not driven.

1967 Firebird, V-8

	6	5	4	3	2	1
2d Cpe	960	2,880	4,800	10,800	16,800	24,000
2d Conv	1,120	3,360	5,600	12,600	19,600	28,000

Note: Deduct 25 percent for 6-cyl. Add 20 percent for 326 HO. Add 10 percent for 4-speed. Add 20 percent for 400 /4V carb. Add 30 percent for the Ram Air 400 Firebird.

1968 Firebird, V-8

	6	5	4	3	2	1
2d Cpe	960	2,880	4,800	10,800	16,800	24,000
2d Conv	1,120	3,360	5,600	12,600	19,600	28,000

Note: Deduct 25 percent for 6-cyl. Add 20 percent for 350 HO. Add 10 percent for 4-speed. Add 25 percent for the Ram Air 400 Firebird.

1969 Firebird, V-8

	6	5	4	3	2	1
2d Cpe	960	2,880	4,800	10,800	16,800	24,000
2d Conv	1,120	3,360	5,600	12,600	19,600	28,000
2d Trans Am Cpe	1,280	3,840	6,400	14,400	22,400	32,000
2d Trans Am Conv	1,560	4,680	7,800	17,550	27,300	39,000

Note: Deduct 25 percent for 6-cyl. Add 25 percent for "HO" 400 Firebird. Add 10 percent for 4-speed. Add 20 percent for Ram Air IV Firebird. Add 50 percent for "303" V-8 SCCA race engine.

1970 Firebird, V-8

	6	5	4	3	2	1
2d Firebird	720	2,160	3,600	8,100	12,600	18,000
2d Esprit	740	2,220	3,700	8,330	12,950	18,500
2d Formula 400	760	2,280	3,800	8,550	13,300	19,000
2d Trans Am	1,120	3,360	5,600	12,600	19,600	28,000

NOTE: Deduct 25 percent for 6-cyl. Add 10 percent for Trans Am with 4-speed. Add 25 percent for Ram Air IV Firebird.

1971 Firebird, V-8

	6	5	4	3	2	1
2d Firebird	740	2,220	3,700	8,330	12,950	18,500
2d Esprit	720	2,160	3,600	8,100	12,600	18,000
2d Formula	760	2,280	3,800	8,550	13,300	19,000
2d Trans Am	1,120	3,360	5,600	12,600	19,600	28,000

Note: Add 25 percent for Formula 455. Deduct 25 percent for 6-cyl. Add 40 percent for 455 HO V-8. Add 10 percent for 4-speed. (Formula Series - 350, 400, 455).

1972 Firebird, V-8

	6	5	4	3	2	1
2d Firebird	640	1,920	3,200	7,200	11,200	16,000
2d Esprit	620	1,860	3,100	6,980	10,850	15,500
2d Formula	660	1,980	3,300	7,430	11,550	16,500
2d Trans Am	780	2,340	3,900	8,780	13,650	19,500

Note: Add 10 percent for Trans Am with 4-speed. Deduct 25 percent for 6-cyl. Add 40 percent for 455 HO V-8.

1973 Firebird, V-8

	6	5	4	3	2	1
2d Cpe	620	1,860	3,100	6,980	10,850	15,500
2d Esprit	640	1,920	3,200	7,200	11,200	16,000
2d Formula	660	1,980	3,300	7,430	11,550	16,500
2d Trans Am	680	2,040	3,400	7,650	11,900	17,000

Note: Add 50 percent for 455 SD V-8 (Formula & Trans Am only). Deduct 25 percent for 6-cyl. Add 10 percent for 4-speed.

1974 Firebird, V-8

	6	5	4	3	2	1
2d Firebird	400	1,200	2,000	4,500	7,000	10,000
2d Esprit	580	1,740	2,900	6,530	10,150	14,500
2d Formula	640	1,920	3,200	7,200	11,200	16,000
2d Trans Am	660	1,980	3,300	7,430	11,550	16,500

Note: Add 40 percent for 455-SD V-8 (Formula & Trans Am only). Deduct 25 percent for 6-cyl. Add 10 percent for 4-speed.

Firebird 1967-1974

Gran Sport

"Buick's marketing people claimed that the Skylark GS was 'a howitzer' with windshield wipers."

■ *Cousin to the Skylark Gran Sport was the Riviera GS option for '66. It included a chrome air cleaner, heavy-duty suspension, a high-performance posi axle, whitewalls and GS ornamentation all for $131.57.*

Doug Mitchell

1965 - 1973
G S / G S X

1965

Buick was struggling to compete with the muscle car insurgency of the early '60s and ultimately took the "if-you-can't-beat-'em-join-'em" approach with a rocket-propelled grenade called the Skylark GS. Now, I drive a '57 Buick Century that has awesome power, but it's more of a high-top-speed car like the state trooper cruiser I own. This was in the Buick tradition of a big, heavy car with buckets of horsepower. The Skylark GS was more about tire-smoking take-offs and getting from 0 to 60 mph in under 8 seconds

With a 400-cid/325-hp V-8, a four-barrel carb and 10.25:1 compression, the Skylark GS tested by *Motor Trend* in May 1965 cranked out .81 hp per cubic inch and fed it through a two-speed Super Turbine 300 automatic transmission with a floor-mounted shifter. (A heavy-duty all-synchromesh floor-mounted three-speed stick shift was standard and a heavy-duty all-synchro four-speed manual was available.) The magazine reported that its 3,720-lb. test car reached the 60-

■ *The first Gran Sport used a beefed-up convertible-type frame that made it sit up higher than other Skylarks and gave a ready-to-run look that blended well with several luxury touches.*

Phil Kunz

1965 1966 1967 1968 1969 1970 1972 1973 1974

1965: Buick unveils its first muscle car with the 401-cid/325-hp Skylark Gran Sport. The cars gain immediate acceptance and almost 16,000 are built.

1966: Redesigned Gran Sports feature sloping roof side panels, new sheet metal and blacked-out grilles.

1967: The GS officially becomes the "GS 400" as a new 400-cid V-8 replaces the "nailhead" 401. Hood scoops now faced forward.

1967: GS 340 introduced as a capable but less-powerful sibling to the GS 400.

1968: "Stage I Special Package," a rare dealer-installed package, increases hp to 345, although actual output was probably closer to 400.

1969: Functional hood scoops are standard.

1970: The Gran Sport reaches its muscle car zenith with the GS 455.

1970: GSX package unveiled and available in Saturn Yellow and Apollo White.

1972: Final year for the Skylark-based GS.

1973: GS based on Century coupe.

1974: GS based on Apollo model. 455-cid engine dropped.

1965 1966 1967 1968 1969 1970 1972 1973 1974

mph mark in a mere 7.8 seconds. It did the quarter-mile in 16.6 seconds at 86 mph and had a top speed of 116 mph. This was not your father's "Roadblaster."

Back in 1965, GM cars had not quite all become clones of each other. There was still a real difference between a Cadillac and a Chevy or an Olds and a Pontiac. Buick emphasized its corporate individuality by going its cousins one better. Its GS muscle car used a beefed-up convertible-type frame that resisted torque flexing. This made it very different from other GM A-body cars, including the standard Buick Specials. As magazine test drivers of the day discovered, the difference made a difference. "It seems to us that Buick has another winner in the Skylark Gran Sport," said Bob McVay, assistant technical editor at Motor Trend. "The point is that better cars are being built—and Buick is building them!"

Naturally, the frame of the Skylark GS was fitted with specially valved shock absorbers and heavy-duty springs at all four corners. A thicker and stiffer anti-roll bar was mounted up front. At the rear, a four-control-arm suspension layout did such a good job handling the tremendous engine power without side sway, that Buick said a rear anti-roll bar was not a necessity. Buick's marketing people claimed that the Skylark GS was "a howitzer with windshield wipers." Today we might call it a Humvee with portholes.

Other features of the first Skylark GS included heavy-duty upper control arm bushings, dual exhausts, 7.75 x 14 tires and a choice of 2.78:1, 3.08:1, 3.23:1, 3.36:1, 3.55:1 and 3.73:1 rear axle ratios. To show what a Skylark Gran Sport could do set up with 4.30 gears and cheater slicks, *Motor Trend* mentioned that Lenny Kennedy's race-prepped example clocked a 13.42-second, 104.46-mph quarter-mile run at the Winternational Drags.

The Gran Sport package cost $256.82 above the price of a regular Skylark with a three-speed transmission. It was sold only with bucket seats, which were $69.94 extra. *Motor Trend's* test car was a "post" coupe with automatic, air conditioning, power steering, radio, PCV system, bucket seats, special exterior trim, two-tone paint and whitewalls, plus miscellaneous small accessories, and went out the door for $3,822.62, plus tax and license. The car got 19.7 mpg at a steady 65 mph and 12.3 mpg in city driving.

■ *Many drivers in the '60s got to know the rear end appearance of the Skylark GS better than its frontal image. After midyear, owners could add the Stage 1 or Stage 2 engine packages for even better performance.*

Tom Glatch

■ *A new-for-'68 body featured a unique S-shaped sweep on the body sides. The grille was a wide, rectangular loop of heavy chrome with a blacked-out insert. A vinyl top was $94.79 extra and Rallye Wheels cost $42.66.*
Doug Mitchel

1966

After one year on the market, the Buick Skylark GS became a separate car line with an all-new body that looked a little more "Big Buick" like and was more heavily sculpted. Where the '65 original looked agile and sporty, the '66 was more "haunched down" and muscular. The black-out grille was separated into four slot-shaped quadrants with a "Gran Sport" nameplate in the lower left-hand corner. Trimming the lower body sides was a full-length chrome molding that arched over the wheel openings and a simulated vertical-slanting chrome air vent behind the front wheels. "Buick" appeared above the center of the grille and simulated air scoops graced the hood. The rear body panel was finished in matte black.

The 1966 Gran Sport was a fairly fancy car for a performance machine. It incorporated many of the plusher features of the Skylark versions of the Special, plus the Gran Sport cosmetic features described above and many mechanical upgrades, including a heavy-duty suspension and a 401-cid/325-hp "Wildcat" V-8 with 10.25:1 compression and a four-barrel carburetor. This engine developed 445 lbs.-ft. of torque at 2800 rpm. To placate the General Motors brass, the engine was advertised as the "400," which made it "GM-legal" for use in an intermediate-sized car. In mid-season, a 340-hp engine option was released. Gran Sport buyers could chose between fat White Line or Red Line tires in size 7.75 x 14.

Inside, the Skylark Gran Sport featured a slick all-vinyl interior with a standard notchback bench seat up front (bucket seats were optional), carpeting and full wheel covers. As in '65, "post" coupe, two-door hardtop and convertible models were marketed. Of the three, the pillared coupe was least popular, the Sport Coupe was most popular and the convertible was the "middle child."

Motor Trend gave the test to a pair of Skylark GS hardtops, both with Super Turbine automatic transmission. One was loaded with options, the other had no options and several mild upgrades, like a 4.30:1 rear axle, racing slicks, headers, shimmed front springs and a transmission kick-down switch. The stock version did 0 to 60 mph in 7.6 seconds and covered the quarter-mile in 15.47 seconds at 90.54 mph. The upgraded car did 0 to 60 in 5.7 seconds and the quarter-mile in 14 seconds at 101 mph! *Car and Driver's* car—also a hardtop—had the 340-hp Wildcat 401 V-8, Super Turbine automatic and other options. It covered the quarter-mile in 14.92 seconds at 95.13 mph.

After driving the '66 Gran Sport, *Motor Trend's* Steve Kelly expressed surprise. "Now and then, we select a car to test which at the outset promises nothing spectacular, but by the conclusion of the testing program, has shown itself to be an automobile of many virtues and few vices," he said. "This is the story, in part, of the Buick Gran Sport."

1967

Buick gave its Specials and Skylarks a quick "facial" for 1967. High-performance versions were changed very little. Although the grille design was similar, the letters "GS" were now used in place of "Gran Sport" name at the left side and they were in the center—not the lower corner. These letters were also repeated on the rear deck lid.

The Skylark Gran Sport series grew by one new model during 1967. This happened when a new GS 340 Sport Coupe was introduced at the Chicago Auto Show on February 25. The original Gran Sport then became the GS 400. Buick called the new model the "GS 400's running mate ... for people who look for a large measure of sporting flavor at a low price." The original still came in three body types: post coupe, two-door hardtop and ragtop.

■ *A large, functional hood scoop was part of the GS equipment. The ragtop retailed for $3,271.* Motor Trend *tested a '68 GS convertible that clocked a 16.3-second quarter-mile at 88 mph.*

Tom Glatch

Buick was smart. Although the GS 340 was aimed at muscle market "bottom feeders," it wasn't cheap. Less than $200 separated it from the GS 400 hardtop. But, it had the snappy appearance of a red-hot chilly pepper, which the GS 400 did not. Among its trademarks were red Ralley stripes along the sides, red non-functional hood scoops, red Ralley wheels and red-accented GS ornamentation. Buyers had to pick Door A or Door B. The GS 340's red-hot image was behind one, and the GS 400's cool-looking muscle motor was behind the other.

What made the GS-340 interesting is that it beat the '68 Plymouth Road Runner to market. Conceptually, both models sprung from the same idea: give young buyers the muscle image without the horsepower so they could not "walk the walk" while saving money on insurance. The Road Runner had more cubes and horses in standard form, but both cars came with plain bench seat interiors and a long list of good things on the options list.

The 340-cid/260-hp V-8 was the same engine a buyer could order for any other mid-size Buick, including wagons, but it come with a standard four-speed manual gearbox. GS 340 options included a Sport Pac suspension with heavy-duty underpinnings, a thick rear stabilizer bar and 15:1 steering.

■ Dual exhausts were standard fare on this 340-hp GS 400 convertible. Other features included GS badges, wheel lip moldings and bright rear deck lid moldings with a "GS 400" call-out just below the trunk lock.

Tom Glatch

■ Interior features of the GS 400 included ashtrays, a heater and defroster, a cigar lighter, a key warning system. Operating console was a $57.93 option and required bucket seats which cost $68.46.

Tom Glatch

■ *The '68 Gran Sport was a well-decorated car with lots of chrome. Simulated air vents behind from wheels had "GS" and engine call-outs just above them. Standard equipment tires were 7.75 x 14 whitewalls.*

Tom Glatch

■ *The '68 Gran Sport was considered a Skylark Custom model, although it came with more powerful engines that regular Customs and without their fender skirts. It did include custom-padded seat cushions.*

Tom Glatch

"While Plymouth hit with the Road Runner in '68, Buick missed with the GS 340. Production was low and the car is a relative rarity today."

While Plymouth hit with the Road Runner in '68, Buick missed with the GS 340. Production was low and the car is a relative rarity today.

GS 400 equipment included a hood with twin simulated air scoops, a thin Ralley stripe along the lower belt line, GS badges, three forward-slanting chrome "vents" behind the front wheel openings, a full-length lower body molding, foam-padded vinyl seats, dual exhausts, White-Line wide oval tires and a heavy-duty suspension. Desirable options included a four-speed manual transmission ($184.31), limited-slip differential ($42.13), front power disc brakes ($147), a tachometer ($47.39), a console ($57.93) and chrome wheels ($90.58).

A brand new 400-cid engine replaced the old 401-cid "nailhead" V-8, which had a pent-roof design that dated back to 1953. The new V-8 blended lightweight construction with airflow to create a potent package. It had a 4.040 x 3.900-inch bore and stroke, a single Rochester four-barrel carburetor and a 10.25:1 compression ratio. It was also available with the variable-pitch-stator Super Turbine 400 transmission, previously used only in big Buicks.

Experts soon realized that the new motor was really potent. "Before the wheels had made their first revolution we immediately noticed that the 1967 GS 400 was going to be an even far stronger performer than its 1966 counterpart—which itself was no slouch," said *Motor Trend* in October 1966. In April 1967, *Motor Trend's* Steve Kelly road tested a well-equipped GS 400 hardtop with automatic and a four-speed GS 400 with fewer options. The automatic version did 0 to 60 mph in 4.6 seconds, one second slower than the four-speed car. Quarter-mile performance was 15.2 seconds for both cars, but the four-speed GS 400 was going 95 mph, as opposed to 93 mph for the car with the Super Turbine 400 gearbox. *Motor Trend* said the car had "the best road behavior of any car we've driven in quite a while."

1968

Totally redesigned, GM A-bodies like the Buick Special now had a separate 112-inch-wheelbase chassis for the sporty two-door models. Sedans and wagons used a longer stance for allow family-size seating arrangements. The new body emphasized the long hood/short rear deck look and Buick designers outdid the corporate pack by adding a distinctive S-shaped sweep to the body

"Motor Trend said the car had 'the best road behavior of any car we've driven in quite a while.' "

■ *The 400-cid/340-hp V-8 blended lightweight construction with airflow to create a potent package. It had a 4.040 x 3.900-inch bore and stroke, a single Rochester four-barrel carburetor and a 10.25:1 compression ratio.*

Tom Glatch

■ *The 1970 GS 455 convertible retailed for $3,469. Standard extras included dual exhaust, functional hood scoops, a floor-mounted gearshift and the 455-cid/350-hp V-8.*

Phil Kunz

sides. The grille was a wide, rectangular loop of heavy chrome with a blacked-out insert. The "coke bottle" profile ended in an almost-bullet-shaped rear end treatment that made long-time Buick fans think of the classic '54 Skylark.

The GS series stayed at four models for 1968, but things were still shuffled around quite a bit. A popular new GS 350 replaced the slow-selling GS 340. It was basically a Skylark Custom two-door hardtop with a more muscular exterior. A GS 350 spin-off was a hybrid called the GS California Special. It was a post-coupe version of the GS 350 with special features. The GS 400 line was cut to two models: sport coupe and convertible

The GS 350 had a pretty impressive array of hot rod industry bolt-ons to set it apart as a supercar. Finned, simulated air intakes decorated the front fenders and a paint stripe replaced chrome trim moldings on the lower edges of the body. Bright wheel lip moldings were in, but fender skirts were out. GS plaques decorated the grille, deck lid and rear fenders. All-vinyl seats were standard. Bucket seats were not, but you could add them. The hood had a scoop at the rear and concealed windshield wipers were new "designer" touch.

Buick's 350-cid V-8 had a 3.8- x 3.85-inch bore and stroke. The four-barrel version used in the GS was also available in Special Deluxe, Skylark Custom and LeSabre models. It ran a 10.25:1 compression ratio and a GM Rochester

Quadrajet carb. Output was advertised as 280 hp at 4600 rpm and 375 lbs.-ft. at 3200 rpm. Your basic GS 350 came with a column-mounted three-speed manual transmission. Options included a two-speed Super Turbine automatic with column or console shifter or three- or four-speed manual gearboxes with a shifter on the column, floor or consolette. The only available axle ratio was 3.23:1.

The unique California GS was a midyear addition to the Skylark line intended for California motorists only. This was the only GS variant to still use the post-coupe body. It was dressed up with a vinyl roof, extra chrome trim, styled wheels, a special steering wheel and "GS California" emblems. The GS 350 V-8 was used, but only with the Super Turbine automatic transmission. Buyers could chose between a column- or console-mounted gear shifter and either a 3.42:1 or 2.93:1 rear axle. There's no record of California GS sales.

The GS 400 reused the 400-cid/340-hp V-8 that debuted in '67 with no changes in horsepower or torque. A three-speed transmission and a 3.42:1 rear axle were standard. A heavy-duty three-speed transmission and a four-speed manual gearbox were available. Stick-shift cars offered 3.64:1 and 3.91:1

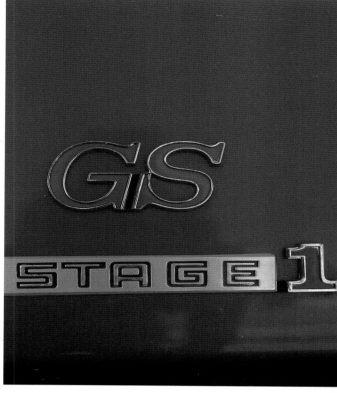

■ *The Stage 1 option was offered again in 1970.* Motor Trend *called it "an engineering tour de force." At just $200 extra, the 360-hp engine was indicated by call-outs placed below the GS monogram.*

Jerry Heasley

■ *Stage 1 stuff included huge stellite valves, big-port heads with special machining and valve relieving, hefty valve springs, a high-lift cam, a tweaked carb, notched and blueprinted pistons and a special distributor.*

Jerry Heasley

■ *GSX badge on left-hand side of center tier of eggcrate grille used in 1971 also featured "GS" letters in red and larger X in white, but the inscription "By Buick" was underneath the badge.*

■ *In 1971, GSX emblems were prominently located on rear fenders above the rectangular side marker lights. The smaller GS monogram was painted red, followed by a larger white-painted X.*

■ *In 1971 the Buick Skylark GS came standard with G78-14 bias-belted black sidewall tires. G60-15 Super Wide white-lettered tires with chrome-plated wheels were part of a $230.65 package.*

rear axles. Turbo-Hydra-Matic cars came standard with a 2.93:1 rear end with automatic, but 3.42:1, 3.64:1 and 3.91:1 axles were optional.

The GS 400 hardtop did 0 to 60 mph in 7.5 seconds. *Motor Trend* tested a '68 GS convertible that clocked a 16.3-second quarter-mile at 88 mph. *Hot Rod's* Eric Dahlquist road tested a hardtop in January 1968. His car, with the air scoop opened for cold-air induction, did the quarter-mile in 14.78 seconds at 94 mph.

On January 1, 1968, Buick released a pair of factory cold-air packages. Called the Stage 1 and Stage 2 options, they included valve train upgrades, forged aluminum pistons, a special intake manifold gasket that blocked the heat riser, oversize rods, fully-grooved main bearings, 6 percent richer carb metering rods, special spark plugs and exhaust headers.

1969

Three high-performance versions of the mid-sized Buick were marketed this year: California GS coupe, GS 350 hardtop and a pair of GS 400s—the hardtop and the convertible. While the GS 400s were the true kick-butt muscle machines, Buick did a good job of promoting all of these fun cars to the enthusiast crowd and stressing their performance attributes compared to standard models. With

■ *A Cortez Gold '71 GSX shows stripes, GSX emblems, black-stripe rocker panel moldings and a color-coordinated rear deck lid spoiler that were included in this very desirable option package.*

Jerry Heasley

■ *The '71 GSX seats were again trimmed in vinyl, but it had a slightly different grain and pattern than was used in 1970. The '71 also had a different type of three-spoke steering wheel. Note the "can-crusher" gearshift.*

Jerry Heasley

the right options, the 350-powered Gran Sports could also provide an awesome blend of go power and handling.

"No wonder Buick owners keep selling Buicks for us," said one ad for the '69 GS 400 Stage 1 hardtop. "When Buick builds a premium machine, even enthusiasts start talking." Overall, the '69 Skylark GS models had just minor styling revisions. A new ice-cube-tray grille carried GS identification on the lower left. The overall exterior appearance was a bit cleaner than in the past, with some extraneous ornamentation deleted.

Exterior trim for the California GS included a custom vinyl top covering, chrome Super Sport wheels, belt reveal and wheel opening moldings, door window, center pillar and rear window scalp moldings, a deluxe steering wheel and California GS trim on the rear fender panel. The standard drive train in this last-year model was a 280-hp version of the Buick 350 with a four-barrel, dual exhausts and Turbo Hydra-Matic drive. Buick put 4,831 of the cars together for the California market. Uncle Tom McCahill tested one and got a 0-to-60 time of 9.5 seconds and a top speed of 110 mph.

"GS 350" grille ornamentation announced the entry-level high-performance sport coupe. It also had similar identification on the rear fender and deck lid. Functional air scoops decorated the hood. The engine used was the same 280-hp job used in the California GS, but in the GS 350 it came standard with a three-speed manual transmission and column-mounted gear shifter. Other equipment included Mirror Magic paint, 14-inch wheels, heavy-duty springs and shocks and a stabilizer bar. Bucket seats were optional.

The GS 400 was similar to the GS 350 with "400" badges on the grille, rear fender, rear deck lid and door trim panel. There were quite a few underhood differences. The standard engine was larger (400-cid) and generated more power (340 hp at 5000 rpm), but the big performance news was a factory Stage 1 option and an even mightier Stage 2 option.

Mentioned in *Hot Rod* as early as January 1968, as part of a Super Performance package, the Stage I and Stage II engine options really hit their stride this year. The magazine described the Stage 1 setup as, "Two 'muffs' reaching up from twin air snorkels on the four-barrel air cleaner, compressing

"For the second year in a row, Car Life found the GS 400 to be the fastest muscle car it tested."

against the hood underside, directing only outside air to the fuel mixer." The cold air passed through a chrome grille on the air scoop.

Both hi-po versions of the 400-cid V-8 offered drag strip-style performance for the serious muscle car freaks. The calmer Stage I was promoted in regular Buick ads, while the "hairier" Stage II hardware had to be ordered from a dealer and installed by the car owner. The Stage I "factory" package was actually designed for dealer installation. It incorporated a high-lift camshaft, tubular push rods, heavy-duty valve springs and dampers and a high-output oil pump. The Stage 1 V-8 was rated for 345 hp at 4800 rpm. When it was ordered, the transmission was equipped with a 5200-rpm governor to protect against over-revving the engine and a 3.64:1 or 3.42:1 positraction rear axle was used. Also included were dual exhausts with big 2 1/4-inch tailpipes and a modified quadrajet carburetor. A heavy-duty Ralley suspension and front power disc brakes were available.

The reported 350-hp Stage II option was a buy-it-from-a-dealer-and-install-it-yourself package for all-out race cars. It was not recommended for use on the street or on cars with mufflers. It included an even wilder cam and all the other goodies.

For the second year in a row, *Car Life* found the GS 400 to be the fastest muscle car it tested. The magazine reported 0 to 60 mph in 6.1 seconds.

■ *The '71 Skylark Gran Sport convertible, model no. 43467, retailed for $3,475. This one is finished in code 75 Fire Red and has the code 155 Pearl White interior.*
Jerry Heasley

■ *Standard engine for the GS Buick was the 350 with 8.5:1 compression, a four-barrel carburetor and a new 260-hp rating. The engine was finished in bright red, which looks great when set off by a chrome air cleaner.*

Jerry Heasley

1970

Although the California GS didn't "make the cut" for the '70 model run, the GS 350 returned ... sort of. Buick changed the name to just "GS." The 350-cid V-8 was still included. Like the GS 350, the '70 GS came only as a sport coupe (hardtop). This year the juiced-up 10.25:1 compression 350-cid four-barrel V-8 got a fairly hefty working over that boosted its output to 315 hp at 4800 rpm. Other than a new black-textured egg-crate grille and minor trim revisions, the GS wasn't changed much from the '69 GS 350 version.

With the cubic-inch race at its apex, Buick decided to make its most muscular mid-size model a GS 455. Its 455-cid V-8 was derived from the earlier 430 and produced 350 hp at 4600 rpm. Torque output was a strong 510 lbs.-ft. at 2800 rpm. It featured a 10.0:1 compression ratio and a Rochester four-barrel carburetor. This engine could push a well-equipped 3,800-lb. Skylark from 0 to 60 mph in about 6.5 seconds. The GS 455 series included a sport coupe and a convertible and the hardtop outsold the ragtop 6 to 1.

Muscle maniacs could still get the Stage I option. *Motor Trend* said: "Buick's Stage I was interesting in 1969, now with the 455 mill it's an engineering tour de force." The $200 360-hp engine was a bargain, too. It included extra-large nickel-

chrome stellite steel valves, big-port cylinder heads with special machining and valve relieving, stronger valve springs, a high-lift cam, a carb with richer jetting, blueprinted pistons (notched for valve clearance) and an advanced-performance distributor. It was available with a special shift-governed Turbo-Hydra-Matic 400 a heavy-duty four-speed manual gearbox with a beefed-up clutch.

A Stage I GS 455 with automatic transmission could do 0 to 60 mph in 5.5 seconds and took just less than 14 seconds to zip down the quarter-mile. One magazine did it in 13.39 seconds at 105.5 mph and *Motor Trend* clocked 13.79 seconds at 104.50 mph as it flew through the traps. The stick-shifted version was just a little slower.

On top of its super performance, the GS 455 was a real handler and hugged the road even better when equipped with Ralley Ride package for $16 extra. This option gave *Motor Trend's* press car extra stability at high speed. The test car had four-wheel manual drum brakes that could slow it from 60 mph in 139.1 ft. Senior editor Bill Sanders said of the brakes: "they held up exquisitely without fade after repeated stops from over 100 mph."

Buick fielded a legendary new muscle car in 1970. The GSX started as a show-car version of the GS that Buick whipped up for the '70 Chicago Auto Show—one of the nation's largest new-car exhibitions. After its appearance at the February event, the decision was made to market it as a limited-production car.

Officially, the GSX package was a $1,196 option for the GS 455. It included a hood-mounted tachometer with available lighting control, G60 x 15 tires on 7-inch-wide chrome wheel rims, a molded plastic front spoiler, a rear spoiler with integral baffle and torsion bar support, twin outside rearview Sport-type mirrors, a four-speed Hurst gear shifter, front disc brakes, a heavy-duty suspension, black vinyl bucket seats, special body graphics with hood stripes and body side stripes, GSX emblems on the grille and dash pad and a special padded steering wheel. The GSX came standard with the 455-cid/350-hp V-8 and the 360-hp Stage I engine kit was a factory option. The GSX came only in Apollo White or Saturn Yellow with Code 188 black interior trim.

"With the cubic-inch race at its apex, Buick decided to make its most muscular mid-size model a GS 455."

■ *Six new colors were available for '71 GSXs including Stratomist Blue. Arctic White, Lime Mist, Platinum Mist, Cortez Gold and Bittersweet Mist were the other "GSX colors." Buyers could, however, get special colors.*

Phil Kunz

Muscle Car

■ *In 1971, buyers could pick the GSX Ornamentation Group and get it all or they could order items separately. Just 124 cars got the complete GSX Ornamentation Group, but many GSs had some GSX features.*

Phil Kunz

■ *Not included in the GSX package, but offered as an option for GS/GSX models was the hood tach.*

Jerry Heasley

"Buick's GSX. A limited edition," said the teaser headline on a Buick ad in the April 1970 issue of *Motor Trend*. The automaker called it "another light-your-fire car from Buick." As things turned out, not too many people had their fires lit, but with a total of 678 copies built, the GSX is really a rarity. Four hundred cars had the Stage 1 engine. All GSXs were built between February and May 1970 and the VIN numbers were randomly assigned.

1971

Buick worked hard to keep high-performance cars alive in 1971, in spite of having to de-tune its engines to satisfy new federal clean-air standards. The Gran Sport and GS 455 were lumped into one series. This resulted in a "gentleman's muscle car" called the Gran Sport Buick. Buick promised "power to please or pass; performance to believe in."

More than ever before, Buick's sales brochure pushed comfort and convenience items like Comfort-Flo ventilation and a smoking set (which most collectors wish the original owner never used). But the brochure also spoke about GS features "to get excited about," such as a blacked-out grille with bright trim, bright wheel house moldings, bright rocker panel moldings with red-filled accents, dual functional hood scoops and GS monograms on the front fenders, deck and grille. Cars equipped with the 455 or 455 Stage 1 options had additional engine identification emblems.

The standard engine for the GS Buick was the 350 with 8.5:1 compression, a four-barrel carburetor and a new 260-hp rating. The GS 455-cid V-8 now produced 330 hp and the 455-cid Stage 1 engine had a 345-hp rating. A functional Ram-Air induction system was used again and helped feed the engine cold air. Buick's trademark—a high-torque rating—was also down. In the case of the Stage 1 engine, it dropped from 510 lbs.-ft. at 2800 rpm in 1970 to 460 lbs.-ft. at 3000 rpm for 1971. Some reference books will show net horsepower and torque ratings, which make things look even worse. Actually, if you average all 1971 GS 455 road tests, the elapsed time for the quarter-mile is 14.25, which compares pretty favorably to an average ET of 14.02 for the not-de-tuned 1970 model.

Muscle Car

■ *The 1972 Gran Sport appearance enhancements included wide rocker moldings, wheelhouse moldings and GS monograms on the front fenders and rear deck. A front bench seat was standard. This is a GS 455 Sport Coupe.*

Phil Kunz

Now you could add the GSX package to a GS Sport Coupe with *any* GS engine. They included the 260-hp 350, the 315-hp 455 V-8 or the 345-hp 455 Stage 1. The package, which was featured in the '71 sales catalog, included body side stripes, hood paint, GSX emblems, painted headlight bezels, black-stripe rocker panel moldings and a color-coordinated rear deck lid spoiler. This year the GSX was available in Stratomist Blue, Artic White, Lime Mist, Bittersweet Mist, Cortez Gold or Platinum Mist. Special-order colors were also a possibility.

The package was merchandised differently than in 1970. GSX buyers could order the GSX Ornamentation Group and get everything. They could also order various components separately. For instance, the hood-mounted tachometer was now a separate option for any GSX. The seats were again trimmed in black vinyl, but it had a slightly different grain and pattern. The '71 also had a different type of steering wheel. The sales catalog indicated that the package could be added to any GS, but history suggests that all 124 were sport coupes.

1972

This year, Buick offered gearheads a choice of 350- and 455-powered Skylarks that were available with the Gran Sport package. This package included dual exhausts, functional dual hood scoops, heavy-duty springs, heavy-duty shocks and a stabilizer bar. Appearance enhancements included wide rocker moldings, wheelhouse moldings and GS monograms on the front fenders and rear deck. A black vinyl interior with a front bench seat was standard.

The first level of power was the 350-cid four-barrel V-8. It came in a base 190-nhp version, as well as an optional 195-nhp version. Both hardtop and convertible models were marketed. Both "GS 350s" made nice, all-around street performance cars, but Buick had a couple of better things up its corporate sleeve for buyers who wanted more muscle—at least as much as Uncle Sam would allow you to have in '72.

The first pigeon to flutter out of Houdini's tux was the Gran Sport 455. The bigger mill came with the same 8.5:1 compression ratio and four-barrel carb as the 350, but its added cubic inches translated into a massive amount of extra torque and improved off-the-line performance. This engine produced 225 nhp at 4000 rpm.

Buick again offered the GS 455 with a Stage 1 engine kit and this version copped *Cars Magazine's* "Top Performance Car of the Year" award. "In the opinion of our test staff—who spent more than an aggregate of six weeks on the road covering thousands of miles in approximately 20 cars—the GS 455 offers the best combination of handling, ride, braking, quality control, engine performance and tasteful styling of all the '72 intermediate models offering optional or standard high performance packages," said editor Marty Schorr.

The '72 Stage 1 version of the 455 was a gutsy 270-nhp performer that romp-romped a little rougher than the standard 455. It included a performance-modified Rochester Quadrajet, a specially tuned distributor, a hotter cam, special valve springs, direct ram-air induction and 3.42 gearing. The Stage 1 was available with either stick shift or a THM 400 automatic, but *Cars Magazine* got better performance from the THM car. It moved out from 0 to 60 in 7.5 seconds and did the quarter-mile in the mid-14s at over 100 mph. "It's not the kind of performance the Gran Sports of two years ago were turning in," said Schorr. "But those days are gone forever."

"Both hardtop and convertible models were marketed. Both 'GS 350s' made nice all-around street performance cars, but Buick had a couple of better things up its corporate sleeve for buyers who wanted more muscle ..."

Muscle Car

■ *Base price for the 1972 Skylark Gran Sport convertible was $3,406. This is one of just 81 ragtops put together with the 455 Stage 1 engine option. Buick also built 656 GS 350 ragtops and 126 GS 455 convertibles.*

Jerry Heasley

A sedate-looking '72 Buick Gran Sport picked up a bunch of enviable timing slips at the National Hot Rod Association's "Winternationals" drag fest in Pomona, California. Though the car looked like your average "grocery getter," it was definitely in the "fast food" category according to *Motor Trend's* A. B. Shuman. "Buick, it seems, has an indisputable knack for making singularly sneaky cars," he said, in June 1972, about the Buick GS Stage 1. The red GS with a white vinyl top and automatic looked nothing like a drag racer.

The Skylark-based muscle car was champion in the Stock Eliminator category and went on to beat all the other stock class winners to become overall category winner. In Shuman's hands, it did 0 to 60 mph in 5.8 seconds, while the quarter-mile took 14.10 seconds (with a 97-mph terminal speed). With open exhausts, fatter tires and a few "tweaks" allowed by NHRA rules, weekend drag racer Dave Benisek set an elapsed time record of 13.38 seconds, at Pomona, with the same car.

Although it was getting rarer and rarer, the GSX-optioned Skylark hardtop was still available in 1972. Buick built 44 of them. The GSX was available with all three GS engines. The 350-cid version came with three- or four-speed manual gear boxes or the Turbo-Hydra-Matic 350. The 455-cid four-barrel came with three- or four-speed manual gearboxes, or the Turbo-Hydra-Matic 400. The 455-cid Stage 1 version was also available with three- or four-speed manual gear boxes or the Turbo-Hydra-Matic 400. No breakouts are available indicating how many of these cars were built with each drive train combination and it is impossible to say if examples of all combinations were actually manufactured.

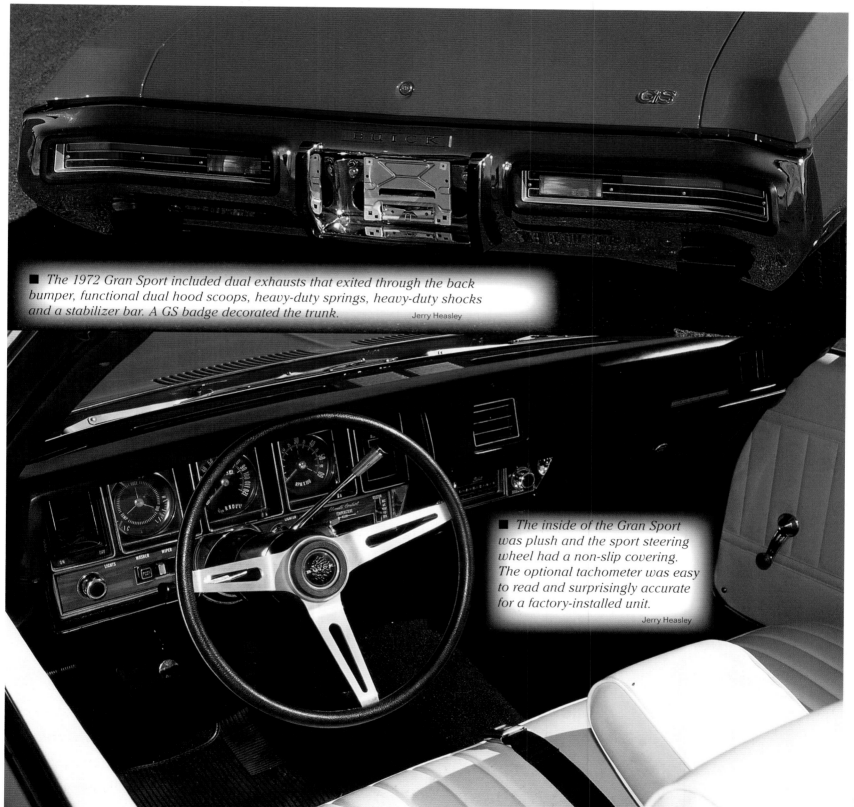

■ *The 1972 Gran Sport included dual exhausts that exited through the back bumper, functional dual hood scoops, heavy-duty springs, heavy-duty shocks and a stabilizer bar. A GS badge decorated the trunk.* Jerry Heasley

■ *The inside of the Gran Sport was plush and the sport steering wheel had a non-slip covering. The optional tachometer was easy to read and surprisingly accurate for a factory-installed unit.*

Jerry Heasley

■ *Cars Magazine editor Marty Schorr said,*
"The GS 455 offers the best combination
of handling, ride, braking, quality control,
engine performance and tasteful styling
of all the '72 intermediate models."

Jerry Heasley

GRAN SPORT YEAR-BY-YEAR SPEC'S

1965

Engine	Bore/Str.	Comp. Ratio	CID	BHP	WT.	W.B.	O.L.	Width	HT
V-8	4.1875 x 3.640	10.25	401	325 @4400	3,720	115.0	203.4	73.9	54.0

1966

Engine	Bore/Str.	Comp. Ratio	CID	BHP	WT.	W.B.	O.L.	Width	HT
V-8	4.1875 x 3.640	10.25	401	325 @4400	3,388	115.0	204.0	75.5	54.0

1967

Engine	Bore/Str.	Comp. Ratio	CID	BHP	WT.	W.B.	O.L.	Width	HT
GS 340									
V-8	3.75 x 3.850	10.25	340	260 @4200	3,271	115.0	205.0	75.4	54.1
GS 400									
V-8	4.040 x 3.90	10.25	400	340 @5000	3,413	115.0	205.0	75.4	54.1
V-8	4.040 x 3.90	10.25	400	340 @5000	3,413	115.0	205.0	75.4	54.1

1968

Engine	Bore/Str.	Comp. Ratio	CID	BHP	WT.	W.B.	O.L.	Width	HT
GS 350									
V-8	3.800 x 3.850	10.25	350	280 @4800	3,375	112.0	200.6	75.6	52.8
GS CALIFORNIA									
V-8	3.800 x 3.850	10.25	350	280 @4800	3,244	112.0	200.6	75.6	52.8
GS 400									
V-8	4.040 x 3.90	10.25	400	340 @5000	3,514	112.0	200.6	75.6	52.8

1969

Engine	Bore/Str.	Comp. Ratio	CID	BHP	WT.	W.B.	O.L.	Width	HT
GS 350									
V-8	3.800 x 3.850	10.25	350	280 @4800	3,406	112.0	200.7	75.6	53.4
GS CALIFORNIA									
V-8	3.800 x 3.850	10.25	350	280 @4800	3,341	112.0	200.7	75.6	53.4
GS 400									
V-8	4.040 x 3.90	10.25	400	340 @5000	3,549	112.0	200.7	75.6	53.4
GS 400 Stage I									
V-8	4.040 x 3.90	10.25	400	345 @5000	3,549	112.0	200.7	75.6	53.4
GS 400 Stage II									
V-8	4.040 x 3.90	10.25	400	350 @5000	3,549	112.0	200.7	75.6	53.4

1970

Engine	Bore/Str.	Comp. Ratio	CID	BHP	WT.	W.B.	O.L.	Width	HT
GS 350									
V-8	3.800 x 3.850	10.25	350	315 @4800	3,434	112.0	202.2	77.3	53.0
GS CALIFORNIA									
V-8	3.800 x 3.850	10.25	350	315 @4800	3,255	112.0	202.2	77.3	53.0
GS 455/GSX									
V-8	4.3125 x 3.90	10.00	455	350 @4600	3,562	112.0	202.2	77.3	53.0
GS 455 Stage I/GSX									
V-8	4.3125 x 3.90	10.00	455	360 @4600	3,562	112.0	202.2	77.3	53.0
GS 455 Stage II/GSX									
V-8	4.3125 x 3.90	10.00	455	370 @4600	3,562	112.0	202.2	77.3	53.0

1973

High-performance cars may have been out of fashion in '73, but Buick could still sell you a Gran Sport-optioned Century that would screech its tires fairly loudly. The Century name, last used in 1958, was dusted off and used to replace the Skylark designation. The '73 Buick Century Regal sported GM's new "Colonnade" styling with single headlights in sweeping front fenders, low, wide feature lines, a

1971

Engine	Bore/Str.	Comp. Ratio	CID	BHP	WT.	W.B.	O.L.	Width	HT
GS 350									
V-8	3.800 x 3.850	8.50	350	260 @4600	3,461	112.0	203.2	75.6	53.4
GS 455/GSX									
V-8	4.3125 x 3.90	8.50	455	315 @4600	—	112.0	203.2	75.6	53.4
GS 455 Stage I/GSX									
V-8	4.3125 x 3.90	8.50	455	345 @4600	—	112.0	203.2	75.6	53.4

1972

Engine	Bore/Str.	Comp. Ratio	CID	BHP	WT.	W.B.	O.L.	Width	HT
GS 350									
V-8	3.800 x 3.850	8.50	350	260 @4600	3,461	112.0	203.3	75.6	53.4
GS 455/GSX									
V-8	4.3125 x 3.90	8.50	455	315 @4600	—	112.0	203.3	75.6	53.4
GS 455 Stage I/GSX									
V-8	4.3125 x 3.90	8.50	455	345 @4600	—	112.0	203.3	75.6	53.4

1973

Engine	Bore/Str.	Comp. Ratio	CID	BHP	WT.	W.B.	O.L.	Width	HT
GS 350									
V-8	3.800 x 3.850	8.50	350	260 @4600	3,487	112.0	210.7	—	—
GS 455/GSX									
V-8	4.3125 x 3.90	8.50	455	315 @4600	—	112.0	210.7	—	—
GS 455 Stage I/GSX									
V-8	4.3125 x 3.90	8.50	455	345 @4600	—	112.0	210.7	—	—

Note: Compiled from a variety of contemporary sources. Minor differences in measurements are due to the way the car was measured, rather than changes in the car itself or related to the fact that different body styles were used as the basis for factory specifications tables. Weight is for lightest model.

torpedo-shaped rear end and low-cut limousine-style window treatments. It had a distinctive grille with a vertically segmented insert and also had special crest emblems on the front fender sides.

The $173 Gran Sport package, with special styling and a max-handling suspension, was available as a sports-performance option. It included an electric clock, wheel opening moldings, full instrumentation, a glovebox light, an ashtray light and courtesy lights. Simply ordering the package did not give you a muscle car, but it got you started down that road.

The base Gran Sport engine was a mild-mannered "no-lead" 350 with 190 nhp that was nothing to get excited about. Factory upgrades started with a high-output 455 V-8 with an 8.5:1 compression ratio, a four-barrel carb and160 nhp. But, the big banana was a Stage 1 version of the Buick 455 that the company managed to cling to for one more year. It produced a hefty 270 nhp at 4400 rpm and 390 lbs.-ft. of torque at 3000 rpm.

While this latest—and last—mid-sized Gran Sport lacked a Ram Air hood setup, it didn't lack a lot in the go-fast department, and it was a rarity. Of the 56,154 Century coupes built in '73, only 979 cars had a high-output 455 four-barrel V-8 and only 728 had the Stage 1 package.

PRODUCTION STATISTICS AND BREAKOUTS

1965 GRAN SPORT

Year	Body Code	Body Type	Engine Type	MSP Price	Model Yr. Prod.
65	STD07	2CP	V-8	$2,608	NA
65	STD17	2HT	V-8	$2,748	NA
65	STD67	2CV	V-8	$2,898	NA
TOTAL					**NA**

* *Motor Trend's* post coupe with options weighed 3720 lbs.

ALL GS TOTAL					**NA**

1966 GRAN SPORT

Year	Body Code	Body Type	Engine Type	MSP Price	Model Yr. Prod.
66	STD07	2CP	V-8	$2,956	1,835
66	STD17	2HT	V-8	$3,019	9,934
66	STD67	2CV	V-8	$3,167	2,047
TOTAL					**13,816**
ALL GS TOTAL					**13,816**

1967 GRAN SPORT

Year	Body Code	Body Type	Engine Type	MSP Price	Model Yr. Prod.
GS 340					
67	STD17	2HT	V-8	$2,845	3,692
GS 400					
67	STD07	2CP	V-8	$2,956	1,014
67	STD17	2HT	V-8	$3,019	10,659
67	STD67	2CV	V-8	$3,167	2,140
TOTAL					**13,813**
ALL GS TOTAL					**17,505**

1968 GRAN SPORT

Year	Body Code	Body Type	Engine Type	MSP Price	Model Yr. Prod.
GS 350					
68	STD37	2HT	V-8	$2,845	8,317
CALIFORNIA GS 350					
68	STD27	2CP	V-8	NA	NA
GS 400					
68	STD37	2HT	V-8	$3,019	10,659
68	STD67	2CV	V-8	$3,167	2,140
TOTAL					**12,799**
GS 350 + GS 400 TOTAL					**21,116**

(CALIFORNIA GS NOT INCLUDED)

1969 GRAN SPORT

Year	Body Code	Body Type	Engine Type	MSP Price	Model Yr. Prod.
GS 350					
69	STD37	2HT	V-8	$2,980	4,933
GS 400					
69	STD37	2HT	V-8	$3,181	6,356
69	STD67	2CV	V-8	$3,325	1,176
TOTAL					**7,532**
GS 350 + GS 400 TOTAL					**12,465**

1970 GRAN SPORT

Year	Body Code	Body Type	Engine Type	MSP Price	Model Yr. Prod.
GS					
70	STD37	2HT	V-8	$3,098	9,948
GS 455					
70	STD37	2HT	V-8	$3,283	8,732
70	STD67	2CV	V-8	$3,469	1,416
TOTAL					**10,148**
GSX					
70	STD37	2HT	V-8	4,479	*

* 678 cars in the GS 455 line had GSX option

GS + GS 455 TOTAL					**20,096**

(INCLUDES 678 GSX)

1971 GRAN SPORT

Year	Body Code	Body Type	Engine Type	MSP Price	Model Yr. Prod.
GS					
71	STD37	2HT	V-8	$3,285	8144
71	STD67	2CV	V-8	$3,476	1416
GS 455					
71	STD37	2HT	V-8	$3,449	*
71	STD67	2CV	V-8	$3,639	*
GS 455 Stage 1					
71	STD37	2HT	V-8	$3,774	*
71	STD67	2CV	V-8	$3,964	*
GSX					
71	STD37	2HT	V-8	—	124

* Included in GS production

TOTAL (ALL)					**9,684**

1972 GRAN SPORT

Year	Body Code	Body Type	Engine Type	MSP Price	Model Yr. Prod.
GS					
72	STD37	2HT	V-8	$3,406	645
GS 455					
72	STD37	2HT	V-8	—	1,099
72	STD67	2CV	V-8	—	126
GS 455 Stage 1					
72	STD37	2HT	V-8	—	728
72	STD67	2CV	V-8	—	81
GSX					
72	STD37	2HT	V-8	—	44*

* Included in GS production

TOTAL (ALL)					**8,619**

1973 CENTURY REGAL GRAN SPORT

Year	Body Code	Body Type	Engine Type	MSP Price	Model Yr. Prod.
CENTURY REGAL + GS (GS 350)					
73	STD37	2HT	V-8	$3,470	NA
CENTURY REGAL + GS+ 455 HO (GS 455)					
73	STD37	2HT	V-8	$3,643	979
CENTURY REGAL + GS + 455 Stage 1 (GS 455 Stage 1)					
73	STD37	2HT	V-8	$4,189	728

Note: 1965-1968 tables are from recently released General Motors 1955-1968 production data records.

The 1971 Buick sales catalog indicated that the latest GSX package could be added to any Skylark Gran Sport, but marque historians believe that all 124 cars built were Sport Coupes.

Jerry Heasley

PRICE GUIDE

Vehicle Condition Scale

6 — Parts car:
May or may not be running, but is weathered, wrecked and/or stripped to the point of being useful primarily for parts.

5 — Restorable:
Needs complete restoration of body, chassis and interior. May or may not be running, but isn't weathered, wrecked or stripped to the point of being useful only for parts.

4 — Good:
A driveable vehicle needing no or only minor work to be functional. Also, a deteriorated restoration or a very poor amateur restoration. All components may need restoration to be "excellent," but the car is mostly useable "as is."

3 — Very Good:
Complete operable original or older restoration. Also, a very good amateur restoration, all presentable and serviceable inside and out. Plus, a combination of well-done restoration and good operable components or a partially restored car with all parts necessary to compete and/or valuable NOS parts.

2 — Fine:
Well-restored or a combination of superior restoration and excellent original parts. Also, extremely well-maintained original vehicle showing minimal wear.

1 — Excellent:
Restored to current maximum professional standards of quality in every area, or perfect original with components operating and apearing as new. A 95-plus point show car that is not driven.

1965 Skylark

4d Sed	532	1,596	2,660	5,990	9,310	13,300
2d Cpe	580	1,740	2,900	6,530	10,150	14,500
2d HT	620	1,860	3,100	6,980	10,850	15,500
2d Conv	880	2,640	4,400	9,900	15,400	22,000

NOTE: Add 20 percent for Skylark Gran Sport Series (400 cid/325hp V-8). Deduct 5 percent for V-6.

1966 Skylark Gran Sport

2d Cpe	720	2,160	3,600	8,100	12,600	18,000
2d HT	960	2,880	4,800	10,800	16,800	24,000
2d Conv	1,080	3,240	5,400	12,150	18,900	27,000

1967 Gran Sport 340

2d HT	760	2,280	3,800	8,550	13,300	19,000

1967 Gran Sport 400

2d Cpe	680	2,040	3,400	7,650	11,900	17,000
2d HT	780	2,340	3,900	8,780	13,650	19,500
2d Conv	960	2,880	4,800	10,800	16,800	24,000

1968 Gran Sport GS 350

2d HT	780	2,340	3,900	8,780	13,650	19,500

1968 Gran Sport GS 400

2d HT	800	2,400	4,000	9,000	14,000	20,000
2d Conv	920	2,760	4,600	10,350	16,100	23,000

NOTE: Add 15 percent for Skylark GS Calif. Spl.

1969 Gran Sport GS 350

2d Calif GS	760	2,280	3,800	8,550	13,300	19,000
2d HT	800	2,400	4,000	9,000	14,000	20,000

1969 Gran Sport GS 400

2d HT	840	2,520	4,200	9,450	14,700	21,000
2d Conv	1,000	3,000	5,000	11,250	17,500	25,000

NOTE: Add 40 percent for Stage I option.

1970 Gran Sport GS 350

2d HT	800	2,400	4,000	9,000	14,000	20,000

1970 Gran Sport GS 455

2d HT	840	2,520	4,200	9,450	14,700	21,000
2d Conv	1,040	3,120	5,200	11,700	18,200	26,000

1970 GSX 455

2d HT	1,600	4,800	8,000	18,000	28,000	40,000

NOTE: Add 40 percent for Stage I 455.

1971-72 Gran Sport 350

2d HT	760	2,280	3,800	8,550	13,300	19,000
2d Conv	960	2,880	4,800	10,800	16,800	24,000
2d HT GSX	1,440	4,320	7,200	16,200	25,200	36,000

NOTE: Add 40 percent for Stage I & 20 percent for GS-455 options. Add 15 percent for folding sunroof (1972).

1971-72 Riviera

2d HT GS	500	1,500	2,500	5,630	8,750	12,500

1973 Riviera

2d HT GS	460	1,380	2,300	5,180	8,050	11,500

GTO

1964 1/2

The 1964 1/2 Pontiac GTO was America's first true "muscle car." Cases could be made for giving that title to the '50 Olds 88, the '55 Chrysler C300, the '57 Chevy "fuelie" or the '61 Chevy Super Sport. However, the classic definition of muscle car comes down to a mid-size production car with a big engine shoehorned into it. Created by stuffing the full-sized Pontiac's 389-cid V-8 into the new, 115-inch wheelbase Tempest LeMans, the "Goat" was unique in concept and execution.

The objective of Pontiac Motor Division's '64 Tempest program was to provide a line of cars that would be larger in size and provide greater roominess, passenger comfort and utility than earlier Tempests. The '64 also had to provide maximum manufacturing and service interchangeability so it could be built in different plants. By making it easier to interchange parts between larger Pontiacs and the Tempest, PMD virtually *invited* hot rodders to drop a big Pontiac V-8 into its mid-size car.

■ *The 1964 1/2 GTO is generally considered the first true American muscle car—a midsize sedan with rather pedestrian looks that had a big motor stuffed under the hood.*
Jerry Heasley

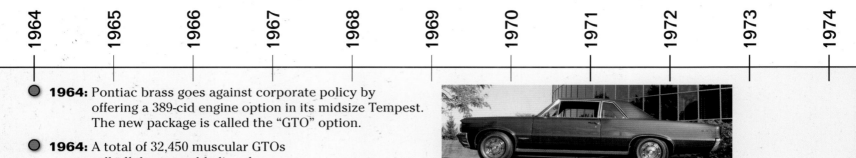

1964 1965 1966 1967 1968 1969 1970 1971 1972 1973 1974

1964: Pontiac brass goes against corporate policy by offering a 389-cid engine option in its midsize Tempest. The new package is called the "GTO" option.

1964: A total of 32,450 muscular GTOs roll off the assembly line, far exceeding sales expectations.

1965: Modest redesign includes stacked headlights and different front and rear treatments.

1966: The restyled GTO becomes its own model. Sales soar to nearly 97,000 cars.

1967: Tri-Power is replaced by the 400-cid V-8.

1968: Drastic redesign produces a beautiful, curvy new car with a stylish rubber bumper.

1969: The "Judge" package is introduced. The bold styling is accompanied by a new Ram Air III engine and Ram Air IV package that took Pontiac horsepower to new heights.

1970: Another big redesign featuring four exposed headlights.

1971: Last year for the GTO as a separate model.

1972: The GTO is reduced to an option package on the LeMans and LeMans Sport.

1974: The GTO takes a final bow as an option package on the Ventura.

■ *Ace Wilson's Royal Pontiac dealership, located in Royal Oak, Michigan, helped design special "Royal Bobcat" GTOs, one of which* Car and Driver *used as a test vehicle for a magazine story about the model's durability and performance.*

■ *"GTO" lettering in the lower left-hand grille helped identify the first-year GTO package.* Jerry Heasley

■ *The GTO had numerous chassis upgrades and a definite performance car feel.* Jerry Heasley

"The General"—GM—had a corporate rule dictating that cars have a minimum of 10 lbs. of vehicle weight per cubic inch. The heaviest LeMans had a curb weight of 3,232 lbs., so Pontiac's 326 was the largest allowable V-8, at least until JZD—John Zachary Delorean—came on the scene.

Delorean had little patience for corporate rules. According to one story told by auto writer Jim Dunn, JZD bent one rule by taking the corporate jet to Hollywood on many weekends to hobnob with movie stars. A strict GM bean counter discovered that JZD had 90 new zone cars loaned out to his

Hollywood friends. Delorean shortstopped the audit by taking the accountant out to Hollywood the next week. After that, he stopped counting beans. Eventually, GM got the most of the loaner cars back, except for six that wound up in Mexico and stayed there!

In a similar manner, JZD and his "Young Turk" Pontiac engineers—guys like Bill Collins and Russ Gee—found a way to do an end run around the 10-pounds-per-cube requirement. They discovered that GM's Engineering Policy Committee was concerned only with approving *new* models. That meant that a larger V-8 could be sold as a factory *option* for existing LeMans two-door models. This would bypass the policy committee's approval process. They worked it out so that Pontiac buyers could just check a box on the LeMans order form, pay $295 extra and get the GTO option.

The '64 LeMans version of the Tempest was no Yugo. It already wore extra jewelry like ribbed décor plates and badges on the rear deck, simulated slanting louvers ahead of the rear wheel cutouts and a LeMans script on the dashboard. There were three LeMans models and, just to be sure everyone understood they were supposed to be sporty, they all had only two doors. Vinyl bucket seats—people loved vinyl back then—were standard. No one cared if they got hot in the sun.

Of course, the GTO package didn't launch with promo man Jim Wangers singing up a storm with Ronnie & the Daytonas or selling "GTO" shoe concepts to Thom McCann. Get real! Delorean and his crew were *sneaking* the whole works out to the Woodward Avenue warriors. They didn't want The General to know what was going down. If the word got out, the jig was up. So, along about midyear, the GTO package discreetly appeared on the Tempest LeMans order form. It included the big 389-cube V-8 and some special appearance items in place of regular LeMans trim. The badges on the grille, fender, deck lid and glove box door emblems said "GTO." Simulated engine-turned aluminum panels decorated the dash. The hood was "performancized" with dummy air vents.

While it resembled a Star Chief/Bonneville four-barrel V-8 on factory spec sheets, the GTO engine was of special construction. It had the 421 H.O. V-8's 10.75:1 compression heads, big valves, a hotter-than-standard cam, a H-D

■ *The beautiful first-year GTO coupe in Skyline Blue.*

Dan Lyons

■ *The three-speed on the column was standard for the 1964 GTO, but you could order a floor-shifted version as well.*

Jerry Heasley

■ *The 389-cid Tri-Power V-8 gave Pontiac drivers horsepower to burn for 1964.*

Jerry Heasley

■ *The vertically stacked headlights were one of the main changes to the 1965 Tempest/ GTO lineup.* Dan Lyons

cooling system, H-D starter, H-D battery and a low-restriction dual exhaust system. It delivered 325 hp at 4800 rpm, which was pretty heady stuff in mid-'64. Tri-Power was optional on the same block. With three deuces, the GTO 389 made 348 hp at 4900 rpm.

The GTO was cool as they came in '64. In addition to added under-hood hardware and special exterior and interior trimmings, the option included a three-speed manual transmission with column-mounted shifter, special 6-inch-wide wheels and premium 7.50 x 15 red-stripe nylon cord tires of a new

low-profile design. The GTO could also be ordered with a heavy-duty three-speed manual gearbox or a Muncie close-ratio four-speed manual gearbox with linkage a' la Hurst.

GTO stands for "Grand Turismo Omologato." That's a term derived from the Italian language that applies to grand touring (GT) coupes that are approved for road racing. In his memoir *Glory Days*, Wangers credits JZD with coining the European name. American car enthusiasts—at least those who were GM fans—preferred to call the car the "GTO," the "Goat," the "Great One," the "GeeTO" or the "Tiger." Ford and Mopar enthusiasts may have applied their own terms to the GTO, while European sports car fans surely went the purist route and insisted that it wasn't a "real" GT.

■ *1965 GTO survivors in this condition are definite collector prizes.* Dan Lyons

Wangers was the PR guy who put the GTO on the map. He was a drag racing nut with a talent for expressing the high-performance drive in the King's English. One of his bosses, who shall go unnamed, once told me that Wangers spent all day on the phone talking to his racing buddies. " I had a big project he had to get finished and he wasn't doing anything on it," said the executive. "So I had his phone taken out until it was completed, and it was done the next day and it was totally fantastic!" In addition to getting the GTO featured in many enthusiast magazines, Wangers did several outstanding promotions. One that we already alluded to revolved around a record called "GTO" that a young Nashville music publisher named John Wilkins dreamed up. A group of musicians recorded the tune under the name Ronnie & the Daytonas. It rose to fourth place on the national charts, lasted 17 weeks and sold a million copies. When it counted, Wangers was always a winner.

In 1964 terms, the GTO was fast. A GTO convertible with the four-barrel V-8 recorded a 7.7-second 0-to-60 time and ran down the quarter-mile in 15.8 seconds at 93 mph. It could hit 115 mph flat out. A Tri-Power GTO hardtop hit 60 mph in just 6.6 seconds and did the quarter-mile in 14.8 seconds. Some magazines—perhaps with a little "live feed" from "Gentleman" Jim Wangers—got even better performance numbers. And the numbers added up to sales. By late-1963, GTO customer deliveries were way past the initial projections of 5,000 cars. In March 1964, *Car & Driver* gave "The Great One" a great writeup. By then, it was already a winner.

1965

One-on-top-of-the-other headlights were an instant giveaway that the second GTO had changed a bit for 1965, but the re-tailoring wasn't in any way drastic. At the rear, the tail lights wrapped around the body. The fenders were actually taller and made the car look slimmer and longer. The basic GTO option now cost $296. It included the heated-up 389-cid V-8, GTO lettering on the left-hand grille, rear fenders and deck lid, a new middle-of-the-hood dummy air scoop and V-shaped front fender side badges.

"By late-1963, GTO customer deliveries were way past the initial projections of 5,000 cars."

Two 389-cid engines were once again available in the GTO-optioned LeMans. As in 1964, one carried a four-barrel carb and one carried three two-barrel carbs with a progressive linkage. The base engine put out 335 hp at 5000 rpm and the optional V-8, with a 10.75:1 compression ratio and Tri Power, produced 360 hp at 5200 rpm. The Tri-Power motor added $116 to the price tag. Technical improvements included a new camshaft, better heads and a revised intake manifold design.

The 335-hp '65 GTO convertible did 0-to-60 mph in 7.2 seconds and covered the quarter-mile in 16.1 seconds. Late in the year a 389-cid Ram Air engine with Tri-Power arrived. This rare motor was installed in about 200 GTOs. It also carried a 360-hp rating, although it could out-perform the standard Tri-Power engine.

Several chassis items were upgraded for 1965. Rally wheel rims were a new option. PMD promoted another record called "The GEETO Tiger" by the Tigers. It didn't catch on like "GTO," but led to a tie-in with Hurst. In a contest, a Hurst Gold GTO hardtop with gold wheels was given away. This special one-of-a-kind car still exists.

■ The Tempest series was fully redesigned for 1966. The cars featured smoother, rounder bodies, stacked headlights, and distinctive ornamentation. The GTOs, the one shown here is a convertible with 389-cid Tri-Power, were again the high-performance machines of the series. Jerry Heasley

■ *Palmetto Green was a somewhat offbeat
color choice for a muscle car, but it was
the color worn by this 1966 GTO hardtop.*
Phil Kunz

By 1965, the GTO was a rage. Royal Bobcat GTOs, a "tuner" version of the
GTO created by Royal Pontiac, of Royal Oak, Michigan, made appearances in
many car magazines. Milt Shorneck, of Royal, was one of the best GTO mechanics
in the country. Today a Royal Bobcat GTO is worth its weight in gold.

1966

PMD gave the GTO full-fledged "model" status in 1966. This meant that the
mid-size muscle car was no longer a LeMans. It was still a Tempest-based model
and the '66 Tempest body was completely and smoothly restyled. The "venturi,"
or "wasp-waist," look was in and the GTO wore it well. Once again the headlights
were stacked. The car retained a 115-inch wheelbase and, at 206.4 inches, was
about the same length as in '65. However, Pontiac's new "A-body" had a heavier
look to it, even though some body styles were actually a few pounds lighter in
weight than before.

A cross-hatched wire mesh grille had one rectangular parking light on
each side and a GTO nameplate in the left-hand grille cavity. As in '65, a single
air scoop appeared on the hood and trademark V-shaped badges were seen

behind the front wheel openings. GTO lettering appeared on the deck lid and rear fenders. The upper belt line contour was pinstriped using a new process that PMD had pioneered on big cars a year earlier. At the rear there were slinky-looking twin-slot tail lights similar to those showcased on several GM dream cars of that era.

Standard GTO equipment included walnut grain dash panel inserts, dual exhausts, heavy-duty shock absorbers and springs, a fat stabilizer bar and fat 7.75 x 14 Red Line or White Line low-profile tires. The standard '66 GTO V-8 had a 10.75:1 compression ratio, a four-barrel Carter AFB carburetor, hydraulic valve lifters and 335 hp at 5,000 rpm. GTO power train options were the same as in 1965. This was the last year for factory Tri-Power. Some popular options included a Ride and Handling package ($16), Rally wheels ($40) and a Safe-T-Track rear axle ($37).

In magazine road tests, the 1966 Pontiac 335-hp GTO coupe was found to go 0-to-60 mph in 6.8 seconds and cover the quarter-mile in 15.4 seconds. The 360-hp GTO convertible had the same 0-to-60 mph time and did the quarter-mile in 15.5 seconds at 93 mph.

■ *Fontain Blue with red pinstriping and a white top made for a striking combination on this 1966 GTO.* Daniel B. Lyons

■ *The 1967 GTO convertible was hard to beat as an all-around muscle car. It was a great-looking car with a 400-cid, 335-hp V-8, dual exhausts and a ragtop—all for about $3,200!*
Phil Kunz

1967

Why mess with success? The styling of the '67 "Goat" didn't change much. The mesh in the radiator grille had a diagonally crisscrossing pattern. A molding along the "lip" of the upper grille opening dipped down around the vertical center divider. Wide, bright metal underscores highlighted the rocker panels. The V-shaped badges behind the front wheel openings were now on these underscore moldings. The "GTO" designation was carried in the left-hand grille and on the rear fenders. New tail lights took the form of four thin rectangles at each side. GTOs included all LeMans features, plus a hood scoop, fake walnut dash inserts, heavy-duty shock absorbers, hefty springs, a fat stabilizer bar and F70 x 14 Red or White line tires.

If the '66 looked sensational, the '67 went one better, but for the first time in GTO history model-year production tumbled. I don't think there was a darn thing wrong with the car—a lot of GTO buyers were marching off to Vietnam. My high school friend, Tony Cruz, left behind a gorgeous, pale green GTO hardtop that I'll never forget as long as I live. Overall, the GTO's popularity was down about 15 percent.

Four versions of a new 400-cid V-8 (a bored-out 389) went in '67 GTOs. Three used a 10.75:1 compression ratio and a single four-barrel Rochester carb. The 335-hp version was standard. A 360-hp HO version was optional. A second option was the Ram Air 400. It also carried a 360-hp rating, but the power peak came at 5400 rpm. A 255-hp version of the 400 with 8.6:1 compression and a two-barrel carburetor was a market-niche-expanding, no-cost economy option. The base 335-hp GTO hardtop went 0-to-60 mph in 6.6 seconds and did the quarter-mile in 15.5 seconds.

On TV, the "Monkeemobile" GTO phaeton was a big hit. Wangers recalls this car was made for a Kellogg's contest in which participants could win a role on the television show and a GTO convertible. Second prize was one of 15 GTO hardtops. MPC produced a Monkeemobile model. One Monkeemobile wound up carrying tourists at a Puerto Rican resort. It was later purchased for $500 by a collector.

■ *The hood tachometer was an $84.26 option in 1967.*   Jerry Heasley

■ *The 1967 GTO came in coupe, hardtop and ragtop varieties. The hardtop was by far the most popular, outselling the two other body styles combined by about a 4 to 1 margin.*
Doug Mitchel

■ *With its radically different front end, the 1968 GTO was easy to distinguish from its predecessors.* Phil Kunz

 Muscle Car

■ *Dark Blue vinyl was one of eight different interior choices on the 1967 GTO.* Jerry Heasley

1968

From many standpoints, the '68 GTO was a winner. *Motor Trend* named it "Car of the Year." At *Car Life* it pulled down a "10 Best Cars" award. "The GTO has become a classic in its own time," said *Car Life*. "It's an unmistakable car, slightly erotic, highly romantic, full of verve, optimism, grace and beauty." In Pontiac dealerships, where the numbers counted most, model year production rose to 87,684 GTOs.

You could say the '68 GTO won by its nose. This part of the vehicle was dominated by a steel-reinforced "Endura" rubber front bumper. Endura was a new material developed in conjunction with the Dayton Rubber Company. It could be molded into an endless array of shapes and it "remembered" its original shape after modest impact. In one ad, JZD battered a GTO's nose with a sledgehammer (Shades of Henry Ford and his WWII-era soybean sedan!). Nothing happened. Endura rubber could be painted to match a car's body. The Endura bumper allowed Pontiac designers to better integrate the bumper into the GTO's overall design.

Like any change, the Endura nose scared people, especially those worried about safety or a bumper-less appearance. So the GTO's Endura nose could be replaced with a conventional LeMans bumper if the buyer preferred. Relatively few did.

For the '68 model year, two wheelbases were used for Tempests. Like other two-door models, the GTO rode the shorter 112-inch stance. Overall length was about six inches shorter. In spite of this, the weight increased slightly, which had a negative effect on high performance. The front and rear tread widths were both 60 inches.

Standard GTO equipment was expanded a bit and now included hidden headlights. The new hood reverted back to a twin-air-scoop hood like the '64 Goat. A three-speed manual transmission with Hurst shifter was included. Sports type springs and shock absorbers were used. Among other GTO features were "fastback" Red Line tires, bucket or notch back armrest seats, disappearing windshield wipers and a choice of three 400-cid V-8s. The new GTO came only in two-door hardtop and convertible models.

"The GTO has become a classic in its own time."

— Car Life

■ *Badging was found behind the front wheel openings on the 1968 GTO. The Endura nose was billed as safer and more durable than anything previously used by Pontiac.* Jerry Heasley

■ *A deluxe steering wheel and Hurst shifter were among the standard features on the 1968 GTO.* Jerry Heasley

The base GTO V-8 had a 4.12 x 3.75-inch bore and stroke. With a 10.75:1 compression ratio and one Rochester four-barrel carb it generated 350 hp at 5,000 rpm. As in 1967, two options with matching carburetor and compression specifications were offered. The HO version produced 360 hp at 5100 rpm and the Ram Air version produced 360 hp at 5400 rpm. In the '68 Ram Air system, the air scoops sat higher on the hood and drew in more cold air. Late in the year, a new 366-hp Ram Air II option with round-port cylinder heads replaced the Ram Air 400.

1969

Pontiac promoted the 1969 Goat as the "Humbler" and called it a "Wide-Track Breakaway" car. A honeycomb grille with a horizontal divider was new for '69 and hidden headlights were standard equipment. GTO lettering was seen on the left grille, the right side of the deck lid and behind the front wheel openings. The tail lights were now above the bumpers and carried lenses surrounded by bright metal moldings.

Standard GTO equipment included a 400-cid/350-hp V-8 with dual exhausts, a heavy-duty clutch, a three-speed manual gear box with floor shift, a Power-Flex fan, sports-type springs and shock absorbers, Red Line wide-oval tires, carpeting, a deluxe steering wheel, GTO identification features and a choice of bucket or notchback seats.

The GTO could be ordered with an optional 400-cid economy engine running an 8.6:1 compression ratio, a single two-barrel carburetor and 265 hp. There were two other 400-cid options. Both of them had a 10.75:1 compression ratio and a single Rochester four-barrel carburetor. The Ram Air III version produced 366 hp and the Ram Air IV version was good for 370 hp.

A special high-performance "The Judge" option was released December 19, 1968. The Judge was aimed at the Plymouth Road Runner, a model that combined a bare-bones body and trim package with some serious hardware. Though more expensive than a base GTO, "The Judge" was the least expensive of several super-high-performance models with comparable equipment on the market in 1969.

Bold decals on the sides of the front fenders read "The Judge." Bright Carousel Red paint (an orange color) was used on about 80 percent of all Judges built. The Judge cost about $400 more than a regular GTO, but you got a lot for the money. The go-fast stuff included the 366-hp Ram Air (III) V-8, a three-speed

■ *The Ram Air III option replaced the H.O. in the Pontiac lineup for 1969. This 366-hp setup could be upgraded to 370 hp with the Ram Air IV option.* Phil Kunz

GTO 1964½-1974

manual stick-shift transmission and functional, driver-controlled air intake scoops on the hood. The cars were decorated with tri-color vinyl tape stripes and had a rear "airfoil" type spoiler.

The Ram Air III Judge was a fast car, and the Ram Air IV version was even faster. *Mechanix IIllustrated* tested a standard Judge and reported a 5.9 second 0-to-60 time. Later, *High-Performance Pontiac* published a time of 5.1 seconds for a Ram Air IV version.

Pontiac built 8,491 GTOs and Judges (362 convertibles) with Ram Air III V-8s and 759 GTOs and Judges (59 convertibles) with Ram Air IV V-8s.

1970

"The quick way out of the little leagues," read an ad showing a 1970 GTO with six young, sports-minded admirers. There's no doubt that the Goat was a slugger in the super-car World Series, but the ballgame was in its final innings by 1970. Government safety and anti-pollution mandates, congressional criticism and rising insurance premiums were teaming up to choke off the wave of muscle cars.

Once again, Pontiac blended the Tempest two-door body with an Endura rubber nose to make the GTO. A "snouty" new frontal treatment featured two oval "nostrils" housing recessed grilles with GTO lettering on the left-hand side.

■ *"The Judge" was originally planned as a no-frills muscle car, but by the time it debuted it was a flashy, unmistakable American classic, either in convertible or hardtop form.*

Jerry Heasley

■ *"The Judge" package was identified by decals in several locations, including the airfoil.*

Jerry Heasley

■ *The parchment and black color combination made for a suitably eye-catching interior on the Judge.*

Jerry Heasley

■ *The hood tachometer was on the options list for the GTO. The Ram Air engine was identified by a hood decal.*

Jerry Heasley

This 1970 Judge is decked out in Palisade Green with tri-color accents.
Dan Lyons

There was also GTO lettering on the sides of the flared, crease-sculptured front fenders. Standard equipment included bucket seats, a padded vinyl dash, a twin air scoop hood, a heavy-duty clutch, a Sports suspension, carpeting, courtesy lamps, dual exhausts, a deluxe steering wheel, a three-speed manual floor shift and fat G78 x 14 tires.

"The Judge" option was available again at $337 over base price. It included a 400-cid Ram Air V-8, Rally II wheels, G70 x 14 fiberglass black sidewall tires, a rear-deck air foil, side stripes, Judge stripes and decals, black-textured grilles and T-handle shifters (on cars with manual gearboxes).

■ *Atoll Blue was one of 16 base color choices on the 1970 Judge.*
Phil Kunz

■ *Only 168 Judge convertibles were built for 1970.*
Dan Lyons

It's pretty difficult to confuse a second-generation GTO Judge with any other muscle car. The wild colors, twin hood scoops, prominent rear spoiler and trademark "eyebrows" made for one of the most outrageous cars seen in any era.
Doug Mitchel

Pontiac lost third place in U.S. sales for the first time in 10 years in 1970. Production of GTO hardtops fell to 32,737 and only 3,615 convertibles were built. The Judge hardtop had a production run of 3,629, along with just 168 Judge convertibles. Ram Air III V-8s went into 4,356 GTO and Judge hardtops and 288 convertibles. Ram Air IV V-8s were put in 767 GTO and Judge hardtops and 37 convertibles.

The 366-hp GTO did 0-to-60 mph in 6 seconds. The quarter-mile took 14.6 seconds.

1971

Some said the king of the muscle cars was showing some "middle-age spread" by '71. It was still The Goat, but it was more of an old "Billy" than a newborn kid. The already-hefty weight of the GTO was trimmed just slightly, but standard power was noticeably lower. The base engine for GTOs was now a de-tuned 400-cid four-barrel V-8 with an 8.2:1 compression ratio and 300 hp—a loss of 50 ponies from '70.

A new Endura nose piece identified the fish-mouth '71 GTO. The twin grille cavities were larger in size and had a new insert with a wide-spaced diagonal mesh. The traditional "GTO" nameplate still sat in the driver's-side grille, but it was positioned more toward the bottom outer corner. Round parking lamps filled the circular protrusions just below the side-by-side dual headlights. Between the headlights and parking lights were integral body-colored bumpers.

Twin air slots were sliced into the hood towards the front, replacing the twin scoops near the middle of the '70 hood. GTO decals decorated the front fender sides, behind the wheel openings, and the right-hand edge of the rear deck lid. Standard equipment included all LeMans items plus engine-turned aluminum dash inserts, dual exhausts with through-the-valance-panel extensions, a Power-Flex cooling fan, heavy-duty stabilizers, heavy-duty shocks, heavy-duty springs and fat G70-14 tires.

■ *The Tempest GT-37 was a close relative of the GTO as option code 334. It was available only as a hardtop (shown is a 1971 model) and was a less-expensive, de-contented version GTO that was a pretty capable muscle car for the money.* Phil Kunz

"Some said the king of the muscle cars was showing some 'middle-age spread' by '71."

"This 455 Judge can still deal out some judicial action on the street."

— Muscle Car Review

The number of engine and transmission combos available in the '70 GTO was cut from 17 to 10. Engines included the base 400-cid V-8, a 455-cid V-8 that developed 325 hp at 4800 rpm and a 455-cid HO engine that produced 335 hp at 4800 rpm. Transmission options included a heavy-duty three-speed manual gearbox with floor shift, a four-speed manual gearbox with floor shift and Turbo Hydra-Matic.

While the jury may have been out on whether the muscle car era would survive high insurance rates and restrictive government regulations, there was no denying that the GTO Judge knew how to make rulings with decisive zeal. "This 455 HO Judge can still deal out some judicial action on the street," said Paul Zazarine in *Musclecar Review* in 1990.

"The Judge" option—available for the two-door hardtop and the convertible only—added the 455-cid HO engine, Rally II wheels less trim rings, a hood air inlet, a T-handle shifter (only with manual transmission), a rear deck lid airfoil, specific body side stripes, "The Judge" decals, Ram Air decals and a black texture in the grille. A low-as-you-could-go Judge hardtop cost about $3,840. The very rare ragtop version—17 were actually built—sold for as little as $4,070. On both models the RPO 621 "ride & handling" shock absorber and

spring package, which had a suggested retail price of $9.48, was a mandatory option.

A stock '71 GTO with the 300-hp V-8 did the quarter-mile in 14.4 seconds and was traveling 98 mph when it passed through the traps. The GTO was still an exciting car, but sales were about a third of what they started at in 1964, and no wonder! The muscle car market was shriveling due to stricter government anti-pollution and safety standards. In addition, insurance companies were making it prohibitive to buy coverage for muscle cars.

1972

The clean air Gestapo and the insurance industry ganged up to bring an end to the GTO model in 1972. But Jim Wangers and his honchos at PMD found an old trick to keep their beloved GTO alive. They recreated the GTO option for the LeMans a' la 1964 and it worked like gangbusters. The GTO survived

■ *The GTO was starting to decline in popularity by 1972. Only about 5,800 GTOs were produced for that model year, and the Judge was not offered.* Phil Kunz

■ *As they were on the Firebird, the honeycomb wheels were a hip option for the GTO in 1972. This car was dressed in Sundance Orange.*   Doug Mitchel

"The GTO survived for three more years in several different formats, although the convertible body style and The Judge option package did not make the cut."

for three more years in several different formats, although the convertible body style and The Judge option package did not make the cut.

Looks-wise, the '72 Goat was very '71-like. It had a revised grille mesh and new front-fender air extractors. It was still characterized by an Endura front end and a special hood with dual air scoops opening at the front. However, this treatment was no longer exclusive to the "Goat." You could order it as an option for any LeMans or LeMans Sport model with a V-8.

The GTO option itself was offered for the LeMans coupe and hardtop and shared its interior with those models. Engine-turned aluminum lower instrument panel trim and GTO door panel identification was added. There were GTO decals on the rear quarters and deck lid, a grille with the GTO name, a scooped hood, an Endura front bumper, concealed wipers on hardtops and air extractors on the front fenders.

PMD felt that it was making the GTO more obtainable by changing it from a model to an option, so buyers could order it in various configurations from "stripper" to luxury-sports car. "You'll be seeing a lot more of Pontiac's great GTO this year, because Pontiac has made the GTO easier to own," the '72 sales

catalog said, "by letting you decide how grand you want your Grand Turisimo Omologato to be." But, the change didn't help sales.

The base engine for the GTO was the 400-cid with its 4.12 x 3.75-inch bore and stroke. With an 8.2:1 compression ratio and a four-barrel carburetor, it generated 250 hp. There were two optional 455s with a 4.15 x 4.21-inch bore and stroke and four-barrel. The first, with an 8.2:1 compression ratio, cranked out 250 hp. The most powerful option was the 455 HO, which had an 8.4:1 compression ratio and a four-barrel carb. It was good for 300 hp. Gearbox choices included a heavy-duty three-speed, four-speed manual, close-ratio four-speed manual and Turbo-Hydra-Matic. Manual drum brakes, fat stabilizer bars, heavy-duty shocks, dual exhausts with side splitters behind the rear wheels, fat tires and a Power-Flex cooling fan were standard. Extras included a tachometer and a full gauge package.

■ *Pontiac's whole A-body intermediate line had a completely new look for 1973, and the GTO was an obvious example. The GTO option was available on the LeMans hardtop or sport coupe and featured drastically different Colonnade styling with a longer tail end, blacked-out grille and 400-cid four-barrel V-8 under the hood.* Phil Kunz

A 1972 GTO hardtop with the regular 455 V-8 carried 13 lbs. per horsepower and its performance really suffered for it. It required 7.1 seconds to scoot from 0-to-60 mph and the quarter-mile took 15.4 seconds. Despite Pontiac's attempt to give GTO buyers choices that could make the "Goat" both more affordable and fancier at the same time, only 5,807 cars with the option left the factory.

1973

In 1973, all GM intermediates got completely new Colonnade styling with torpedo-shaped body lines and limo-like windows. The cars looked like a cross between one designer's idea of a "Star Wars" spaceship and a second designer's concept for a high-speed boat. The LeMans was also reskinned and got the sharp new looks, too. So did cars with the GTO option package—but only for this one year. That makes them pretty unique.

Design traits of the '73 Goat included a ship's-prow nose, twin rectangular grilles on either side of the "beak," single headlamps mounted in square housings, highly sculptured fenders and a "Colonnade"-style roof with heavy pillars designed to meet federal rollover standards. The large door windows were deep-cut into the beltline as on a limousine.

"Even our legendary GTO is alive and well as an option," said a 1973 sales catalog section covering the LeMans Sport Coupe, a model with bucket seats

and louvered rear quarter windows. The next page, featuring the base LeMans, said, "You can turn LeMans into Pontiac's legendary GTO just by ordering the GTO package. You get a scooped hood, blacked-out grille, firm suspension, wide tires and a lot of performance." A small picture of an Ascot Silver LeMans Colonnade hardtop with the $368 GTO package was at the bottom of the page. The option also included fat stabilizer bars, rear sway bars, baby moon hubcaps, 15 x 7-inch wheel rims and special body striping.

Mechanically, the GTO package included a 400-cid four-barrel V-8 and heavy-duty three-speed manual transmission with floor shift. The dual-exhaust outlets were brightened with chrome tailpipe tips. A standard 455-cid V-8 was available as optional equipment. Unfortunately, the GTO did not get an exciting new engine that had been promised for it.

At the press preview for the '73 GTO in the summer of 1972, PMD announced a new Super-Duty 455 V-8 to replace the 455 HO. The Super-Duty or "SD" designation dated back to the early '60s (before that hot Pontiac engines were called "NASCAR V-8s" and "Tempest 425 NASCAR V-8s"). The '73 Super-Duty was an awesome motor that incorporated practically all of the 455 HO goodies, plus goodies like dry sump oiling provisions and high-flow heads. The SD 455 was scheduled for use in GTOs, Grand Ams, Formulas and Trans Ams.

CARS magazine picked the SD 455 GTO as its "Top Performance Car of the Year." Photos exist of "pilot" models of the new GTO and Grand Am with SD-455 badges on the body sides, but this true high-performance V-8 was never used in any production cars other than Firebird Trans Ams and Formulas.

On October 1, 1972, Martin J. Caserio became PMD's general manager and killed the SD 455 program for A-bodies. Only 4,806 LeMans and LeMans Sport Colonnade hardtops combined were built with the GTO option in 1973. None of these cars were Super-Dutys, unless they had an unauthorized engine swap.

1974

This was the 11th, and last, GTO. For 1974, a GTO option was offered for Ventura and Ventura Custom coupes. It cost $195 to turn one of the "senior compacts" into a Goat. The package included a 350-cid four-barrel V-8, front

"CARS magazine picked the SD 55 GTO as its 'Top Performance Car of the Year.'"

GTO YEAR-BY-YEAR SPEC'S

1964

Engine	Bore/Str.	Comp. Ratio	CID	BHP	WT.	W.B.	O.L.	Width	HT
V-8*	4.06 x 3.75	10.75	389	325 @ 4800	3,106	115.0	203	73.3	54.0
V-8**	4.06 x 3.75	10.75	389	348 @ 4900	3,106	115.0	203	73.3	54.0

* Base four-barrel
** Optional Tri-Power

1965

Engine	Bore/Str.	Comp. Ratio	CID	BHP	WT.	W.B.	O.L.	Width	HT
V-8*	4.06 x 3.75	10.75	389	335 @ 5000	3,444	115.0	206.1	73.1	54.0
V-8**	4.06 x 3.75	10.75	389	360 @ 5200	3,444	115.0	206.1	73.1	54.0
V-8***	4.06 x 3.75	10.75	389	360 @ 5200	3,444	115.0	206.1	73.1	54.0

* Base four-barrel
** Optional Tri-Power
*** Optional RA I

1966

Engine	Bore/Str.	Comp. Ratio	CID	BHP	WT.	W.B.	O.L.	Width	HT
V-8*	4.06 x 3.75	10.75	389	335 @ 5000	3,445	115.0	206.4	74.4	54.0
V-8**	4.06 x 3.75	10.75	389	360 @ 5200	3,445	115.0	206.4	74.4	54.0
V-8***	4.06 x 3.75	10.75	389	360 @ 5200	3,445	115.0	206.1	74.4	54.0

* Base four-barrel
** Optional Tri-Power

1967

Engine	Bore/Str.	Comp. Ratio	CID	BHP	WT.	W.B.	O.L.	Width	HT
V-8*	4.12 x 3.75	10.75	400	335 @ 5000	3,425	115.0	206.6	74.7	53.7
V-8**	4.12 x 3.75	8.6	400	255 @ 4400	3,425	115.0	206.6	74.7	53.7
V-8***	4.12 x 3.75	10.75	400	360 @ 5100	3,425	115.0	206.6	74.7	53.7
V-8****	4.12 x 3.75	10.75	400	360 @ 5100	3,425	115.0	206.6	74.7	53.7

* Base four-barrel
** Optional low-compression two-barrel V-8
*** Optional HO V-8
**** Optional Ram Air V-8

1968

Engine	Bore/Str.	Comp. Ratio	CID	BHP	WT.	W.B.	O.L.	Width	HT
V-8*	4.12 x 3.75	10.50	400	350 @ 5000	3,506	112.0	200.7	74.8	52.2
V-8**	4.12 x 3.75	8.6	400	265 @ 4600	3,506	112.0	200.7	74.8	52.2
V-8***	4.12 x 3.75	10.75	400	360 @ 5100	3,506	112.0	200.7	74.8	52.2
V-8****	4.12 x 3.75	10.75	400	360 @ 5400	3,506	112.0	200.7	74.8	52.2

* Base four-barrel
** Optional low-compression two-barrel V-8
*** Optional Ram Air V-8
**** Optional Ram Air II V-8

■ A 1970 Judge convertible in Sierra Yellow.

Jerry Heasley

1969

Engine	Bore/Str.	Comp. Ratio	CID	BHP	WT.	W.B.	O.L.	Width	HT
V-8*	4.12 x 3.75	10.75	400	350 @ 5000	3,503	112.0	201.5	75.8	52.3
V-8**	4.12 x 3.75	8.6	400	265 @ 4600	3,503	112.0	201.5	75.8	52.3
V-8***	4.12 x 3.75	10.75	400	366 @ 5100	3,503	112.0	201.5	75.8	52.3
V-8****	4.12 x 3.75	10.75	400	370 @ 5500	3,503	112.0	201.5	75.8	52.3

* Base four-barrel
** Optional low-compression two-barrel V-8
*** Optional Ram Air V-8
**** Optional Ram Air II V-8

1970

Engine	Bore/Str.	Comp. Ratio	CID	BHP	WT.	W.B.	O.L.	Width	HT
V-8*	4.12 x 3.75	10.25	400	350 @ 5000	3,638	112.0	202.9	76.7	52.6
V-8**	4.12 x 3.75	10.50	400	366 @ 5100	3,638	112.0	202.9	76.7	52.6
V-8***	4.12 x 3.75	10.50	400	370 @ 5500	3,638	112.0	202.9	76.7	52.6

* Base four-barrel
** Optional Ram Air III V-8
*** Optional Ram Air IIV V-8

1971

Engine	Bore/Str.	Comp. Ratio	CID	BHP	WT.	W.B.	O.L.	Width	HT
V-8*	4.12 x 3.75	8.2:1	400	300 @ 4800	3,619	112.0	202.9	76.7	52.6
V-8**	4.15 x 4.21	8.2:1	455	325 @ 4400	3,619	112.0	202.9	76.7	52.6
V-8**	4.15 x 4.21	8.4:1	455	335 @ 4800	3,619	112.0	202.9	76.7	52.6

* Base four-barrel
** Optional V-8
*** Optional HO V-8

1972

Engine	Bore/Str.	Comp. Ratio	CID	BHP	WT.	W.B.	O.L.	Width	HT
V-8*	4.12 x 3.75	8.2:1	400	250 @ 4400	3,619	112.0	202.7	76.7	52.6
V-8**	4.15 x 4.21	8.2:1	455	250 @ 3600	3,619	112.0	202.7	76.7	52.6
V-8**	4.15 x 4.21	8.4:1	455	300 @ 4000	3,619	112.0	202.7	76.7	52.6

* Base four-barrel
** Optional V-8
*** Optional HO V-8

(Note: Compiled from a variety of contemporary sources. Minor differences in measurements are due to the way the car was measured, rather than changes in the car itself or related to the fact that different body styles were used as the basis for factory specifications tables. Weight is for lightest model.)

"For 1974, a GTO option was offered for Ventura and Ventura Custom coupes. It cost $195 to turn one of the 'senior compacts' into a Goat."

and rear stabilizer bars, a radial-tuned suspension, Pliacell shocks, power steering, drum brakes, E78-14 tires, a heavy-duty three-speed manual gearbox, dual exhausts with splitters, a 3.08:1 axle, Rally II rims less trim rings, special grille driving lights, a rear-facing "shaker" air scoop and computer selected high-rate rear springs.

The code J engine included in the Ventura GTO package was a 350-cid V-8 with a four-barrel carburetor and 7.6:1 compression ratio. It developed 185 hp. The X-body Ventura had a 111-inch wheelbase and an overall length of 199.4 inches. It was the smallest GTO and the only non-A-body GTO.

For years, these cars were ignored by GTO enthusiasts, but they are now beginning to catch on with a younger generation of collectors.

PRODUCTION STATISTICS AND BREAKOUTS

1964 TEMPEST + GTO

Year	Body Code	Body Type	Engine Type	MSP Price	Model Yr. Prod.
64	STD27	2CP	V-8	$2,852	7,384
64	STD37	2HT	V-8	$2,963	18,422
64	STD67	2CV	V-8	$3,081	6,644
ALL GTO TOTAL					**32,450**

1965 TEMPEST + GTO

Year	Body Code	Body Type	Engine Type	MSP Price	Model Yr. Prod.
65	STD27	2CP	V-8	$2,727	8,319
65	STD37	2HT	V-8	$2791	55,722
65	STD67	2CV	V-8	$3,026	11,311
ALL GTO TOTAL					**75,352**

1966 GTO

Year	Body Code	Body Type	Engine Type	MSP Price	Model Yr. Prod.
66	STD07	2CP	V-8	$2,783	10,363
66	STD17	2HT	V-8	$2,847	73,785
66	STD67	2CV	V-8	$3,082	12,798
ALL GTO TOTAL					**96,946**

1967 GTO

Year	Body Code	Body Type	Engine Type	MSP Price	Model Yr. Prod.
67	STD07	2CP	V-8	$2,871	7,029
67	STD17	2HT	V-8	$2,935	65,176
67	STD67	2CV	V-8	$3,165	9,517
ALL GTO TOTAL					**81,722**

1968 GTO

Year	Body Code	Body Type	Engine Type	MSP Price	Model Yr. Prod.
68	STD37	2HT	V-8	$3,101	77,704
68	STD67	2CV	V-8	$3,327	9,980
ALL GTO TOTAL					**87,684**

1969 GTO

Year	Body Code	Body Type	Engine Type	MSP Price	Model Yr. Prod.
69	STD37	2HT	V-8	$3,139	77,704
69	STD67	2CV	V-8	$3,365	9,980
ALL TOTAL					**87,684**

1970 GTO

Year	Body Code	Body Type	Engine Type	MSP Price	Model Yr. Prod.
BASE GTO					
70	STD37	2HT	V-8	$3,267	32,737
70	STD67	2CV	V-8	$3,492	3,615
GTO + "THE JUDGE"					
70	STD37	2HT	V-8	$3,604	3,629
70	STD67	2CV	V-8	$3,829	168
ALL GTO TOTAL					**40,149**

1971 GTO

Year	Body Code	Body Type	Engine Type	MSP Price	Model Yr. Prod.
BASE GTO					
71	STD37	2HT	V-8	$3,446	9,497
71	STD67	2CV	V-8	$3,676	661
GTO + "THE JUDGE"					
71	STD37	2HT	V-8	$3,840	357
71	STD67	2CV	V-8	$4,070	17
ALL GTO TOTAL					**10,532**

1972 GTO

Year	Body Code	Body Type	Engine Type	MSP Price	Model Yr. Prod.
BASE GTO					
72	STD27	2CP	V-8	$3,066	134
72	STD37	2HT	V-8	$3,195	5,673
ALL GTO TOTAL					**5,807**

1973 GTO

Year	Body Code	Body Type	Engine Type	MSP Price	Model Yr. Prod.
LEMANS					
73	STD37	2CP	V-8	$3,288	494
LEMANS SPORT					
73	STD37	2CP	V-8	$3,810	4,312
ALL GTO TOTAL					**4,806**

1974 VENTURA + GTO

Year	Body Code	Body Type	Engine Type	MSP Price	Model Yr. Prod.
VENTURA					
74	STD27	2CP	V-8	$3,035	2,487
74	STD17	2HB	V-8	$3,186	687
LEMANS SPORT					
74	STD27	2CP	V-8	$3,183	2,848
74	STD17	2HB	V-8	$3,344	1,036
ALL GTO TOTAL					**7,058**

Note: 1964-1968 tables are from recently released General Motors 1955-1968 production data records.

■ *The 1965 GTO got a new grille, hood, and rear end.*   Jerry Heasley

PRICE GUIDE

Vehicle Condition Scale

6 — Parts car:
May or may not be running, but is weathered, wrecked and/or stripped to the point of being useful primarily for parts.

5 — Restorable:
Needs complete restoration of body, chassis and interior. May or may not be running, but isn't weathered, wrecked or stripped to the point of being useful only for parts.

4 — Good:
A driveable vehicle needing no or only minor work to be functional. Also, a deteriorated restoration or a very poor amateur restoration. All components may need restoration to be "excellent," but the car is mostly useable "as is."

3 — Very Good:
Complete operable original or older restoration. Also, a very good amateur restoration, all presentable and serviceable inside and out. Plus, a combination of well-done restoration and good operable components or a partially restored car with all parts necessary to compete and/or valuable NOS parts.

2 — Fine:
Well-restored or a combination of superior restoration and excellent original parts. Also, extremely well-maintained original vehicle showing minimal wear.

1 — Excellent:
Restored to current maximum professional standards of quality in every area, or perfect original with components operating and apearing as new. A 95-plus point show car that is not driven.

1964 LeMans

	6	5	4	3	2	1
2d HT	720	2,160	3,600	8,100	12,600	18,000
2d Cpe	660	1,980	3,300	7,430	11,550	16,500
2d Conv	760	2,280	3,800	8,550	13,300	19,000
2d GTO Cpe	1,520	4,560	7,600	17,100	26,600	38,000
2d GTO Conv	2,000	6,000	10,000	22,500	35,000	50,000
2d GTO HT	1,560	4,680	7,800	17,550	27,300	39,000

Deduct 20 percent for Tempest 6-cyl.

1965 LeMans

	6	5	4	3	2	1
4d Sed	440	1,320	2,200	4,950	7,700	11,000
2d Cpe	500	1,500	2,500	5,630	8,750	12,500
2d HT	660	1,980	3,300	7,430	11,550	16,500
2d Conv	840	2,520	4,200	9,450	14,700	21,000
2d GTO Conv	2,040	6,120	10,200	22,950	35,700	51,000
2d GTO HT	1,600	4,800	8,000	18,000	28,000	40,000
2d GTO Cpe	1,560	4,680	7,800	17,550	27,300	39,000

Deduct 20 percent for 6-cyl. where available. Add 5 percent for 4-speed.

1966 GTO

	6	5	4	3	2	1
2d HT	1,600	4,800	8,000	18,000	28,000	40,000
2d Cpe	1,560	4,680	7,800	17,550	27,300	39,000
2d Conv	2,040	6,120	10,200	22,950	35,700	51,000

Add 5 percent for 4-speed. Add 30 percent for tri power option.

1967 GTO

	6	5	4	3	2	1
2d Cpe	1,560	4,680	7,800	17,550	27,300	39,000
2d HT	1,600	4,800	8,000	18,000	28,000	40,000
2d Conv	2,040	6,120	10,200	22,950	35,700	51,000

Add 25 percent for Ram Air 400 GTO.

1968 GTO

	6	5	4	3	2	1
2d HT	1,320	3,960	6,600	14,850	23,100	33,000
2d Conv	1,480	4,440	7,400	16,650	25,900	37,000

Add 25 percent for Ram Air I, 40 percent for Ram Air II.

1969 GTO

	6	5	4	3	2	1
2d HT	1,280	3,840	6,400	14,400	22,400	32,000
2d Conv	1,440	4,320	7,200	16,200	25,200	36,000

Add 75 percent for GTO Judge option.

1970 GTO

	6	5	4	3	2	1
2d HT	1,240	3,720	6,200	13,950	21,700	31,000
2d Conv	1,400	4,200	7,000	15,750	24,500	35,000

Add 75 perce3nt for Judge option

1971 GTO

	6	5	4	3	2	1
2d HT	1,120	3,360	5,600	12,600	19,600	28,000
2d Conv	1,280	3,840	6,400	14,400	22,400	32,000

Add 75 percent for Judge option

1972 GTO

	6	5	4	3	2	1
2d HT	740	2,200	3,700	8,330	12,950	18,500
2d Sed	620	1,860	3,100	6,980	10,850	15,500

1973 GTO

	6	5	4	3	2	1
2d Spt Cpe (V-8)	580	1,740	2,900	6,530	10,150	14,500

1974 GTO

	6	5	4	3	2	1
2d Cpe	320	960	1,600	3,600	5,600	8,000

Mustang

1964 1/2

n 1964, the economy was booming. There were plenty of jobs. America was experiencing a "youth movement" as "baby boomers" of the 1950s became young adults. This was the "Mustang Generation" as Ford saw it.

"This (Mustang) generation wants economy and sportiness, handling and performance, all wrapped up in one set of wheels," went the sales pitch. "There is a market searching for a car. Ford committed itself to design that car. It carries four people, weighs under 2,500 pounds and costs less that $2,500."

April 17, 1964, was a big day for the Mustang, which had its official introduction at the New York World's Fair. The previous evening, the car had been unveiled in 9 p.m. commercials on all three TV networks. With nearly 29 million viewers were tuned in, the Mustang media blitz had started. On the first day that it went on sale, more than 22,000 orders were taken. Within one year, Mustang sales reached 417,000. That total established a record for a full year of sales for a brand-new nameplate. As far as we know, that record still stands.

■ *The GT Package was a new addition to the Mustang menu in 1965, and included a bunch of nice upgrades from the base pony car, including a four-barrel A Code 289 engine, special grille with built-in fog lamps, special striping and badging, and a three- or four-speed stick shift.*
Phil Kunz

1964   1965   1966   1967   1968   1969   1970   1971

1964: Mustang debuts at World's Fair in New York on April 17.

1965: "K" Code 289 with 271 hp puts punch in Ford's pony car. Serious speed freaks can opt for a race-ready GT-350 or GT-350R.

1966: GT-350 available in four colors. Paxton superchargers available on GT-350.

1967: Major redesign includes a full fastback roofline. New 390 big block becomes an engine option.

1967: The GT-500 arrives.

1968: The Cobra Jet 428 is unveiled in April. It was rated at 330 hp, but actual output was likely upwards of 400 hp.

1968: GT-500KR replaces the GT-500 at midyear. 302 engine replaces the 289 in the GT-350.

1969: Boss Mustangs debut. Mach 1 body style arrives.

1969: Super Cobra Jet 428 becomes the most lethal engine choice.

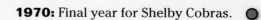

1970: Final year for Shelby Cobras.

1971: Boss 351 replaces Boss 302 and 429.

■ *The open chrome air cleaners were seen on the 271-hp K code V-8s in 1965.*

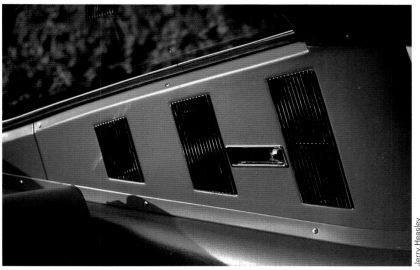

■ *The fastback "2+2" was big news for the Mustang in 1965. Four decades later, Ford would roll out an all-new Mustang with similar styling.*

Two models were offered: a spunky-looking hardtop coupe and a convertible. The standard Mustang engine was a 170-cubic-inch inline six that generated 101 hp, but the Mustang's secret was a "cheap" V-8 that was part of a long list of options and accessories. The V-8 used in early Mustangs was the 260-cubic inch version with 164 hp.

Looks-wise, the Mustang had flair. It sported a long hood and a short rear deck. In 1964, as today, that kind of image said "performance." The Mustang's appeal was so strong that the Dearborn factory, where Falcons were also built, couldn't keep up with demand. By July, Ford's plant in San Jose, California, started building Mustangs. Soon after, the Falcon assembly line at the Ford's Metuchen, New Jersey, factory was converted to Mustang production.

The Mustang's performance theme was further driven home by its selection as "Official Pace Car" for the 1964 Indy 500, although no replica model was made. With the Mustang's midyear launch, there was no time for that. Still, being chosen to pace the race put the car in the public eye again. It also made collector's items of all 230 pace cars that were built. Thirty-five convertible pace cars were sold to dealers after the race and about 190 hardtops were given out to the winners of two contests.

In June 1964, Ford made a 289-cubic inch "Challenger" V-8 available in the Mustang. The two-barrel version with 9.0:1 compression generated 210 hp. A 220-hp version with a four-barrel carburetor and 9.8:1 compression was also offered. A Challenger High-Performance option with a four-barrel carb, solid valve lifters and 10.5:1 compression was good for a whopping 271 hp.

By the end of 1964, the Mustang scored 263,434 sales and many of the cars were loaded with profitable options. A V-8 was used in 73 percent. Nearly half had automatic transmission and nearly 20 percent had a four-speed manual gearbox. Radios were in 77.8 percent, while 99 percent had heaters, 31 percent had power steering and 88 percent had white sidewall tires.

More than half of all Mustang buyers fit into the under-34-years-old bracket, where great popularity had been anticipated, but a sizable 16 percent of the customers fell into the 45- to 55-year-old category. This showed that the Mustang was bridging the generation gap to earn its remarkably strong sales.

A new Mustang 2+2 fastback was introduced on October 1, 1964. On April 17, 1965, the Mustang celebrated its first birthday. By then, it had set a new world's record of more than 418,000 sales in its first year on the market.

1965

October 1, 1964 was introduction day for the 1965 Mustang. In addition to the new 2+2, front disc brakes, luxury interiors and a GT package were released. An alternator replaced the generator used on early cars.

Minor changes marked the transition from early-production 1965 models (often referred to as "1964 1/2 Mustangs") to "regular" 1965 Mustangs. The later cars had the door handles attached with Allen screws, rather than "C" clips.

"...The Mustang had flair. It sported a long hood and a short rear deck. In 1964, as today, that kind of image said 'performance.'"

The Mustang nameplates on the body sides were 1/4 inch longer (approximately 5 inches total length) and chome-plated inside door lock buttons were used.

Any Mustang could be made more luxurious by ordering the luxury interior option. It included an instrument panel with wood-grained vinyl trim, new bucket seats with handsome, embossed inserts, a sports-steering wheel with chromed "rivets" and more little niceties like integral door arm rests and door courtesy lights. The embossed bucket seats became known as the "pony" interior, as the embossment showed herds of stylized wild mustangs.

The GT kit included the 225-hp V-8, a three-speed synchro stick shift, a special grille with built-in fog lamps, GT front fender insignia, a GT five-dial instrument cluster, a GT paint stripe (deletable), dual exhausts with "trumpet" extensions, front disc brakes and a special handling package. A 271-hp, solid-lifter, high-performance V-8 and four-speed tranny could be substituted.

"Cobra Kits" were also available for Mustangs from Ford's Genuine Parts division. Kits for the 221-, 260- and 289-cubic-inch V-8s were marketed. They included extras from simple packages, such as chrome dress-up parts and a

■ *Ford took the muscle car world to another level when it rolled out the GT-350, a brainchild of performance car whiz Carroll Shelby. These cars have since become some of the most collectible and coveted cars to ever roll out of Detroit.* Phil Kunz

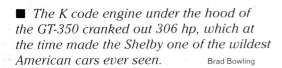
■ *The no-frills grille and Guardsman Blue stripes made the GT-350 instantly recognizable, although the stripes were actually optional.* Brad Bowling

■ *The K code engine under the hood of the GT-350 cranked out 306 hp, which at the time made the Shelby one of the wildest American cars ever seen.* Brad Bowling

Cobra distributor kit, to harder-to-install engine performance kits, dual exhaust kits, cam kits, heavy-duty clutch kits and induction kits with single four-barrel, dual four-barrel and triple two-barrel carburetor set ups.

Ford proved itself a capable promoter. Ads stressed how the Mustang could be "factory-customized" to a buyer's taste. One told how "Wolfgang" the harpsichord player had his life changed by his sporty Mustang. After winning a "Tiffany Award" in 1964, the '65 Mustang took a Bronze Medal Award from the Industrial Design Institute. Calendar year registrations hit 518,252 Mustangs.

1966

The '66 Mustang was changed only modestly. The instrument panel looked less like the Falcon's. The grille now had the pony "floating" in its center "corral" with no horizontal or vertical dividing bars. A wind split ornament was added at the end of the "cove" on the body sides. Federally mandated safety features including seat belts, a padded instrument panel, emergency flashers, electric windshield wipers (with washers) and dual padded sun visors were made standard. Prices increased accordingly.

The GT Equipment Group continued to be available in 1966 as a $152.50 option package for Mustangs with high-performance V-8 power plants. The GT Equipment Group included a dual exhaust system, front fog lamps, special body ornamentation, front disc brakes, GT racing stripes (in place of rocker panel moldings) and handling package components. The handling package (normally $30.84 extra by itself) included increased-rate front and rear springs, larger-diameter front and rear shock absorbers, a steering system with a 22:1 overall ratio and a large-diameter stabilizer bar.

■ *Travelers who really wanted to fly could rent one of a 936 special GT-350H cars that were made available to the Hertz rental car company in 1966. These hairy rental cars were so fast that some customers apparently took them straight to the track, rolling up $17 a day and 17 cents a mile while they were burning rubber.* Phil Kunz

The Mustang's base V-8 engine for 1966 was the Code "G" 4.00 x 2.87-inch bore and stroke 289-cid with a 9.3:1 compression ratio and an Autolite two-barrel carburetor. It generated 200 hp at 4400 rpm. The performance options included the Code "A" 289-cid Challenger V-8 with a 10.1:1 compression ratio and four-barrel Autclite carburetor, which produced 225 hp at 4800 and the Code "K" Challenger High-Performance V-8. This version of the "289" featured a 10.5:1 compression ratio, a four-barrel Autolite carburetor and solid valve lifters, which helped it to make 271 hp at 6000 rpm.

A Mustang 2+2 with the Challenger High-Performance V-8 could do 0 to 60 mph in 7.6 seconds and needed about 15.9 seconds to make it down the quarter-mile.

The GT package proved to be twice as popular as it had been in 1965 and its sales increased from about 15,000 the earlier year to approximately 30,000.

A motorized Mustang GT toy car was available from Ford dealers in 1966. It cost just $4.95 back then. A full-page ad showed a young boy pushing the car under his Christmas tree. By the end of the year, there had been a total of 1,288,557 Mustangs built since the mid-1964—quite an amazing number!

1967

Ford's pony car had caught other companies unprepared in 1964, but now they were poised to catch up. Mercury introduced a new car that was virtually a fancy Mustang, calling it Cougar. Chevrolet launched its own, entirely new Camaro sports-compact model. The Firebird was Pontiac's version of the Camaro. It bowed in mid-1967, six months after the Chevrolet pony car.

Ford was hard-pressed to improve on its now "classic" Mustang, but it had to. Lee Iacocca and company did a great job with a tough assignment. The 1967 Mustang got a jazzy new body, a wider tread for better road grip and a bigger engine bay designed to accommodate a wider range of engines.

Option choices were widened, too. They now included a Tilt-Away steering wheel, a built-in heater/air conditioner, an overhead console, a Stereo-Sonic tape system, a SelectShift automatic transmission that also worked manually, a bench seat, an AM/FM radio, Fingertip speed control, custom exterior trim group, and front power disk brakes.

"Usually, second-generation cars lose a lot of the flavor of the original. Not so with the Gen II Mustangs."

Styling followed the same theme, but in a larger size. That was, absolutely, a wise move. Usually, second-generation cars lose a lot of the flavor of the original. Not so with the Gen II Mustangs. They had stronger new styling that recalled the original, plus a handsome new interior.

On the exterior, the 1967 Mustang was heftier and more full fendered. Especially low and sleek was the new 2+2, which featured all new sheet metal. The fastback roofline had a clean, unbroken sweep downward to a distinctive, concave rear panel. Functional air louvers in the roof rear quarters were thinner than before. The wheelbase was unchanged, but overall length grew by nearly two inches. Front and rear tracks went up by 2.1 inches, as did the width.

Sheet metal sculpturing was more obvious, with lots of rounded contours. "Hairy" is how many enthusiasts described it back then. The larger, snout-like grille looked ready to take a bite out of all the "Johnny-come-lately" sporty cars. The same three body styles were offered, but the Mustang did not really have different "models." The GT option was still available.

All Mustangs had bigger engine bays to accommodate a new 390-cid/315-hp big-block V-8. This small-bore/long-stroke power plant was related to the

■ *The 1968 High Country Special Mustang was sold in Colorado and has since become a very sought-after collector car. The Shelby-influenced cars were similar to the California Specials of the same year, and were most easily identified by their rear deck lid spoiler and plain blacked-out grille.* Brad Bowling

■ *The ribbed tail panel was part of the Exterior Décor Group in 1968.* Brad Bowling

■ *The special GT wheel covers were part of the $147 GT Package.* Jerry Heasley

Ford "FE" engine, introduced way back in 1958. It provided a good street-performance option with lots of low-end performance and plenty of torque.

All '66 engines were carried over and a new 200-hp "Challenger 289" V-8 with a two-barrel carburetor was standard in cars with the GT option. A GTA designation was used on cars with automatic transmission and GT equipment.

Other technical changes included front suspension improvements. A Competition Handling package was released. It cost quite a bit extra and didn't go into too many cars, due to its steep price.

While engine choices grew, most Mustangs were slower because the added size and weight hurt performance. Cars with the 390 were the exception. They were larger and heavier, too, but *not* slower. The 390s could move!

Automakers had predicted another hot, 9-million-unit sales season, but 1967 wound up with the industry losing 1 million sales from 1966 levels. This occurred despite the fact that new cars were introduced two weeks earlier than usual to give them extra selling time. Model-year production of Mustangs wound up at 472,121. This was a drop of 135,447 cars from 1966.

1968

"Only Mustang makes it happen!" said a '68 ad showing Sidney, a white-shirt-and-tie type, "seashelling at the seashore." Sidney then purchased a red Mustang 2 + 2. A time-sequence photo showed him being "transformed" into a lifeguard with three beach bunnies clinging on his muscular arms.

If the ad theme sounded familiar, the car looked similar, too. Only subtle changes took place. Bucket seats, a floor-mounted stick shift, a sports steering wheel and rich, loop-pile carpeting remained standard. Minor trim updates included a front end with the Mustang emblem "floating" in the grille, script-style (instead of block letter) Mustang body side nameplates and cleaner-looking bright metal trim on the cove. There was a new "2-tone" hood.

The $147 GT option included a choice of stripes. Either rocker panel stripes or reflecting "C" stripes could be specified. Other GT goodies included fog lights in the grille, a GT gas cap and GT wheel covers. The fog lights no longer had a bar separating them from the "corral" in the grille.

Disc brakes made the standard equipment list when big-block V-8s were ordered. A total of 17,458 GTs were made in 1968. The 390 GT is considered a very desirable collector's car today.

New engines were offered in 1968. There were no options for the base 289

■ The new 335-hp Cobra-Jet V-8 went in 2,817 1968 Mustangs, including this GT.   Phil Kunz

■ The 1969 Mustangs were the only first-generation cars that had four headlights.   Brad Bowling

V-8. Instead, a 302-cubic-inch V-8 was offered. This was initially seen with a four-barrel carburetor and 230 hp rating. Later on, a 220-hp two-barrel version came out. Big-block options included two "FE" series engines, the 390 (with 320/325 horsepower) and the 427 (with 390 hp). This engine was used in only a handful of cars before it was phased out in December 1967. Starting in April 1968, a new 428 Cobra-Jet 335-hp V-8 went into about 2,817 Mustangs. Cars with a four-speed included strengthened front shock absorber towers and revised rear shock absorber mountings. Ram Air induction was available.

About 5,000 GT/CS "California Specials" were produced in 1968. Their features included a Shelby-style deck lid with a spoiler, sequential tail lights and a blacked-out grille. They had no Mustang grille emblem. Their wheel covers were the same ones used on 1968 GTs, but without GT identification.

Production fell again. With 317,404 units built, the Mustang slipped from second place in domestic auto production in 1965, to seventh place in 1968. However, it was still the best-selling pony car.

1969

In 1969, the Mustang got its third major restyling. The new body retained the Mustang image, but grew 3.8 inches. There was no change in wheelbase. The windshield was more sharply raked. The quad headlights had the outer lenses deeply recessed into the fenders and the inner lenses in the grille.

The body sides were no longer "indented." A feature line ran from the tip of the front fender to just behind the rear most door-seam, at a level just above the front wheel opening. Convertibles and hardtops had a rear-facing, simulated air vent just in front of the rear wheel opening on each side of the body. Fastbacks had a "backwards-C" air scoop above the main feature line.

The fastback became the SportsRoof or Sports Roof (various Ford ads spelled the term differently). It had a 0.9-inch lower roofline than the 2+2. The rear quarter louvers were replaced with a small window next to the door glass.

Though the styling remained Ford-like, the Mustang adopted a GM-like marketing program with distinctive "models" to suit the tastes of different buyers. Mustangs now came in basic, luxury, sporty and high-performance

■ *The Boss 429 burst onto the scene in 1969 as Ford attempted to legalize the 429-cid V-8 for use in NASCAR races.* Jerry Heasley

formats. This may have reflected the influence of Semon "Bunkie" Knudsen, a long-time GM executive who became president of Ford after resigning at GM.

Two new models were introduced in the fall. The Grande was a dressed-up notchback hardtop with a vinyl roof and a plush interior. The Mach 1 was a performance car based on the SportsRoof. Knudsen brought famed GM designer Larry Shinoda to Ford with him. While the introductory Mustang designs were finished, Shinoda quickly created the Boss 302 model.

For $147, the GT Equipment Group could be ordered. Base engine in the GT was a 351-cid "Windsor" V-8 with 250 hp. GT buyers also got a special handling package, lower body racing stripes, dual exhausts, pin-type hood lock latches, a simulated hood scoop with integral turn indicators (a "shaker" scoop with the 428CJ Ram Air V-8), a three-speed manual transmission, four-wheel drum brakes, glass-belted whitewall Wide-Oval tires and styled steel wheels with

Argent Silver trim and GT hubcaps. Only 4,973 Mustang GTs were sold in 1969, so the package was a lot less popular than it had been in the past.

The Mach 1 was stealing the show. "Mustang Mach 1 - holder of 295 land speed records," said Ford's *1969 Performance Buyer's Guide*. "This is the one that Mickey Thompson started with. From its wide-oval, belted tires to its wind tunnel designed SportsRoof, the word is 'go.'" Ford said the production car had "the same wind-splitting sheet metal as the specially modified Mach 1 that screamed around Bonneville clocking over 155, hour after hour, to break some 295 USAC speed and endurance records."

Standard on Mach 1s was a spoiler, a matte black hood, a simulated hood scoop and exposed NASCAR-style hood lock pins (that could be deleted). A reflective side stripe and rear stripes carried the model name behind the front wheel arches and above the chrome pop-up gas cap. Chrome styled steel wheels and chrome exhausts tips (with optional four-barrel carburetor) were other bright touches. Also featured were dual color-keyed racing mirrors and a handling suspension. Mach 1s also had the fanciest high-back bucket seat interior, black carpets, a Rim-Blow wheel, a center console, a clock, sound deadening insulation and teakwood-grained doors, dash and console trim.

The base engine was a 351-cid two-barrel Windsor V-8… essentially a stroked 302 with raised deck height. It made a great street performance mill. Options included a 351-cid/290-hp four-barrel V-8 and a 390 with 320 hp.

The CJ 428 became optional for Mustang GT or Mach 1 on April 1, 1968. It came in Cobra Jet or Super Cobra Jet versions. The former was referred to as the "standard Cobra engine." It generated 335 hp at 5200 rpm and 440 lb.-ft. of torque at 3400 rpm. The SCJ was the same engine with Ram Air induction, a hardened steel cast crankshaft, special "LeMans" con-rods and improved balancing for drag racing. It advertised the same horsepower. Hot Rod magazine called the SCJ "the fastest running pure stock in the history of man."

Introduced late in the 1969, the Boss 302 also received high acclaim from the performance crowd. Mustang expert Jerry Heasley says. "This little fastback coupe could blow the doors off almost anything around town in 1969 and 1970, including many of the big-block muscle cars roaming the streets."

"Hot Rod magazine called the SCJ 'the fastest running pure stock in the history of man.'"

The black striping and callouts, blacked-out hood, slatted rear window and the rear deck spoiler made the 1969 Boss 302 look fast, and it was. The car was designed to run in the SCCA Trans-Am racing series. Jerry Heasley

Hot Rod reported that the car out-classed "most of the world's big-engined muscle cars." The Boss 302 went head-to-head with the Camaro Z28 on the Trans-Am racing circuit and the showroom floor. The main asset of a Boss 302 was its high-performance small-block V-8, which was essentially a stroked version of the famous 289. Special cylinder heads gave it a performance advantage over previous small-blocks. Sometimes called "Cleveland" heads (because of their similarity to those used on the 351-cubic-inch engine made in Ford's Cleveland, Ohio foundry), the Boss 302 heads had canted intake and exhaust valves that acommodated bigger ports and valves. Another benefit was a straighter-flowing fuel/air mixture, giving better volumetric efficiency, especially with a little "improvement" to the stock exhaust system.

The used a mechanical camshaft with a duration of 290-degrees for both intake and exhaust cycles and a .290-inch lobe lift. The forged steel crank was balanced both statically and dynamically and anchored in place with five main bearings. The three center bearings had four-bolt caps. Forged steel con rods were also used. A high-rise, aluminum intake manifold carried a single 780-cfm four-barrel Holley carb. Other goodies included pop-up pistons, a dual-point

distributor, a high-pressure oil pump, lightweight, stamped rocker arms, screw-in rocker arm studs and push rod guide plates (with specially hardened push rods), an oil pan windage baffle and screw-in freeze plugs.

A four-speed transmission with Hurst shifter was provided. For street performance and drag strip use, the wide-ratio gearbox worked best. At low rpms, the lower speed, first-gear ratio of the wide-ratio gear box helped the Boss 302 get moving faster. The close-ratio option was best for road racing.

Ford offered the Boss 302 with three axle ratios, including the standard 3.50 non-locking version, plus the Traction-Lok 3.50 and 3.91. Also available was a No-Spin axle with a 4.30 ratio built by Detroit Automotive. With each of these ratios, Ford installed fully machined axle shafts that helped prevent build up of stress points via larger axle shaft splines, an extra-strength cast nodular iron center section and larger wheel seals.

The Boss 302 front suspension used high-rate (350 inch-pounds) springs with heavy-duty, direct-acting Gabriel shock absorbers and a special steel stabilizer bar with specifically calibrated rubber mounts. The rear suspension was of the Hotchkiss type, with 150 inch-pounds leaf springs and used a staggered shock absorber arrangement. Ford added a rear stabilizer bar to help keep the rear end from swaying. Power front disc brakes were standard. The stock manual

"The Boss 302 went head-to-head with the Camaro Z28 on the Trans-Am racing circuit and the showroom floor."

Mustang 1964-1971

Pony car fans without big bank accounts could still drive off in a new 1969 GT-500 for about $5,000. The 1,534 fastbacks built for that year are worth considerably more these days. Doug Mitchel

steering had a quick 16:1 ratio and power steering was optionally available. Power steering is desirable with the fat F60-15 tires.

A long list of muscle car goodies were included on the Boss 302—black tail light bezels, a black backlight molding, black headlight castings, color-keyed, dual racing mirrors, hood, rear deck lid and lower back panel black finish, dual exhausts, hub caps with trim rings, black tape identification on the front fender and front spoiler, a 45-amp battery and a Space-Saver spare tire.

On the inside, the Boss 302 used the basic layout of other Mustangs. Circular gauges were used, with "idiot lights" to monitor oil pressure and electrics. A tachometer was provided and easily visible. An adjustable rear deck lid spoiler and rear window SportSlats ("venetian blinds") were optional.

Ford had to build 1,000 Boss 302 Mustangs to qualify the package as "production" so that it could meet SCCA Trans-Am racing series guidelines. The model proved to be more popular than expected and 1,934 were built.

In a similar vein, Ford hoped to qualify its new-for-1969 429-cid "semi-hemi" V-8 for NASCAR racing by offering it in a street-performance car and building 500 copies. Although the Mustang wasn't used in stock car racing, the strong sales of the Boss 302 indicated that it would be easier to sell 500 big-block Mustangs than to sell that many Torino Talladegas with the "429."

Ford worked around the rules and built the Talladegas with "351 Windsor" engines. The company gave an aftermarket firm called Kar Kraft, in Brighton, Michigan, the job of building Boss 429 Mustangs. Technically an option, the Boss 429 listed for just under $5,000 with all the performance goodies. Horsepower was advertised at 375. There were two versions of the 429 installed, one with mechanical lifters and one with hydraulic lifters.

It was not an easy job to squeeze the big 429 into the Mustang. Kar Kraft did many suspension changes and chassis modifications. A total of 1,358 Boss 429s were constructed during the calendar year. This included 857

■ *The heart of the 1970 Boss 429.*
Tom Glatch

of the 1969 models and 499 of the 1970 models. These cars cost $4,932 and included engine bay bracing, inner wheel well sheet metal work and flared wheel housings (to accommodate a widened track and the use of seven-inch Magnum 500 wheel rims). A huge, functional scoop was installed on the hood and a special spoiler underlined the front bumper. Power steering and brakes, a Traction-Lok axle with 3.91 gears, and a Boss 302 rear spoiler were also included. All of the cars had the Decor Group interior option, high-back bucket seats, deluxe seat belts, a wood-trimmed dash and console and a Visibility Group. Automatic transmission and air conditioning were not available.

1970

The '70 Mustang was basically a continuation of the '69. The new models were introduced in September 1969, but "Bunkie" Knudsen did not see them introduced. Henry Ford II fired him, on short notice, in August 1969. "HFII" never explained his firing of Knudsen, but some believe that Ford wanted to move away from muscle cars and racing, which Knudsen loved. Others said he simply that Knudsen had too often tried to overstep the limits of his power.

■ *The Boss 429 remained a limited edition model in 1970, with only 499 built for the model year.* Brad Bowling

■ 1970 Mach 1's had a black stripe down the center of the hood. A shaker hood scoop was available on the 302- and 351-equipped cars. Phil Kunz

■ The Shaker hood scoop was a functional item on the 1970 Mustangs. It was standard on the 428-cid engines. Jerry Heasley

■ *1970 was the last year for the Shelby GT cars. This example wears the Black Jade paint.*
Doug Mitchel

Knudsen was initially replaced by three executives. Lee Iacocca became executive vice president and president of North American Operations. Robert L. Stevenson held the same titles for International Operations. Robert J. Hampson was executive vice president and president of Non-Automotive Operations. Within a year, Iacocca would become Ford's overall president.

The biggest change for 1970 was the return to single headlights. They were located inside a larger, new grille opening. Simulated air intakes were seen where the outboard headlights were on the 1969 models. The rear end was also slightly restyled. Six Mustangs models were offered. They included the hot Mach 1, luxurious Grande and race-bred Boss 302. Hardtop, convertible and a SportsRoof body styles were marketed again.

The lineup of nine engines was almost the same as 1969, but the 390-cid V-8 was discontinued. Standard features included wall-to-wall carpeting, front bucket seats, a locking steering column, a fully synchronized manual transmission a sporty floor shift and a rear deck spoiler on SportsRoof models.

The 1970 Mach 1 featured the new front end, tail lights recessed in a flat panel with honeycomb trim between them, ribbed aluminum rocker panel moldings (with big Mach 1 call-outs) and a cleaner upper rear quarter treatment without simulated air scoops at the end of the main feature line. A black-striped hood with standard fake scoop was new and twist-in hood pins held the hood down. You could get now a shaker hood scoop with the 351. The steering wheel was redesigned. A larger rear stripe, larger rear call-out, mag-type hubcaps, wide 14 x 7-inch wheels and bright oval exhaust tips were also new.

"Hot Rod said that the new Boss 302 was 'definitely the best handling car Ford has ever built.'"

The 1971 Mach 1 had a prominent chin spoiler, Ram Air hood and honeycomb grille all standard.

Brad Bowling

The Boss 302 was back, also with minor improvements. They included the revised front and rear styling, new Grabber paint colors and a "hockey stick" striping treatment with the words "Boss 302" above and on the blade of the hockey stick on the upper front fender. Wide 15 x 7-inch steel wheels with hubcaps and trim rings were standard. The shaker hood became optional. High-back bucket seats were added to the standard features list. Smaller diameter valves and a new crankshaft were used in the small-block performance V-8 and most Boss 302s used finned aluminum valve covers. A rear sway bar was added to the suspension and the front one was thickened.

Hot Rod said that the new Boss 302 was "definitely the best handling car

■ *The 1970 429 Mach 1 could clock a 14.09-second quarter-mile if it came with a stick shift and 3.91:1 rear axle.* Phil Kunz

■ *The Boss 351 of 1971 was a hit with speed-loving buyers. It was hard to argue with a hot car that cost only a little over four grand and could get to 60 in less than 6 seconds and run sub-14-second quarter-miles right out of the lot.* Phil Kunz

Ford has ever built." On the other hand, the practical-thinking *Consumer Guide* labeled it "uncomfortable at any speed over anything but the smoothest surface." The passing of the Boss 302 at the end of the 1970 model-year was mourned by the performance crowd, even though a Boss 351 replaced it. They knew that the years of the high-compression, high-performance Detroit muscle car were ending. *Speed and Supercar* called the Boss 302, "probably the most advanced non-hemi (engine) design ever to emanate from Detroit."

1971

The '71 Mustang continued the long hood/short deck look that had established the industry trend for pony cars. A restyled body with a different front end appeared. The new design was most apparent in the unique, flatter roof shape of the SportsRoof models. Hardtops had what Ford called a "tunnel backlight" (rear window). All models featured flush door handles and hidden windshield wipers. The closed cars had thinner roof sections for an airier look.

Mustangs had a slightly longer wheelbase and gained 2.1 inches of length. They were also 2.4 inches wider than the '70 model and 5.9 inches wider than a '65. Weights were up about 500 pounds from the year earlier. The '71s were designed by Larry Shinoda before Bunkie Knudsen left Ford. The Sportsroof's "Kammback" look reflected an interest in racing aerodynamics.

The same base models were available, but the Boss 302 and Boss 429 were gone. A new Boss 351 filled the gap. Its 351-cid/330-hp "Cleveland" engine became the Mustang's small-block, high-performance V-8. As in 1970, there was no GT option. The "Twister Special" Mach 1 was also gone.

Ford's designers again did a marvelous job of retaining the classic Mustang "look," while revising just about the entire vehicle. A full-width grille incorporated the headlights at each end. On standard models, the famous "corral" returned to the center of the grille. It had a large, chrome pony inside it. Optional was a honeycomb-textured grille insert with sportlamps. It did not have a "corral." Instead, the center had a smaller galloping pony emblem on a red, white and blue colored bar. A chrome bumper and chrome fender and hood moldings was standard, except on Mach 1's and Boss 351s.

Standard equipment for Mustangs was similar to past years. Grandes came with the same basic equipment as Mustangs, plus a deluxe interior, more brightwork, dual accent paint stripes and color-keyed dual racing mirrors.

Mach 1 buyers got all the basics, plus a color-keyed spoiler/bumper with color-keyed hood and front fender moldings. Also color-keyed were the dual racing mirrors, with the left-hand mirror featuring remote-control operation. Mach 1s also had the unique grille with sportlamps; competition suspension, hubcaps and trim rings, a black, honeycomb-textured back panel applique, a pop-open gas cap, a deck lid paint stripe, black or Argent Silver lower body side finish with bright moldings at the upper edge, E70-14 whitewalls, and the base 302-cid V-8. NASA style hood scoops were optional at no extra charge.

The Boss 351 was the car with the most appeal to street performance buffs. It was a better-balanced car than the big-block Fords. Standard equipment included all of the Mustang basics, plus a functional NASA style hood with black or Argent Silver full hood paint treatment, hood lock pins and Ram Air engine

"The Boss 351 was the car with the most appeal to street performance buffs. It was a better-balanced car than the big-block Fords."

■ *Almost 25 percent of Mustang buyers in 1971 opted for the Mach 1. This example carried the 429-cid Ram Air V-8.*
Brad Bowling

decals. Also featured were the racing mirrors, the unique grille with sportlamps, hubcaps and trim rings, black or Argent Silver body side tape stripes (these also became optional on Mach 1s late in the year), color-keyed hood and front fender moldings, Boss 351 nomenclature, dual exhausts, power front disk brakes, a Space-Saver spare tire, a competition suspension with staggered rear shocks, a 3.91 axle ratio with Traction-Lok differential, a functional black spoiler (shipped "knocked-down" inside the car for dealer installation), an 80-ampere battery, Ford's Instrumentation Group option, an electronic rpm-limiter, high-back bucket seats, a special cooling package, a wide-ratio four-speed manual transmission with Hurst shifter, the 351-cubic-inch H.O. (high-output) V-8 with 330 horsepower, and F60-15 belted blackwall tires. Apparently, a chrome bumper was standard on Boss 351s, while the Mach 1-style color-keyed bumper was an option.

An emphasis on more power was evident in that the 200-cubic-inch six was dropped. The 250-cubic-inch six became the smallest Mustang engine. The standard V-8 was a mild version of the 302-cubic-inch motor with 210 horsepower. Other small-block options included 240- and 285-horsepower versions of the 351-cubic-inch V-8, plus the Boss 351 power plant.

For Mustang buyers who demanded big-block muscle, there was a new 429 Cobra Jet (429CJ) engine for $372 more than the cost of the base V-8. A 429 Cobra

Jet Ram Air (429CJ-R) option was $436 above the base V-8. They were both rated at 370 and 370 horsepower. A 429 Super Cobra Jet with Dual Ram Air induction was also available, for $531 over a base V-8. It had 375 horsepower.

The 429CJ-R had hydraulic valve lifters, four-bolt main caps, dress-up aluminum valve covers and a GM Quadrajet four-barrel carburetor. The 429SCJ-R featured mechanical lifters, adjustable rocker arms, a larger Holley four-barrel carburetor and forged pistons.

Mustangs with the 429CJ-R engine came with a competition suspension, Mach 1 hood, 80-ampere battery, 55-ampere alternator, dual exhausts, extra-cooling package, bright engine dress-up kit with cast aluminum rocker covers and a 3.25 ratio, non-locking rear axle. It was not available with air conditioning combined with the Drag Pak option or with the dual Ram Induction option. A C-6 Cruise-O-Matic or close-ratio four-speed manual transmission was required, along with disk brakes. Power steering was required on air-conditioned cars. The 429SCJ engine required the Drag Pak option and a 3.91 or 4.11 high-ratio rear axle.

The new 429s were not the same as the Boss 429, which had been derived from Ford's "semi-hemi" NASCAR racing engine. Instead, they were actually de-stroked versions of the "wedge head" 460-cubic-inch V-8 used in Thunderbirds and Lincolns. They were available in all models: hardtop, SportsRoof and convertible and seem to be worth most in ragtops and Mach 1's.

■ *For 1971, Mach 1 Mustangs sported the SportsRoof "flatback" body style.* Jerry Heasley

MUSTANG YEAR-BY-YEAR SPEC'S

1964

Engine	Bore/Str.	Comp. Ratio	CID	BHP	WT.	W.B.	O.L.	Width	HT
I6	3.50 x 2.94	8.70	170	101 @ 4400	2,449	108.0	181.6	68.2	51.1
V-8	3.80 x 2.87	8.80	260	164 @ 4400	2,615	108.0	181.6	68.2	51.1
V-8	4.00 x 2.87	9.00	289	210 @ 4400	2,615	108.0	181.6	68.2	51.1
V-8	4.00 x 2.87	10.50	289	271 @ 6000	2,615	108.0	181.6	68.2	51.1

1965

Engine	Bore/Str.	Comp. Ratio	CID	BHP	WT.	W.B.	O.L.	Width	HT
I6	3.68 x 3.13	9.20	200	120 @ 4400	2,465	108.0	181.6	68.2	51.1
V-8	4.00 x 2.87	9.30	289	200 @ 4400	2,735	108.0	181.6	68.2	51.1
V-8	4.00 x 2.87	10.00	289	225 @ 4800	2,735	108.0	181.6	68.2	51.1
V-8	4.00 x 2.87	10.50	289	271 @ 6000	2,735	108.0	181.6	68.2	51.1

1966

Engine	Bore/Str.	Comp. Ratio	CID	BHP	WT.	W.B.	O.L.	Width	HT
I6	3.68 x 3.13	9.20	200	120 @ 4400	2,488	108.0	181.6	68.2	51.5
V-8	4.00 x 2.87	9.30	289	200 @ 4400	2,733	108.0	181.6	68.2	51.5
V-8	4.00 x 2.87	10.00	289	225 @ 4800	2,733	108.0	181.6	68.2	51.5
V-8	4.00 x 2.87	10.50	289	271 @ 6000	2,733	108.0	181.6	68.2	51.5

1967

Engine	Bore/Str.	Comp. Ratio	CID	BHP	WT.	W.B.	O.L.	Width	HT
I6	3.68 x 3.13	9.20	200	120 @ 4400	2,578	108.0	183.6	70.9	51.6
V-8	4.00 x 2.87	9.30	289	200 @ 4400	2,766	108.0	183.6	70.9	51.6
V-8	4.00 x 2.87	10.00	289	225 @ 4800	2,766	108.0	183.6	70.9	51.6
V-8	4.00 x 2.87	10.50	289	271 @ 6000	2,766	108.0	183.6	70.9	51.6
V-8	4.05 x 3.78	10.50	390	320 @ 4600	2,766	108.0	183.6	70.9	51.6

1968

Engine	Bore/Str.	Comp. Ratio	CID	BHP	WT.	W.B.	O.L.	Width	HT
I6	3.68 x 3.13	8.80	200	115 @ 3800	2,666	108.0	183.6	70.9	51.6
V-8	4.00 x 2.87	8.70	289	195 @ 4600	2,861	108.0	183.6	70.9	51.6
V-8	4.00 x 3.00	9.50	302	220 @ 4600	2,861	108.0	183.6	70.9	51.6
V-8	4.00 x 3.00	10.00	302	230 @ 4800	2,861	108.0	183.6	70.9	51.6
V-8	4.05 x 3.78	10.50	390	325 @ 4600	2,861	108.0	183.6	70.9	51.6
V-8	4.13 x 3.98	10.70	428	335 @ 5600	2,861	108.0	183.6	70.9	51.6

In 1971, Sports Car Graphic tested both a CJ-powered Mach 1 and a Boss 351. The big-block car was only marginally faster. It won 0-to-60 miles per hour at 6.3 seconds versus 6.6 and did the quarter-mile in 14.6 seconds at 99.4 miles per hour against 14.7 seconds and 96.2 miles per hour. Considering the 351's less cubes and 330 advertised horsepower, it performed quite well against the nose heavy Mach 1 with the big-block.

With the high-performance era winding to a close and the government and insurance companies ganging up on muscle cars, Ford stayed out of factory involvement in racing this year. Mustang production for 1971 continued to decline. It dropped to 149,678. Of this total, about 1,800 were made with 429 Cobra Jet V-8s. These were the last of the big-block Mustangs ever built.

Engine	Bore/Str.	Comp. Ratio	CID	BHP	WT.	W.B.	O.L.	Width	HT
I6	3.68 x 3.13	8.80	200	115 @ 3800	2,713	108.0	187.4	71.3	51.2
I6	3.68 x 3.91	9.00	250	155 @ 4400	2,948	108.0	187.4	71.3	51.2
V-8	4.00 x 3.00	9.50	302	220 @ 4600	2,948	108.0	187.4	71.3	51.2
Boss V-8	4.00 x 3.00	10.50	302	290 @ 5000	2,948	108.0	187.4	71.3	51.2
V-8	4.00 x 3.50	9.50	351	250 @ 4600	2,948	108.0	187.4	71.3	51.2
V-8	4.00 x 3.50	10.70	351	290 @ 4800	2,948	108.0	187.4	71.3	51.2
V-8	4.05 x 3.78	10.50	390	320 @ 4600	2,948	108.0	187.4	71.3	51.2
CJ V-8	4.13 x 3.98	10.60	428	335 @ 5200	2,948	108.0	187.4	71.3	51.2
SCJ V-8	4.13 x 3.98	10.50	428	360 @ 5400	2,948	108.0	187.4	71.3	51.2
Boss V-8	4.36 x 3.59	11.30	428	370 @ 5600	2,948	108.0	187.4	71.3	51.2

CJ = Cobra Jet
SCJ= Super Cobra Jet

Engine	Bore/Str.	Comp. Ratio	CID	BHP	WT.	W.B.	O.L.	Width	HT
I6	3.68 x 3.13	8.80	200	115 @ 3800	2,721	108.0	187.4	71.7	51.5
I6	3.68 x 3.91	9.00	250	155 @ 4400	2,721	108.0	187.4	71.7	51.5
V-8	4.00 x 3.00	9.50	302	220 @ 4600	2,923	108.0	187.4	71.7	51.5
Boss V-8	4.00 x 3.00	10.50	302	290 @ 5800	2,923	108.0	187.4	71.7	51.5
V-8	4.00 x 3.50	9.50	351	250 @ 4600	2,923	108.0	187.4	71.7	51.5
V-8	4.00 x 3.50	11.00	351	300 @ 5400	2,923	108.0	187.4	71.7	51.5
CJ V-8	4.13 x 3.98	10.60	428	335 @ 5400	2,923	108.0	187.4	71.7	51.5
SCJ V-8	4.13 x 3.98	10.50	428	360 @ 5400	2,923	108.0	187.4	71.7	51.5
Boss V-8	4.36 x 3.59	11.30	429	375 @ 5600	2,923	108.0	187.4	71.7	51.5

CJ = Cobra Jet
SCJ= Super Cobra Jet

Engine	Bore/Str.	Comp. Ratio	CID	BHP	WT.	W.B.	O.L.	Width	HT
I6	3.68 x 3.91	9.00	250	145 @ 4000	2,721	108.0	187.4	71.7	51.5
V-8	4.00 x 3.00	9.00	302	210 @ 4600	2,923	108.0	187.4	71.7	51.5
V-8	4.00 x 3.50	9.00	351	240 @ 4600	2,923	108.0	187.4	71.7	51.5
V-8 *	4.00 x 3.50	10.70	351	285 @ 5400	2,923	108.0	187.4	71.7	51.5
CJ V-8	4.00 x 3.50	10.70	351	280 @ 5400	2,923	108.0	187.4	71.7	51.5
Boss V-8	4.00 x 3.50	11.10	351	330 @ 5400	2,923	108.0	187.4	71.7	51.5
CJ V-8	4.36 x 3.59	11.30	429	370 @ 5400	2,923	108.0	187.4	71.7	51.5
SCJ V-8	4.36 x 3.59	11.50	429	375 @ 5600	2,923	108.0	187.4	71.7	51.5

CJ = Cobra Jet
SCJ= Super Cobra Jet
* This engine became the 351 Cobra Jet V-8 in May 1971 and the horsepower rating was lowered at the same time.

■ *The GT-500 was a new addition to the Ford lineup in 1967. It packed a 428-cid big block under the hood. Like the GT-350, it was available only as a coupe.* Phil Kunz

PRODUCTION STATISTICS AND BREAKOUTS

1964 MUSTANG

Year	Body Code	Body Type	Engine Type	MSP Price	Model Yr. Prod.
MUSTANG SIX					
64	65	2HT	Six	$2,345	27,430
64	76	2CV	Six	$2,587	5,255
TOTAL					**32,685**
MUSTANG V-8					
64	65	2HT	V-8	$2,461	65,275
64	76	2CV	V-8	$2,703	23,578
TOTAL					**88,853**
ALL MUSTANG TOTAL					**121,538**

* 1964 (a.k.a .1964 1/2) Mustangs carry 1965 model codes, but have distinctive features.

1965 MUSTANG

Year	Body Code	Body Type	Engine Type	MSP Price	Model Yr. Prod.
MUSTANG SIX					
65	65	2HT	Six	$2,345	167,025
65	63	2FB	Six	$2,345	12,271
65	76	2CV	Six	$2,587	19,595
TOTAL					**198,891**
MUSTANG V-8					
65	65	2HT	V-8	$2,427	242,235
65	63	2FB	V-8	$2,639	64,808
65	76	2CV	V-8	$2,663	53,517
TOTAL					**360,560**
ALL MUSTANG TOTAL					**559,451**

1966 MUSTANG

Year	Body Code	Body Type	Engine Type	MSP Price	Model Yr. Prod.
MUSTANG SIX					
66	65	2HT	Six	$2,416	224,942
66	63	2FB	Six	$2,607	4,403
66	76	2CV	Six	$2,653	23,867
TOTAL					**253,212**
MUSTANG V-8					
66	65	2HT	V-8	$2,522	274,809
66	63	2FB	V-8	$2,713	31,295
66	76	2CV	V-8	$2,653	48,252
TOTAL					**354,356**
ALL MUSTANG TOTAL					**607,568**

1967 MUSTANG

Year	Body Code	Body Type	Engine Type	MSP Price	Model Yr. Prod.
MUSTANG SIX					
67	65	2HT	Six	$2,461	126,583
67	63	2FB	Six	$2,592	4,192
67	76	2CV	Six	$2,698	10,782
TOTAL					**141,557**
MUSTANG V-8					
67	65	2HT	V-8	$2,567	229,688
67	63	2FB	V-8	$2,698	66,850
67	76	2CV	V-8	$2,804	34,026
TOTAL					**330,564**
ALL MUSTANG TOTAL					**472,121**

1968 MUSTANG

Year	Body Code	Body Type	Engine Type	MSP Price	Model Yr. Prod.
MUSTANG SIX					
68	65	2HT	Six	$2,602	84,175
68	63	2FB	Six	$2,712	2,360
68	76	2CV	Six	$2,814	5,241
TOTAL					**91,776**
MUSTANG V-8					
68	65	2HT	V-8	$2,707	155,410
68	63	2FB	V-8	$2,818	32,304
68	76	2CV	V-8	$2,920	16,796
TOTAL					
MUSTANG TOTAL					
MUSTANG DE LUXE SIX					
68	65	2HT	Six	$2,726	870
68	63	2FB	Six	$2,836	98
68	76	2CV	Six	$2,924	145
Total					**1,113**
MUSTANG DE LUXE V-8					
68	65	2HT	V-8	$2,831	8,992
68	63	2FB	V-8	$2,942	7,819
68	76	2CV	V-8	$3,030	3,194
TOTAL					**20,005**
MUSTANG DELUXE TOTAL					**21,118**
ALL MUSTANG TOTAL					**317,404**

1969 MUSTANG

Year	Body Code	Body Type	Engine Type	MSP Price	Model Yr. Prod.
MUSTANG SIX					
69	65	2HT	Six	$2,618	Note 1
69	63	2FB	Six	$2,618	Note 2
69	76	2CV	Six	$2,832	Note 3
MUSTANG V-8					
69	65	2HT	V-8	$2,723	Note 1
69	63	2FB	V-8	$2,723	Note 2
69	76	2CV	V-8	$2,937	Note 3
MUSTANG TOTAL					
MUSTANG GRANDE SIX					
69	65	2HT	Six	$2,849	Note 4
MUSTANG GRANDE V-8					
69	65	2HT	V-8	$2,954	Note 4
MUSTANG GRANDE TOTAL					**22,182**
MUSTANG MACH 1 V-8					
69	63	2FB	V-8	$3,122	72458
MUSTANG MACH 1 TOTAL					**72,458**
ALL MUSTANG TOTAL					**299,320**

Note 1: Total base Mustang hardtop production (all engines) was 127,954.
Note 2: Total base Mustang fastback production (all engines) was 61,980.
Note 3: Total base Mustang convertible production (all engines) was 14,746.
Note 4: Total Mustang Grande production (all engines) was 22,182.

1970 MUSTANG

Year	Body Code	Body Type	Engine Type	MSP Price	Model Yr. Prod.
MUSTANG SIX					
70	65	2HT	Six	$2,721	Note 1
70	63	2FB	Six	$2,771	Note 2
70	76	2CV	Six	$3,025	Note 3
MUSTANG V-8					
70	65	2HT	V-8	$2,822	Note 1
70	63	2FB	V-8	$2,872	Note 2
70	76	2CV	V-8	$3,126	Note 3
MUSTANG TOTAL					**136,176**
MUSTANG GRANDE SIX					
70	65	2HT	Six	$2,849	Note 4
MUSTANG GRANDE V-8					
70	65	2HT	V-8	$2,954	Note 4
MUSTANG GRANDE TOTAL					**13,581**
MUSTANG MACH 1 V-8					
70	63	2FB	V-8	$3,271	40,970
MUSTANG MACH 1 TOTAL					**40,970**
MUSTANG BOSS 302 V-8					
70	63	2FB	V-8	$3,720	6,318
MUSTANG BOSS 302 TOTAL					**6,318**
ALL MUSTANG TOTAL					**197,045**

Note 1: Total base Mustang hardtop production (all engines) was 82,569.
Note 2: Total base Mustang fastback production (all engines) was 45,934.
Note 3: Total base Mustang convertible production (all engines) was 76,73.
Note 4: Total Mustang Grande production (all engines) was 13,581.

1971 MUSTANG

Year	Body Code	Body Type	Engine Type	MSP Price	Model Yr. Prod.
MUSTANG SIX					
71	65	2HT	Six	$2,911	Note 1
71	63	2FB	Six	$2,973	Note 2
71	76	2CV	Six	$3,227	Note 3
MUSTANG V-8					
71	65	2HT	V-8	$3,006	Note 1
71	63	2FB	V-8	$3,068	Note 2
71	76	2CV	V-8	$3,322	Note 3
MUSTANG TOTAL					**95,773**
MUSTANG GRANDE SIX,					
71	65	2HT	Six	$3,117	Note 4
MUSTANG GRANDE V-8					
71	65	2HT	V-8	$3,212	Note 4
MUSTANG GRANDE TOTAL					**17,406**
MUSTANG MACH 1 V-8					
71	63	2FB	V-8	$3,268	36,449
MUSTANG MACH 1 TOTAL					**36,449**
MUSTANG BOSS 351 V-8					
71	63	2FB	V-8	$4,124	1,800
MUSTANG BOSS 302 TOTAL					**1,800**
ALL MUSTANG TOTAL					**151,428**

Note 1: Total base Mustang Hardtop production (all engines) was 65,696.
Note 2: Total base Mustang Fastback production (all engines) was 23,956.
Note 3: Total base Mustang Convertible production (all engines) was 6,121.
Note 4: Total Mustang Grande production (all engines) was 17,406.

Price Guide

Vehicle Condition Scale

6 — Parts car:
May or may not be running, but is weathered, wrecked and/or stripped to the point of being useful primarily for parts.

5 — Restorable:
Needs complete restoration of body, chassis and interior. May or may not be running, but isn't weathered, wrecked or stripped to the point of being useful only for parts.

4 — Good:
A driveable vehicle needing no or only minor work to be functional. Also, a deteriorated restoration or a very poor amateur restoration. All components may need restoration to be "excellent," but the car is mostly useable "as is."

3 — Very Good:
Complete operable original or older restoration. Also, a very good amateur restoration, all presentable and serviceable inside and out. Plus, a combination of well-done restoration and good operable components or a partially restored car with all parts necessary to compete and/or valuable NOS parts.

2 — Fine:
Well-restored or a combination of superior restoration and excellent original parts. Also, extremely well-maintained original vehicle showing minimal wear.

1 — Excellent:
Restored to current maximum professional standards of quality in every area, or perfect original with components operating and apearing as new. A 95-plus point show car that is not driven.

1964 Mustang

	6	5	4	3	2	1
2d HT	1,020	3,060	5,100	11,480	17,850	25,500
Conv	1,400	4,200	7,000	15,750	24,500	35,000

Note: Deduct 20 percent for 6-cyl. Add 20 percent for Challenger

1965 Mustang

	6	5	4	3	2	1
2d HT	1,020	3,060	5,100	11,480	17,850	25,500
Conv	1,400	4,200	7,000	15,750	24,500	35,000
FBk	1,200	3,600	6,000	13,500	21,000	30,000

Note: Add 30 percent for 271 hp Hi-perf engine. Add 10 percent for "GT" Package. Add 10 percent for "original pony interior." Deduct 20 percent for 6-cyl.

1965 Shelby GT

	6	5	4	3	2	1
350 FBk	3,400	10,200	17,000	38,250	59,500	85,000

1966 Mustang

	6	5	4	3	2	1
2d HT	1,020	3,060	5,100	11,480	17,850	25,500
Conv	1,440	4,320	7,200	16,200	25,200	36,000
FBk	1,280	3,840	6,400	14,400	22,400	32,000

Note: Same as 1965.

1966 Shelby GT

	6	5	4	3	2	1
350 FBk	3,280	9,840	16,400	36,900	57,400	82,000
350H FBk	3,520	10,560	17,600	39,600	61,600	88,000
350 Conv	3,800	11,400	19,000	42,750	66,500	95,000

1967 Mustang

	6	5	4	3	2	1
2d HT	940	2,820	4,700	10,580	16,450	23,500
Conv	1,280	3,840	6,400	14,400	22,400	32,000
FBk	1,060	3,180	5,300	11,930	18,550	26,500

Note: Same as 1964-65 plus. Add 10 percent for 390 cid V-8 (code "S"). Deduct 15 percent for 6-cyl.

1967 Shelby GT

	6	5	4	3	2	1
350 FBk	3,240	9,720	16,200	36,450	56,700	81,000
500 FBk	3,600	10,800	18,000	40,500	63,000	90,000

1968 Mustang

	6	5	4	3	2	1
2d HT	940	2,820	4,700	10,580	16,450	23,500
Conv	1,280	3,840	6,400	14,400	22,400	32,000
FBk	1,060	3,180	5,300	11,930	18,550	26,500

Note: Same as 1964-67 plus. Add 10 percent for GT-390. Add 30 percent for 428 cid V-8 (code "R"). Add 15 percent for "California Special" trim. Add 200 percent for 135 Series.

1968 Shelby GT

	6	5	4	3	2	1
350 Conv	3,600	10,800	18,000	40,500	63,000	90,000
350 FBk	3,200	9,600	16,000	36,000	56,000	80,000
500 Conv	3,800	11,400	19,000	42,750	66,500	95,000
500 FBk	3,400	10,200	17,000	38,250	59,500	85,000

Note: Add 50 percent for KR models.

1969 Mustang

	6	5	4	3	2	1
2d HT	900	2,700	4,500	10,130	15,750	22,500
Conv	1,060	3,180	5,300	11,930	18,550	26,500
FBk	980	2,940	4,900	11,030	17,150	24,500

Note: Deduct 20 percent for 6-cyl.

	6	5	4	3	2	1
Mach 1	1,200	3,600	6,000	13,500	21,000	30,000
Boss 302	1,760	5,280	8,800	19,800	30,800	44,000
Boss 429	2,640	7,920	13,200	29,700	46,200	66,000
Grande	940	2,820	4,700	10,580	16,450	23,500

Note Same as 1968; plus. Add 30 percent for Cobra Jet V-8. Add 40 percent for "Super Cobra Jet" engine.

1969 Shelby GT

	6	5	4	3	2	1
350 Conv	3,600	10,800	18,000	40,500	63,000	90,000
350 FBk	3,200	9,600	16,000	36,000	56,000	80,000
500 Conv	3,800	11,400	19,000	42,750	66,500	95,000
500 FBk	3,400	10,200	17,000	38,250	59,500	85,000

1970 Mustang

	6	5	4	3	2	1
2d HT	900	2,700	4,500	10,130	15,750	22,500
Conv	1,060	3,180	5,300	11,930	18,550	26,500
FBk	980	2,940	4,900	11,030	17,150	24,500
Mach 1	1,200	3,600	6,000	13,500	21,000	30,000
Boss 302	1,760	5,280	8,800	19,800	30,800	44,000
Boss 429	2,640	7,920	13,200	29,700	46,200	66,000
Grande	940	2,820	4,700	10,580	16,450	23,500

Note: Add 30 percent for Cobra Jet V-8. Add 40 percent for "Super Cobra Jet". Deduct 20 percent for 6-cyl.

1970 Shelby GT

	6	5	4	3	2	1
350 Conv	3,600	10,800	18,000	40,500	63,000	90,000
350 FBk	3,200	9,600	16,000	36,000	56,000	80,000
500 Conv	3,800	11,400	19,000	42,750	66,500	95,000
500 FBk	3,400	10,200	17,000	38,250	59,500	85,000

1971 Mustang

	6	5	4	3	2	1
2d HT	680	2,040	3,400	7,650	11,900	17,000
Grande	700	2,100	3,500	7,880	12,250	17,500
Conv	1,000	3,000	5,000	11,250	17,500	25,000
FBk	920	2,760	4,600	10,350	16,100	23,000
Mach 1	1,080	3,240	5,400	12,150	18,900	27,000
Boss 351	1,720	5,160	8,600	19,350	30,100	43,000

Note: Same as 1970. Deduct 20 percent for 6-cyl. Add 20 percent for HO option where available.

4-4-2 & Hurst/Olds

1964

In a case of extreme irony, a car that probably got chased by the cops many times started life as a squad car. The official price sticker for the '64 Olds 4-4-2 package called it the B-09 Police Apprehender Pursuit option. "Police needed it—Olds built it—pursuit proved it," said the *Product Selling Information* book.

This was all a ploy, of course. Pontiac had "snuck" the GTO to market as an option package. By the time Olds reacted with the 4-4-2 the brass at GM were watching. So the normally staid and conservative Olds crew took an even sneakier approach and made the 4-4-2 a police-car option. Here's the proof:

Originally, the 4-4-2 name meant 4-barrel carb, 4-on-the-floor and dual exhausts. Now, how many police departments do you think ordered a car with a four-speed manual gearbox and floor shift? (Later, the meaning of the name was changed to 400 cubic inches, four-barrel carb and dual exhausts).

■ *Pounding behind this Target Red 1965 4-4-2 hardtop's flat-black grille is a simmering 400-cid 360-hp Tri-Power V-8. The 4-4-2 badge on the left side of the grille spelled "performance."*

Jerry Heasley

Olds 4-4-2 Timeline

1964: The 4-4-2 "B-08 Police Apprehension Package" is made available on the Olds Cutlass and F-85.

1965: Four-door models were eliminated. A new 400-cid/345-hp engine is joined by heavy-duty shocks, underpinnings, tires and clutch to form a great-handling muscle car.

1966: Redesign gives the 4-4-2 a pronounced hump over the rear wheels.

1966: First tri-carb setup with 360 hp is offered.

1967: W-30 forced-air induction system returns to the lineup featuring a host of performance upgrades.

1967: 4-4-2 is made part of the Cutlass Supreme lineup.

1968: The redesigned 4-4-2 becomes its own model.

1968: The Hurst Olds, featuring a 455-cid big block, arrives. All 515 first-year Hurst Olds were painted Peruvian Silver with black trim.

1969: Turnpike Cruiser option discontinued.

1969: Hurst Olds available in Regal Gold and white.

1970: Hurst Olds goes on a two-year hiatus. W-30 package with 455-cid engine makes the 4-4-2 one of the most formidable muscle cars on the street.

1972: 4-4-2 relegated to option status on the Cutlass. A more pedestrian Hurst Olds returns in Cameo White with black and gold accents.

1973: 4-4-2 available as the W-29 package on the Cutlass and Cutlass Supreme S coupes.

■ *Rear view of the '65 coupe with 4-4-2 option captures the car's "attitude" with its squad-car appearance. Olds stuffed a 400-cid V-8 under the hood in year two.*
Doug Mitchel

■ *The Olds 4-4-2 package was also available on the two-door "post" coupe and this '65 edition wears it well. It has a purposeful look with Red Lines and "bottlecaps."*
Doug Mitchel

The 4-4-2 had a high-lift cam to boost the power of its ultra high-compression V-8 to 310 hp. Other Olds 4-4-2 special features included low-back-pressure mufflers, heavy-duty shocks and springs, a rear stabilizer bar, a dual-snorkel air cleaner and extra-high-quality rod and main bearings.

The 4-4-2 tested by *Car Life* in August 1964 registered a 7.4-second 0 to 60-mph time and a 15.6-second quarter-mile. The following month, *Motor Trend* reported 0 to 30 mph in 3.1 seconds and 0 to 60 mph in 7.5 seconds. Its test car did the standing-start quarter-mile in 15.5 seconds at 90 mph.

For a cop car, the 4-4-2 was a steal. An F-85 club coupe with the 4-4-2 package cost less than a Mustang or GTO in 1964. It was fantastic, too. "No better Oldsmobile has rolled off the Lansing assembly line in many a year," said *Car Life*. "Though it isn't quite the sports car that corporate brass likes to think, it doesn't miss by much."

■ *The muscular midsize Olds still had a "ready-to-rumble" rear end. The Mustang had pushed car designers toward the Coke-bottle school off design and the Olds stylists were very good students.*
Jerry Heasley

1965

Don't car books get boring when an author says, "The car was mildly updated when they changed the round headlights to square and they changed the square tail lights to round ones?" Well, I'm not going to lie to you, the '65 Olds 4-4-2 wasn't changed much from the original design. Hell, enthusiasts were just getting used to it, since it hadn't made headlines until the fall of '64. Somebody just gave it a facial and then stuck a new engine under the hood. Reducing the bore of a new 425-cid Oldsmobile engine from 4.125 inches to an even 4.0 produced an engine ideally sized for the 4-4-2 at 400 cid. "Olds joins the bigger-inch crowd with another meaning for that first 4 – 400 cubic inches," said *Car Life*.

■ *Oldsmobile brought the 1964 Olds 4-4-2 package to market as the B-09 Police Apprehender Pursuit option. This two-door hardtop includes the kit, which featured a specially modified 310-hp V-8.*
Phil Kunz

4-4-2 and Hurst/Olds 1964-1973

■ *Something you didn't see everyday —even in 1966: a bench-seat 4-4-2 hardtop with a floor-mounted stick shift. This is what you call an "understatement" in the world of muscle cars—and it's super cool!*

Jerry Heasley

■ *From the standpoints of both performance and rarity, the late-in-the-year-only '66 tri-power 4-4-2 is, without a doubt, the most desirable example of these production years to a real enthusiast.* Jerry Heasley

With the 400, the muscular mid-size Olds generated 345 hp at 4800 rpm and 440 lbs.-ft. of torque at 3200 rpm. The new engine had a 10.25:1 compression ratio and a single Rochester four-barrel carburetor. With a four-speed manual gearbox and a 3.55:1 axle the 4-4-2 did 0 to 60 mph in 5.5 seconds and the quarter-mile took 15.0 seconds at 98 mph.

This year the 4-4-2 package was available with Hydra-Matic transmission. Since the second "4" in the 1964 model designation had stood for "four-speed manual transmission," Oldsmobile had to explain the 4-4-2 name a different way. The company now said that the first four (4) stood for the new 400-cid V-8, the second four (4) meant four-barrel carburetor and the two (2) meant dual exhaust. This sounded a little awkward, since "4" and "400" aren't the same, but who cared?

■ *As in '67, a 400-cid V-8 was standard in '68, but it was a totally new one with a different bore and stroke. There were three four-barrel versions of this 10.5:1 compression including this 360-hp W-30 Forced Air package.* Jerry Heasley

■ *For 1968, the Olds 4-4-2 came in hardtop, coupe and convertible models. Though the ragtop (seen here in Ebony Black) was rare with just 5,142 assemblies, the coupe had an even lower 4,282-unit production run.*

Phil Kunz

Car and Driver said of the 4-4-2, " It really isn't a sports car, and it isn't exactly like the imported sports sedans—even though that seems to have been the aim of its manufacturer—but it does approach a very worthwhile balance of all the qualities we'd like to see incorporated in every American car."

1966

The '66 Olds 4-4-2 looked like a '65 on steroids. The grille had the same basic "barbell" shape, but the "Oldsmobile" name was stamped in the upper molding. Side-by-side headlights were used again, but they were now in trendy square housings. The blacked-out grille was highlighted with a thin molding, an Olds rocket badge in the center and 442 lettering on the lower left.

The body sides were more slab-like with a more massive, creased-edge look. In profile, the car was "Coke bottle" shaped with raised haunches. A vent-like trim piece appeared behind the front wheel openings and the body wore rocker panel and wheel lip moldings, though the use of chrome was quite restrained.

The 4-4-2 was a fairly upscale muscle car with front and rear carpets, chrome roof bow moldings, a deluxe steering wheel, front bucket or custom seats,

■ *The Silver-and-Black Hurst/Olds wasn't the flashiest-looking muscle car, but it carried the mandatory badges to let car enthusiasts know it was something out of the ordinary.*   Tom Glatch

■ *Olds had punched its 425-cube V-8 to 455 inches, but GM rules would not permit cramming the new engine into the 4-4-2. George Hurst didn't have to follow the rules and the result was a nearly 400-hp super Cutlass.*   Tom Glatch

■ *This 1968 Olds 4-4-2 pillared sport coupe had a 112-inch wheelbase and 206-inch overall length. It listed for $3,087 and weighed in at 3,502 lbs., making it the lightest and speediest version of the mid-size muscle machine.*   Tom Glatch

deluxe armrests, a courtesy lamp package and vinyl or cloth upholstery.

Pounding under the 4-4-2's hood was a slightly hotter 400-cid/350-hp V-8. The five extra ponies were due to a higher 10.25:1 compression ratio. Late in the model year, a triple two-barrel carburetor setup was released. The tri-power cars are rare and very desirable to muscle car fans. You could only get

one during the tail end of '66. *Car Life* magazine took one of these screamers from 0 to 60 mph in a mere 6.3 seconds and called it the "civilized supercar." Quarter-mile runs were made in as little as 14.8 seconds with a terminal speed of 97 miles per hour.

From the standpoints of both performance and rarity, the 1966 Olds Cutlass 4-4-2 equipped with the 360-hp factory Tri-Power installation is the most desirable example of these production years to a real muscle car enthusiast. It did, however, shoot down the cop car ploy for once and always. With three deuces, there was no pretending it was intended for civil servant applications.

1967

For '67, Oldsmobile continued to market the F-85 and a fancier Cutlass version. In addition, a new brand new—even fancier car line was introduced. It took the Cutlass Supreme name that had previously identified only a single, more luxurious model.

■ The badges sitting in the white stripe on the front fender sides of this Burgundy Mist '69 Olds 4-4-2 indicate that it carries the hot $264 W-30 kit. The ram-air motor pushed the top speed up to 123 mph.

Phil Kunz

■ A new pitchman named Dr. Olds prescribed "medicine" for the 4-4-2, including a bolder split grille, fat hood stripes and bright, new name badges. This is the coupe model in Saffron.

Jerry Heasley

In a change of merchandising philosophy, the Cutlass Supreme became the only series with the 4-4-2 available. The '67 4-4-2 looked much like the '66 model, although the bumpers, grille and headlight-tail light arrangements were changed. A unique black-out grille with a 4-4-2 emblem on the left was employed on this plush muscle car. The headlights were wider spaced with parking lamps between them.

The chrome fender vents used in '66 were replaced by red 4-4-2 badges and there was now pin striping on the doors and fenders. Size F70 x 14 Red Line tires

set off the red body badges and trim pieces. During this year, 4-4-2s equipped with a W-30 engine option were first fitted with red plastic fender wells, which remained a W-30 trademark through 1971.

Three different body styles could be equipped with the $216 option package this year. They were the two-door sedan (Oldsmobile called the "club coupe" but most enthusiasts know it as the "post coupe"), the two-door hardtop (or sport coupe) and the convertible. The hardtop was the best-selling model, but all three were pretty rare machines and total production was under 25,000.

■ *The 4-4-2's standard single-snorkel air cleaner was painted bright red, which looked pretty dramatic next to the gold-colored Oldsmobile V-8. "Keep your GM car all GM was good advice on the decal. Today an all-original 4-4-2 is a collector's item.*

Jerry Heasley

■ *Strato bucket seats – shown here in Parchment White vinyl trim – were standard inside the '69 Olds 4-4-2. Black, Green, Blue, Gold and Red were other options. Blue and Gold cloth upholstery was also available.*

Tom Glatch

■ *A chrome-plated dual-snorkel air cleaner was seen atop the 400-cid 360-hp W-30 Ram Air V-8. It ran a 10.5:1 compression ratio and carried a four-barrel carb. Engine code was QU with manual and QT with automatic.*

Tom Glatch

The 400-cid was the sole 4-4-2 engine again, but the tri-power setup did not survive GM's crackdown on super-high-performance equipment. With tri-power banned, "Doctor Oldsmobile" whipped up two new engine choices for muscle car fans. The first was a who-wants-it "Turnpike Cruising package" that included a detuned 400-cid engine with a two-barrel carb.

Of greater interest to enthusiasts was a revived W-30 "forced air induction system" with special air scoops and hoses, a shrouded fan, a specific cam, heavy-duty springs, chrome valve covers and an air cleaner with huge ducts running to special air induction slots above and below the parking lights. The W-30, ultimately used on just 502 cars, allowed Olds to continue advertising a 360-hp engine choice.

A special Turbo Hydra-Matic transmission and a stronger 12-bolt rear end teamed up to enhance the 4-4-2's street racing capabilities. The automatic transmission outsold the four-speed manual tranny for the first time. That reflected another trend towards the use of automatics in drag racing at this time. One 4-4-2 set a B/Pure Stock national record at the drag strip. Another street car with the 400-cid/360-hp engine did 0-60 in 6.7 seconds and the quarter-mile in 14.98 seconds at 95 mph.

1968

Oldsmobile's 4-4-2 became a separate model, instead of a Cutlass option, for the first time in '68. Though many engineering features were carried over, it looked pretty much like an all-new car. Even newer and more exciting was the Hurst/Olds, a specialty car based on the Cutlass. The 4-4-2 came in hardtop, coupe and convertible models, while the Hurst/Olds came only in both closed body styles.

All of the hot mid-size Olds products shared a curvier new body with razor-edge fenders, a very "in" long hood/short deck design and a swoopy, boat-like rear end. Big "4-4-2" emblems and dual through-the-bumper exhausts made the 4-4-2 easy to spot. The Hurst/Olds featured a special Silver and Black paint scheme and in-your-face red H/O badges, not to mention a massive "big-car" 455 V-8.

On the 4-4-2 a coil spring front suspension with an anti-roll bar was mated with a coil spring link-coil live axle rear suspension. The recirculating ball gear steering (with integral assist) had a 20.7:1 overall ratio and 4.3 turns lock-to-lock. Brakes were discs up front and drums rear. Tires were F70-14s. As in '67, a 400-cid V-8 was standard, but it was a totally new one with a different bore and stroke. There were three four-barrel versions of this 10.5:1 compression engine, the hottest with the W-30 Force Air package added. They produced 325 hp (automatic), 350 hp (stick) and 360 hp. A milder 290-hp two-barrel "turnpike cruiser" economy engine could be had, too.

Transmissions included a three-speed, and wide- and close-ratio four-speed manual transmissions and THM. A slew of rear axle options were

"All of the hot mid-size (1968) Olds products shared a curvier new body with razor-edge fenders ..."

■ *Stimulated by a special 455-cid 380-hp "Rocket" V-8, the 1969 Hurst/ Olds two-door hardtop (the only available model) was a bit lighter than its '68 counterpart and faster. George Hurst and crew managed to get the 0-to-60 acceleration time dropped to 5.9 seconds.*
Phil Kunz

■ *Accessories are what make muscle cars valuable today. This Gold colored interior includes the under-dash gauge package and wood steering wheel. Another value-plus item is the four-speed stirrer sticking out of the console.*
Jerry Heasley

available. Other popular extras included a high-voltage ignition system, a tilt-away wood-grain steering wheel and a "Rocket Rally Pac." Bucket seats were standard. Forced Air induction included large air scoops below the front bumper, a special cam, modified intake and exhaust ports, a free-flowing exhaust system and low-friction components.

Car Life's 4-4-2 Holiday hardtop had the 350-hp engine and took 15.13 seconds to do the quarter-mile at 92.2 mph. "A true high-performance car and the best handling of today's supercars," the editors wrote.

Super Stock magazine's Jim McCraw called the first Hurst/Olds an "executive supercars." Oldsmobile had a quality-car image that couldn't be beat and Hurst had a high-performance reputation that other aftermarket firms would kill for. When the two companies joined forces they created a high-performance icon.

Olds had punched its 425-cube V-8 to 455 inches, but GM rules would not permit cramming the new engine into the 4-4-2. George Hurst had no such rules to follow. His Hurst Performance Products company could do the dastardly deed. Hurst hooked up with Olds supplier John Demmer, of Lansing, Michigan, to build a limited number of Hurst's car in his factory. The result was the H/O (Hairy Original?)

The beefed-up Toronado big block cranked up almost 400 hp. It featured a special crank, a custom-curved distributor, special carb jets, a 308-degree cam with a .474-inch lift and hand-assembled Ram-Air heads. A modified Turbo Hydra-Matic used a Hurst Dual-Gate shifter. It could be shifted manually or used like an automatic. The heavy-duty rear incorporated a standard 3.91:1 rear axle. Also included as part of the package were special power disc-drum brakes, a H-D suspension, a H-D cooling system with a high-capacity radiator and viscous-drive fan and G70-14 Goodyear polyglas tires. A total of 515 Hurst/Olds were built for 1968. Of these, 451 were based on the 4-4-2 Holiday two-door hardtop and the other were originally 4-4-2 coupes.

In August 1968, *Super Stock* magazine road tested the 4-4-2 and reported a top run of 12.90 seconds for the quarter-mile at 109 mph. The Hurst/Olds partnership proved to an image booster. The two firms teamed up on other Hurst/Olds for years.

"Oldsmobile had a quality-car image that couldn't be beat and Hurst had a high-performance reputation that other aftermarket firms would kill for."

■ *Special Gold-and-White paint made the Hurst/Olds stand out in a crowd—or even on a bridge. You didn't see many of these even in '69—and with good reason. Only 906 were built.*

Phil Kunz

■ *What could be cooler than rolling down the road in 1969 with your white fender stripes and red-stripe tires? F70-14 rubber was factory-mounted all around on the 4-4-2.*

Tom Glatch

Muscle Car

1969

Like the crocodile in "Peter Pan," the '69 Olds 4-4-2 ticked loudly and precisely and was ready to "eat" the competition. A new pitchman named Dr. Olds prescribed "medicine" for the 4-4-2 including a bolder split grille, fat hood stripes and bright, new name badges. The two-barrel V-8 was eliminated to purify the image. Oldsmobile ads said the final product was a car "Built like a 1 3/4-ton watch."

■ *Olds' 1970 "youth market" lineup featured a real muscle car with bold 4-4-2 lettering on the grille divider. This is the W-30 version. Note the W-30 name on the white stripe behind the front wheel opening.*
Phil Kunz

■ *For 1970, the high-performance Olds remained one of the fastest showroom-stock automobiles in America—especially when it was equipped with the W-30 package like this pillared sport coupe model that listed for $3,312.* Phil Kunz

■ *The optional 455-cid Olds W-30 Ram Air engine had a higher 10.5:1 compression ratio that helped it to generate 370 hp. That was five more "ponies" than the regular 4-4-2 mill.* Jerry Heasley

■ *Here's a close-up look at the 1970 4-4-2 fender badges and the W-30 logos. By this time, the 4-4-2 had carved out a well-deserved reputation for performance and handling that was superior to that of other American supercars.*

■ *The W-30 type 4-4-2 maintained Oldsmobile's tradition of good handling, thanks to the front-coil/ rear-leaf spring suspension and rear stabilizer bar that it shared with other 4-4-2s.*

■ *The standard W-30 transmission was "Oldsmobile's version of Chevy's M22 'Rock Crusher.'" A THM 400 was available. The THM 400 had higher rpm shift positions and sharper shifts than a standard THM.*

Jerry Heasley

■ *"Strictly speaking, a muscle car, but one too gentlemanly to display the gutter habits of its competitors," said Car and Driver of the '71 4-4-2. Net rating for the still-available W-30 engine with lowered compression was 300 hp.*

Jerry Heasley

■ *1971 was the 4-4-2's last year as a separate line. Dual exhausts, special springs, stabilizer bars, special engine mounts, bucket seats, heavy-duty wheels, 4-4-2 badges and G70-14 tires were part of the package.*

Phil Kunz

A center divider in the grille, finished in body color, carried big 4-4-2 identifiers. The front parking lights were moved from between the headlights to the front bumper. Strato bucket seats, red-stripe wide-oval tires, a juicy battery, dual exhausts and beefy suspension goodies were included. An anti-spin rear axle was mandatory.

4-4-2s with the $264 W-30 kit had special hood stripes and front fender decal cut-outs. The ram-air motor could push the car to a 123-mph top speed. A new option was a milder W-31 Force Air setup with THM. This "for-the-street" option was aimed at the younger set where heavy breathing and heavy spending didn't mix. At $310, the W-31 package cost more than the W-30 kit, but the car-and-equipment tab was lower.

Like the 4-4-2, the '69 Hurst/Olds also had modestly updated looks. Each pair of lenses in the quad headlight system was brought closer together which, along with some modification of the central grille and bumper area, created a smoother, less-cluttered appearance. The tail lights were more vertical and recessed.

Stimulated by a special 455-cid/380-hp "Rocket" V-8, the H/O was a bit lighter than its '68 counterpart and faster. 0-to-60 acceleration times dropped to 5.9

seconds. A well-tuned H/O could do the quarter in 13.9 seconds at 102.27 mph. Transmission options were unchanged. Hurst shifters again came in stick-shift cars. Turbo Hydra-Matic buyers got a column shift, although a console mounted gearshift was optional.

Total 4-4-2 output included 2,475 coupes, 19,587 hardtops and 4,295 ragtops. About five percent of these cars (1,389) had the W-30 option and only one percent had the W-31 kit. The number of Oldsmobiles that Hurst modified climbed to 906 and all of the Hurst/Olds were based on the 4-4-2 Holiday hardtop body style.

1970

Olds' 1970 "youth market" lineup included a new pseudo muscle car, as well as the real thing in a slightly updated 4-4-2 format. The Rallye 350, newly introduced in February 1970, hit the drawing board as a Hurst/Olds concept, but the Lansing management team wound up marketing it as an option that combined the looks of a limited-edition muscle car with a more "streetable"

■ *Enthusiasts cheered the return of the Hurst/Olds in '72, although it was nothing like the 1968-1969 models. On May 27, a Gold-and-White Hurst/Olds convertible paced the Indy 500. This hardtop has the cool IPC replica treatment.* Doug Mitchel

"The 'Euro' look was in for GM A-bodies in '73 ... The new 'Colonnade' styling seemed wildly modern at the time."

■ *The '73 Hurst/Olds had rather elaborate-looking tail lights with the Olds emblem outlined on them. A Hurst/Olds badge decorated the right-hand rear quarter on the trunk.*

Jerry Heasley

Muscle Car

■ The "Euro" look was in for GM A-bodies in '73, don't call the Hurst/Olds "Frenchy." It was all-American muscle car. The new "Colonnade" styling seemed wildly modern at the time. Jerry Heasley

■ Five approximately one-inch high, gold-painted louvers decorated the stripe on the center of the hood. They were made of fiberglass and riveted on. This was done in Metallic Gold on both Cameo White and Ebony Black cars.
Jerry Heasley

■ *An unusually handsome four-spoke steering wheel dresses up the control panel. Bucket seats and floor shifter gave the cockpit a muscle car look for sure. Note the Hurst/Olds name on the console.*

Jerry Heasley

■ *The W46 option added the 455-cid L77 V-8, which used a hotter cam. It had a dual-snorkel air cleaner with "Oldsmobile Rocket 455" on it. This engine came linked to a 3.23:1 rear axle. It was not available with air conditioning.*

Jerry Heasley

Muscle Car

■ *The new "Colonnade" styling was very modern looking for 1973. Dual exhaust were part of the H/O package.*   Jerry Heasley

power-train package. The Rallye 350 stuff could be added to the F-85 coupe or Cutlass 'S' coupe or hardtop.

The 4-4-2 had carved out a well-deserved reputation for performance and handling that was superior to that of other American supercars. For 1970, the Hi-Po Olds remained one of the fastest showroom-stock automobiles in America —especially when it was equipped with the W-30 package.

While the basic styling of the A-body Olds was very much unchanged, the grille halves were shorter and wider. On the 4-4-2, a dual-air-slot hood was featured, along with "4-4-2" letters on the grille divider. The Rallye 350 was one of the brightest muscle cars, though not the brawniest. Its smart Sebring Yellow paint made it stand out in the crowd. Its urethane-clad bumpers and Rallye spoke wheels were the same color. Bold orange and black stripes trimmed the rear fender tops and backlight area.

The Rallye 350's engine was a 350 V-8 that developed 310 hp at 4200 rpm. The W-31 Force Air package was available for Rallye 350 optioned cars. It boosted compression from 10.25:1 to 10.5:1 and gave 325 hp at 5400 rpm. Also included on W-31s were aluminum intake manifolds, a heavy-duty clutch, front disc brakes,

■ *Like the daddy-of-all-muscle cars Chrysler 300 Letter Car, the Hurst/Olds—at least the '73 edition—came with swiveling seats. It's interesting how the later cars returned to some of the luxury perks used in the hottest '50s cars.*

Jerry Heasley

a special hood and decals, paint stripes and special emblems. Transmission choices included three-on-the-floor or four-on-the-floor (wide- or close-ratio) with Hurst shifters. A three-speed THM 350 came with column or console shifters.

Thanks to a change in corporate thinking, the 455 V-8 (with 365 hp) became base engine in the hotter 4-4-2. An optional W-30 engine had a higher 10.5:1 compression ratio that helped it to generate five additional "ponies."

The W-30 type 4-4-2 maintained Oldsmobile's tradition of good handling, but there was nothing magical about the front-coil/rear-leaf spring suspension and rear stabilizer bar that it shared with other 4-4-2s. *Car Life* (March 1970) said, "At last people who want more power, but still want their car to handle,

■ *The electric-razor grille had five segments on either side of center divider and black-out finish. A spring-loaded stand-up hood ornament seems like a ritzy touch for a muscle machine.* Jerry Heasley

■ A 455-cid V-8 was standard. The W45 option added W-30 springs and valves (L-75 engine) and a 3.08 rear. It had red "Olds 455" lettering on top and just a single snorkel.

Jerry Heasley

■ W45 was the RPO code for the '73 Hurst/Olds option. It was available for selected Cutlass 'S' coupes and 1,097 were put together. Here you see a pretty pair of them.

Jerry Heasley

have a car that does both." Also included in the W-30 package were standard 10.88-inch front power disc (optional on base 4-4-2s) and 9.5 x 2.0-inch rear drum brakes.

Unlike the air ducts installed on W-31s, which were mounted under the front bumper, those for the W-30 4-4-2 were mounted on its special fiberglass hood. The twin intakes rammed a flow of cool air through a mesh filter. They were linked to a low-restriction air intake by a sponge-like material that created a seal with the hood.

The standard W-30 transmission was "Oldsmobile's version of Chevy's M22 'Rock Crusher.'" The THM 400 was available. Compared to a normal Turbo Hydra-Matic transmission, the THM 400 had higher rpm shift positions and sharper shifts. Hurst-built floor shifters were used. A well-tuned 4-4-2 W-30 was capable of 0-to-60 times of under 6 seconds and quarter-mile runs of 14.36 seconds at 100.22 mph.

Like the GTO "Judge," the Rallye 350 was a trendy-looking Olds aimed at a market niche that proved smaller than sales projections forecasted. Only 3,547 of these "yellow perils" were assembled: 2,527 were Cutlass S-based and 1,020 were F-85s. Many of the cars came with an optional ($74 extra) rear deck lid spoiler. In February 1970, *Motor Trend* tested a Rallye 350 with the 310-hp engine, three-speed manual transmission and 3.23:1 rear axle. It did 0 to 60 mph in 7.7 seconds and covered the quarter-mile in 15.4 seconds at 89 mph.

1971

Car & Driver once characterized the '71 Olds 4-4-2 as, "Strictly speaking, a muscle car, but one too gentlemanly to display the gutter habits of its competitors." The year 1971 marked the beginning of the end for American muscle cars, including the Oldsmobile 4-4-2. Compression ratios on all GM cars were lowered to comply with corporate dictates that said all engines had to be made compatible with unleaded gasoline. As a result, the power output went south. Horsepower ratings were now expressed in "net" numbers; they were measured with all road accessories attached. This brought the base 455 V-8's rating down to 270 hp (instead of 340 hp gross). The net rating for the still-available W-30 engine was 300 hp.

■ *Shades of the 1930s GM Art & Design approach to styling with the grille openings "waterfalling" below the chrome bumper! Bill Mitchell probably loved this design. It certainly had a bold, in-your-face look to it.*

Jerry Heasley

■ *The red-black-and-white Hurst/Olds emblem was very cleverly designed, with the "H" being an icon for a four-speed gear shift gate (without reverse of course), the slash representing a shifter and the solid black "O" symbolizing a shifter ball.* Jerry Heasley

All '71 Olds engines had an 8.5:1 compression ratio. The W-30 engine used "dished" top pistons. It also included the Force Air induction system and the hotter type cam introduced in 1970. A unique 1971 feature was the use of valve rotators on the exhaust valves of 4-4-2 and W-30 engines. In addition, valve rotators were fitted on the intake valves. Special alloy exhaust valve seats were installed in the cylinder heads and the valves themselves had aluminum seats and hardened tips. To ensure that the calibrated settings on the Rochester 4MC four-barrel carburetor were locked in, plastic caps were snapped over the idle mixture screws.

This was the 4-4-2's last year as a separate line. Standard equipment again included dual exhausts, carpets, special springs, stabilizer bars, special engine mounts, Strato bucket seats, heavy-duty wheels, special emblems and a deluxe steering wheel. Buyers could select from vinyl or cloth upholstery. The standard tires were size G70-14.

Lowering the compression ratio generated more heat, so the cooling fan speed had to be increased. To counter the noiser fan, Olds used a clutch that

■ *The 455-cid V-8 used in the '73 Hurst Olds had a 4.125 x 4.25-inch bore and stroke. It was painted metallic blue and the Oldsmobile name was embossed on the rocker covers.* Jerry Heasley

released the fan before an objectionable level was hit. The fan increased speed faster from idle.

The rear ends on all Cutlass models had larger pinion bearings and stronger pinion shafts, The clutches in limited-slip differentials developed higher maximum friction torque. Optional on W-30s was a dual-disc, dual-plate clutch that offered 10 percent greater torque capacity, 40 percent less pedal effort and doubled clutch life.

Hot Rod drove a dual-disc equipped W-30 Olds 4-4-2 with a 455-cid engine and four-speed gearbox and found the shifts "startlingly quick and effortless." The writers said, "You really have to get used to using a light foot." A heavy-duty close-ratio four-speed gearbox could be ordered on the W-30s. *Hot Rod* went on record saying, "It isn't recommended for sustained street driving."

> "Enthusiasts cheered the return of the Hurst/ Olds in '72, although it was nothing like the 1968-69 models."

OLDS YEAR-BY-YEAR SPEC'S

1964

Engine	Bore/Str.	Comp. Ratio	CID	BHP	WT.	W.B.	O.L.	Width	HT
V-8	3.938 x 3.385	10.25	330	310 @ 5200	***	115.0	203.0	74.3	54.5

1965

Engine	Bore/Str.	Comp. Ratio	CID	BHP	WT.	W.B.	O.L.	Width	HT
V-8	4.00 x 3.975	10.25	400	345 @ 4800	***	115.0	204.3	73.8	54.5

1966

Engine	Bore/Str.	Comp. Ratio	CID	BHP	WT.	W.B.	O.L.	Width	HT
V-8	4.00 x 3.975	10.50	400	350 @ 4400	***	115.0	204.2	75.4	54.5
V-8 (3x2)	4.00 x 3.975	10.50	400	360 @ 5000	***	115.0	204.2	75.4	54.5

1967

Engine	Bore/Str.	Comp. Ratio	CID	BHP	WT.	W.B.	O.L.	Width	HT
V-8	4.00 x 3.975	10.50	400	350 @ 5000	***	115.0	204.2	76.0	54.4
V-8	4.00 x 3.975	10.50	400	360 @ 5000	***	115.0	204.2	76.0	54.4

1968

Engine	Bore/Str.	Comp. Ratio	CID	BHP	WT.	W.B.	O.L.	Width	HT
V-8	4.00 x 3.975	10.50	400	350 @ 4800	3,450	112.0	201.6	76.8	53.5
V-8	4.00 x 3.975	10.50	400	360 @ 5400	3,450	112.0	201.6	76.8	53.5

1969

Engine	Bore/Str.	Comp. Ratio	CID	BHP	WT.	W.B.	O.L.	Width	HT
V-8	4.00 x 3.975	10.50	400	350 @ 4800	3,665	112.0	201.9	76.2	52.8
V-8	4.00 x 3.975	10.50	400	360 @ 5400	3,665	112.0	201.9	76.2	52.8
V-8	4.06 x 3.39	10.50	350	325 @ 4600	3,665	112.0	201.9	76.2	52.8

1970

Engine	Bore/Str.	Comp. Ratio	CID	BHP	WT.	W.B.	O.L.	Width	HT
V-8	4.06 x 3.39	10.50	350	325 @ 5400	3,667	112.0	203.2	76.2	52.8

1971

Engine	Bore/Str.	Comp. Ratio	CID	BHP	WT.	W.B.	O.L.	Width	HT
V-8	4.126 x 4.250	08.50	455	270 @ 4600 *	3,688	112.0	203.6	77.0	52.8
V-8	4.126 x 4.250	08.50	455	280 @ 4700 *	3,688	112.0	203.6	77.0	52.8

* Net Horsepower Ratings

1972

Engine	Bore/Str.	Comp. Ratio	CID	BHP	WT.	W.B.	O.L.	Width	HT
V-8	4.126 x 4.250	08.50	455	300 @ 4700 *	***	112.0	203.6	77.0	52.8

*Net horsepower ratings
** The 4-4-2 package was available in cars with four different V-8s but only the W-30, for which specifications are shown, was a true performance option.

1973

Engine	Bore/Str.	Comp. Ratio	CID	BHP	WT.	W.B.	O.L.	Width	HT
V-8	4.126 x 4.250	08.50	455	270 @4700 *	***	115.0	207.0	77.0	NA

*Net Horsepower Ratings
** The 4-4-2 package was available in cars with one six and three V-8s but only the 455 four-barrel V-8, for which specifications are shown, was close to being a rea performance option.
*** Weight depends on base model selection.

(Note: Compiled from a variety of contemporary sources. Minor differences in measurements are due to the way the car was measured, rather than changes in the car itself or related to the fact that different body styles were used as the basis for factory specifications tables. Weight is for lightest model.)

W-30 machines also got a full complement of H-D suspension pieces. Disc front brakes were also available.

1972

You could still get a 4-4-2 in '72. It had some of the same ingredients, but it was merchandised as an option package, rather than a separate car line. You could add it to 1972 Cutlass V-8 models. The package contents were now focused towards handling and appearance upgrades. The standard extras included a heavy-duty suspension, fancy wheels and special appearance items.

The base engine was a 350 with 160 hp. There was also a 180-hp version, plus a 455 with 250 hp. For those who still craved performance, the W-30 option was available. It again included a Force Air induction 455 V-8. This one was rated for 300 net horsepower at 4700 rpm and 410 lbs.-ft. of torque at 3200 rpm.

Enthusiasts cheered the return of the Hurst/Olds in '72, although it was nothing like the 1968-1969 models. The specialty muscle car was only available in Cameo White with black and gold accents and could be order with numerous luxury options. The H/O engine was a 455-cid 300-hp V-8 with 370 lbs.-ft. at 2800 rpm.

1973

The "Euro" look was in for GM A-bodies in '73, so just call the Cutlass "Frenchy." The new "Colonnade" styling seemed wildly modern at the time. The W-29 4-4-2 package came only on Cutlass and Cutlass S coupes. Content was unchanged, but the W-30 option was gone. The only real performer left was the latest Hurst/Olds. It came in Cameo White or Ebony Black with gold stripes and a white vinyl roof.

Two engines could be ordered in 4-4-2-optioned cars, the 350-cid/180-hp V-8 and a 455-cid/250-hp V-8. The latter power plant was also found under the hood of the Hurst/Olds, which lost 50 hp due to the ever-toughening emission standards.

Hurst/Olds packages were also offered in 1974, 1975, 1979, 1983 and 1984, but none of these could match the power of the earlier versions. So in a real-world sense, Olds was out of the high-performance market after 1973.

■ *Raised white-letter tires read "B.G. Goodrich Radial T/A." The wheel centers carry the red-and-white Oldsmobile "rocket" logo. The color-keyed SS III wheels are still available today.*

Jerry Heasley

PRODUCTION STATISTICS AND BREAKOUTS

1964 OLDSMOBILE 4-4-2

Year	Body Code	Body Type	Engine Type	MSP Price	Model Yr. Prod.
64	27	2CP	V-8	*	*
64	37	2HT	V-8	*	*
64	67	2CV	V-8	*	*
64	69	4SD	V-8	*	*
TOTAL					**2,999**

Note: The 4-4-2 package cost $136 and was available for any mid-size Oldsmobile except station wagons.
*Production: F-85 Club Coupe (148), F-85 four-door sedan (3), F-85 deluxe four-door sedan (7), Cutlass club coupe (563), Cutlass holiday coupe (1,842) and Cutlass convertible (436).

1965 OLDSMOBILE 4-4-2

Year	Body Code	Body Type	Engine Type	MSP Price	Model Yr. Prod.
65	27	2CP	V-8	*	*
65	37	2HT	V-8	*	*
65	67	2CV	V-8	*	*
TOTAL					**25,003**

Note: The 4-4-2 package cost $156 on Cutlass models and $190 on F-85s. It was available for any mid-size Oldsmobile two-door model.
* Production: F-85 club coupe (1,087), Cutlass club coupe (5,713), Cutlass holiday coupe (14,735) and Cutlass convertible (3,468).

1966 OLDSMOBILE 4-4-2

Year	Body Code	Body Type	Engine Type	MSP Price	Model Yr. Prod.
66	27	2CP	V-8	*	*
66	37	2HT	V-8	*	*
66	67	2CV	V-8	*	*
TOTAL					**21,997**

Note: The 4-4-2 package was available for any mid-size Oldsmobile two-door model.
* Production: F-85 club coupe (647), F-85 Deluxe holiday coupe (1,217), Cutlass sport coupe (3,787), Cutlass holiday coupe (13,493) and Cutlass convertible (2,853).

1967 OLDSMOBILE CUTLASS SUPREME 4-4-2

Year	Body Code	Body Type	Engine Type	MSP Price	Model Yr. Prod.
66	27	2CP	V-8	*	*
66	37	2HT	V-8	*	*
66	67	2CV	V-8	*	*
TOTAL					**24,833**

Note: The 4-4-2 package was available for any mid-size Oldsmobile two-door model.
*Production: Cutlass sport coupe (4,751), Cutlass holiday coupe (16,998) and Cutlass convertible (3,080).

1968 OLDSMOBILE 4-4-2

Year	Body Code	Body Type	Engine Type	MSP Price	Model Yr. Prod.
68	27	2CP	V-8	$3,087	4,726
68	37	2HT	V-8	$3,150	26,773
68	67	2CV	V-8	$3,341	5,142
TOTAL					**36,641**

1969 OLDSMOBILE 4-4-2

Year	Body Code	Body Type	Engine Type	MSP Price	Model Yr. Prod.
69	27	2CP	V-8	$3,141	2,475
69	37	2HT	V-8	$3,204	19,587
69	67	2CV	V-8	$3,395	4,295
TOTAL					**26,357**

1970 OLDSMOBILE 4-4-2

Year	Body Code	Body Type	Engine Type	MSP Price	Model Yr. Prod.
69	27	2CP	V-8	$3,312	1,688
69	37	2HT	V-8	$3,376	14,709
69	67	2CV	V-8	$3,567	2,933
TOTAL					**19,330**

1971 OLDSMOBILE 4-4-2

Year	Body Code	Body Type	Engine Type	MSP Price	Model Yr. Prod.
69	37	2HT	V-8	$3,551	6,285
69	67	2CV	V-8	$3,742	1,304
TOTAL					**7,589**

1972 OLDSMOBILE 4-4-2

Year	Body Code	Body Type	Engine Type	MSP Price	Model Yr. Prod.
72	37	2HT	V-8	*	*
72	67	2CV	V-8	*	*
TOTAL					**9,715**

Note: The 4-4-2 became an option package again. It was actually a handling package and could be ordered with any Cutlass V-8.
*Only when the W-30 engine option was ordered did the 1972 Olds 4-4-2 become a real "muscle car."
*Production (all): Cutlass hardtop (751), Cutlass 'S' sports coupe (123), Cutlass 'S' hardtop (7,800) and Cutlass Supreme convertible (1041)
*Production (with W-30): coupe and hardtop (659), convertible (113)

1973 OLDSMOBILE 4-4-2

Year	Body Code	Body Type	Engine Type	MSP Price	Model Yr. Prod.
73	37	2CP	V-8	*	*
TOTAL					**9,797**

Note: The 4-4-2 was again a handling package and could be ordered with any Cutlass engine – even a six.
*Only when the 455 V-8 engine was ordered did the 1973 Olds 4-4-2 qualify as a "muscle car."
*Production (all): Cutlass (251) and Cutlass 'S' (9,546)

■ *Without counting the cars peeking out of the garage, here are the two color choices that the '73 Hurst/Olds came in.*
Jerry Heasley

PRICE GUIDE

Vehicle Condition Scale

6 — Parts car:
May or may not be running, but is weathered, wrecked and/or stripped to the point of being useful primarily for parts.

5 — Restorable:
Needs complete restoration of body, chassis and interior. May or may not be running, but isn't weathered, wrecked or stripped to the point of being useful only for parts.

4 — Good:
A driveable vehicle needing no or only minor work to be functional. Also, a deteriorated restoration or a very poor amateur restoration. All components may need restoration to be "excellent," but the car is mostly useable "as is."

3 — Very Good:
Complete operable original or older restoration. Also, a very good amateur restoration, all presentable and serviceable inside and out. Plus, a combination of well-done restoration and good operable components or a partially restored car with all parts necessary to compete and/or valuable NOS parts.

2 — Fine:
Well-restored or a combination of superior restoration and excellent original parts. Also, extremely well-maintained original vehicle showing minimal wear.

1 — Excellent:
Restored to current maximum professional standards of quality in every area, or perfect original with components operating and apearing as new. A 95-plus point show car that is not driven.

1964 Cutlass 4-4-2

	6	5	4	3	2	1
2d Sed	760	2,280	3,800	8,550	13,300	19,000
2d HT	840	2,520	4,200	9,450	14,700	21,000
2d Conv	1,040	3,120	5,200	11,700	18,200	26,000

1965 Cutlass 4-4-2

	6	5	4	3	2	1
2d Sed	760	2,280	3,800	8,550	13,300	19,000
2d HT	840	2,520	4,200	9,450	14,700	21,000
2d Conv	1,040	3,120	5,200	11,700	18,200	26,000

1966 Cutlass 4-4-2

	6	5	4	3	2	1
2d Sed	800	2,400	4,000	9,000	14,000	20,000
2d HT	880	2,640	4,400	9,900	15,400	22,000
2d Conv	1,160	3,480	5,800	13,050	20,300	29,000

NOTE: Add 30 percent for triple two-barrel carbs. Add 90 percent for W-30.

1967 Cutlass 4-4-2

	6	5	4	3	2	1
2d Sed	800	2,400	4,000	9,000	14,000	20,000
2d HT	880	2,640	4,400	9,900	15,400	22,000
2d Conv	1,160	3,480	5,800	13,050	20,300	29,000

NOTE: Add 70 percent for W-30.

1968 4-4-2

	6	5	4	3	2	1
2d Cpe	880	2,640	4,400	9,900	15,400	22,000
2d HT	960	2,880	4,800	10,800	16,800	24,000
2d Conv	1,120	3,360	5,600	12,600	19,600	28,000

1968 Hurst/Olds

	6	5	4	3	2	1
2d HT	1,560	4,680	7,800	17,550	27,300	39,000
2d Sed	1,440	4,320	7,200	16,200	25,200	36,000

1969 4-4-2

	6	5	4	3	2	1
2d Cpe	880	2,640	4,400	9,900	15,400	22,000
2d HT	960	2,880	4,800	10,800	16,800	24,000
2d Conv	1,120	3,360	5,600	12,600	19,600	28,000

1969 Hurst/Olds

	6	5	4	3	2	1
2d HT	1,600	4,800	8,000	18,000	28,000	40,000

1970 4-4-2

	6	5	4	3	2	1
2d Cpe	920	2,760	4,600	10,350	16,100	23,000
2d HT	1,200	3,600	6,000	13,500	21,000	30,000
2d Conv	1,280	3,840	6,400	14,400	22,400	32,000

1971 4-4-2

	6	5	4	3	2	1
2d HT	1,000	3,000	5,000	11,250	17,500	25,000
2d Conv	1,160	3,480	5,800	13,050	20,300	29,000

1972 Cutlass

	6	5	4	3	2	1
4d Sed	300	900	1,500	3,380	5,250	7,500
2d HT	680	2,040	3,400	7,650	11,900	17,000
4d Sta Wag	304	912	1,520	3,420	5,320	7,600

1972 Cutlass S

	6	5	4	3	2	1
2d Cpe	480	1,440	2,400	5,400	8,400	12,000
2d HT	680	2,040	3,400	7,650	11,900	17,000

NOTE: Deduct 5 percent for 6-cyl. Add 35 percent for 4-4-2 option.

1972 Cutlass Supreme

	6	5	4	3	2	1
4d HT	460	1,380	2,300	5,180	8,050	11,500
2d HT	800	2,400	4,000	9,000	14,000	20,000
2d Conv	960	2,880	4,800	10,800	16,800	24,000

NOTE: Add 35 percent for Hurst option.

1973 Cutlass S

	6	5	4	3	2	1
2d Cpe	356	1,068	1,780	4,010	6,230	8,900

NOTE: Add 25 percent for 4-4-2 option. Add 50 percent for Hurst option.

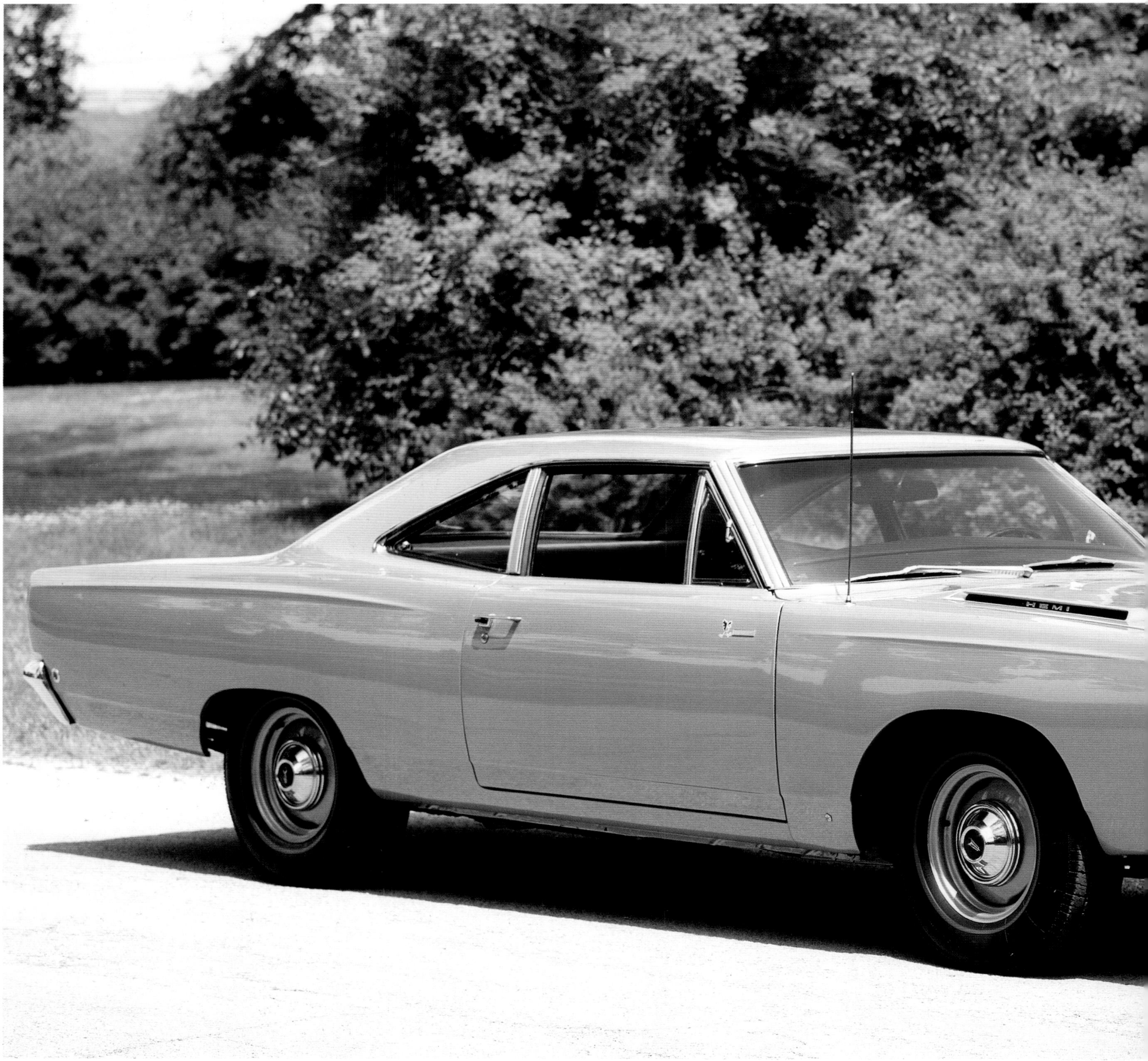
HEMI

Road Runner

1968

Plymouth, once best known for putting flathead sixes in taxicab-like grocery getters, was forced to go the V-8 route in 1955. By the '60s, the V-8s were getting pretty hot and hefty with trick cross-ram manifolds and dual four-barrel carbs. Let's face it, an automaker that dubs its top-horsepower mill the "Golden Commando Sonoramic Ram Induction V-8" is trying pretty hard to let you know its got something special. By '62, the most exotic of the offerings was extracting 420 hp from 413 cubic inches.

That particular engine was more or less a drag-racing-only rarity and marked the apex of 413 development. The next year, the same "Wedge Head" motor was bored out the 4.25 inches (from 4.19). That bumped the displacement number up to 426 cubes and added another five horsepower. This "Max Wedge" V-8 could propel a stock, full-size Plymouth down the quarter-mile in just over 15 seconds. Racing versions were running in the high 11s. Early in February of '64, Mopar upped the ante with a "Super Commando" 426 Hemi V-8 for competition use only. In the Plymouth stable, it was an option for Belvedere II and Satellite models.

■ *The first Road Runner arrived in 1968 full of "attitude." and this came from reveling in its bargain-basement-car image. The Warner Bros. cartoon character that served as its namesake was seen on a door decal.*
Doug Mitchel

1968 **1969** **1970** **1971** **1972**

1968: Plymouth unveils the no-frills Road Runner for less than $3,000.

1968: 426 Hemi is immediately made available for the new car.

1969: Convertible and pillared coupe body styles added to Road Runner menu. 440-cid engine choices also added.

1969: Decals in color.

1970: Air Grabber hoods become optional. Road Runner gets redesign.

1971: The one-year-only SuperBird bows. Based on the Road Runner, the new extreme 'Bird has loud colors, a two-foot-high spoiler and 19-inch nose piece.

1971: Last year for 426 Hemi.

1971: Two-door hardtop lone remaining Road Runner body style.

1972: A new 400-cid engine rated at 255 hp is introduced for the Road Runner.

1968 **1969** **1970** **1971** **1972**

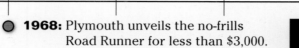

Though it had the same displacement and horsepower as the "Max Wedge" V-8, this mighty mass of muscle was unmatchable and put the Mopars miles ahead at NASCAR superspeedways and drag strips coast to coast. Richard Petty took the flag in the '64 Daytona 500 with his Electric Blue Hemi-powered Plymouth.

When Plymouth released its "Roaring '65s," the Belvedere was the *roaringest* of them all. While retaining the 116-inch wheelbase of all full-size '64 Plymouths, the updated Belvedere lost about three inches of overall length. (The Fury/Sport Fury models grew to a 119-inch wheelbase and gained almost three inches of length.) This made the Belvedere a mid-size car, but one big enough to swallow a Race Hemi in its engine compartment. At the top of the Belvedere offerings were the Satellite hardtop and convertible, which were aimed directly at the muscle car set.

Naturally, John Q. Public clamored for the chance to get a Hemi, so it wasn't long before a non-racing version in a milder state of tune was released. This "Street Hemi" was also a 426-cid/425-hp job on paper. The $1,800 option package included the Hemi engine, a heavy-duty suspension and over-sized brakes. Late in 1966, Plymouth decided it was silly to limit the two Satellites to earthy 383-type performance and decided to shoot for the stars by making

■ *The cartoon bird was also on the right-hand corner of the trunk lid. Red stripe tires and dual exhausts were standard equipment. Priced at just $2,870, the Road Runner was aimed at the youth market.*
Doug Mitchel

■ *For a little extra money you could add trunk trim and full wheel covers to the Road Runner and dress it up with a vinyl top that was all the rage in '68.* Jerry Heasley

■ *The Road Runner name was written out on a small plaque on each door. Fat F70-14 rubber was included as part of the Road Runner's standard equipment list.* Jerry Heasley

■ *The base engine was a special high-performance version of the 383-cid Mopar big-block that cranked up 335 horses, though you could get a 290-hp substitute if buying 30-cents-a-gallon gas was a big problem.*

Jerry Heasley

the Street Hemi package a check-the-box-and-order-a-rocket ship option. The engine package came with a heavy-duty underpinnings, massive drum-type binders and beefy 7.75 x 14 Goodyear high-speed tires. Since 3-on-the-tree shifting couldn't handle Hemi twisting, a four-speed manual box or TorqueFlite automatic was required. The automatic also required a tranny cooler.

While it became the basis for the awesome Road Runner, the Belvedere Satellite was no "stripper" car. Standard features included all the mandatory muscle goodies like bucket seats, a center console, full wheel covers, vinyl upholstery and many bright metal accents. This made it a nice, glittery machine, but it also added pounds and bucks, two things that young buyers didn't need in their '60s supercar.

The '67 GTX—Plymouth's attempt to one-up the Pontiac GTO—failed to hit the nail on the head again. It was a gorgeous muscle car with two awesome engine options—the 426 Street Hemi and the 440 Wedge—and everything from fake hood scoops to a chrome-plated pit-stop gas cap. Naturally, the price tag climbed even higher. The GTX cost about $400 more than the Satellite, and that was a lot of money in '67. Only 12,500 GTX hardtops and ragtops combined were sold. Case closed! A fancy muscle car could tack on a few extra sales, but it wasn't turning the tides. Enter the Road Runner!

"(The Road Runner) included the stuff that most young buyers were captivated with in the '60s, while excluding things that they just didn't care all the much about."

■ *While a ragtop didn't seem to fit the Road Runner's serious-about-performance attitude, it did broaden the model range so Plymouth could better compete with Ford and GM competitors.*

Jerry Heasley

■ *Plymouth was no mass producer of ragtops, but added a Road Runner version in '69. This Scorch Red open-air muscle car is one of only 2,128 made. When new, it cost $3,313, but the fancy wheels were extra.*

Jerry Heasley

■ *This gorgeous '69 sums up the quintessential Road Runner image, which was fairly plain-Jane but still allowed for the addition of certain popular options like a vinyl top.*

Doug Mitchel

The idea of putting a powerful V-8 in the cheapest, lightest car available was not a new one. True performance buyers had been doing it for years. What Plymouth did with the Road Runner was take this idea and do all the work for the customer at the factory. The company standardized the big-block 383 V-8, but stripped out some convenience features to give the car a "value" price. In other words, the Road Runner wasn't exactly a giveaway, but you got a lot for your money. It included the stuff that most young buyers were captivated with in the '60s, while excluding things that they just didn't care all that much about.

The Road Runner had to have "attitude" and this came from reveling in its bargain-basement-car image. It appealed to the young by poking fun at itself because of the way that Plymouth wrapped this "serious" muscle car up in cartoon decals and gave it a beep-beep horn. It seemed as cute and carefree and speedy as the popular Warner Bros. cartoon character that served as its

■ *Collecting factory-issued "stuff" like the Road Runner wheel protector on this Honey Bronze Metallic '69 hardtop is all part of the muscle-car-collecting game.* Jerry Heasley

"toy" image, you had to dig deeper into your pockets for the 426-cid 425-hp Street Hemi.

Car Life said the Road Runner "emulates what a young, performance-minded buyer might do on his own if properly experienced and motivated." It was the *J.C. Whitney Catalog* on wheels. Even with its base 383-cid/335-hp V-8, the Road Runner turned a 7.3-second 0-to-60 and a 15.37-second quarter-mile at 91.4 mph. And there were three steps up from there! To make things better, a hardtop was added at midyear. Plymouth made 29,240 coupes and 15,359 hardtops. Hemis went into 1,019.

1969

The '69 Road Runner had a new grin and a new butt. The year's big news was a really rare ragtop. Serious muscle car lovers interested in street racing and weekend dragging had little use for a heavy convertible with lousy aerodynamics. Only 2,128 of them were made. The hardtop quickly became

the most popular Road Runner with production of 48,549 being counted. The original coupe dropped off to 33,743 assemblies.

Standard no-nonsense Road Runner features like an unsilenced air cleaner, heavy-duty suspension, heavy-duty brakes, heavy-duty shocks, a four-speed gearbox and a Hurst gear shifter made it an "I-mean-business" super car, but Plymouth wasn't beyond dressing it up just a little to give it a "cool" identity. Neat touches included dashboard, deck lid and door nameplates, top-opening hood scoops, chrome engine parts, red- or white-streak tires, a fake walnut shift knob, back-up lights and a deluxe steering wheel.

Standard engine for the Road Runner was the 383-cid V-8 with a Carter AVS four-barrel carb and 10.0:1 compression ratio. This combo produced 335 hp at 4600 rpm. Options included the 440-cid V-8 or the 426-cid Street Hemi. The Hemi

■ *Muscle car lovers interested in street racing and weekend dragging preferred the hardtop. It quickly became the most popular Road Runner. The original coupe shown here dropped to second place.* Jerry Heasley

■ *The '69 Road Runner had a big new grin like the Cheshire Cat. There was no extraneous chrome on the body to ruin the "taxicab" look.*   Jerry Heasley

■ *The '69 Road Runner also had a new rear end. Heavy-duty rear leaf springs were standard, as were heavy-duty brakes all around. All engines offered were big-block V-8s with dual exhaust systems.*   Jerry Heasley

had a 10.25:1 compression ratio and dual four-barrel Carter carbs that helped boost its output to 425 hp at 5000 rpm and 490 lbs.-ft. at 4000 rpm. *Car and Driver* tested a Hemi Road Runner and recorded 0 to 60 mph in 5.1 seconds. The quarter-mile was covered in 13.54 seconds with a trap speed of 105.14 mph. It had an estimated top speed of 142 mph.

"To say that the Road Runner scored heavily in the performance part of the test is Anglo Saxon understatement in the best tradition," said the magazine. "It was the quickest in acceleration, stopped in the shortest distance and ranked second in handling. That's a pretty tough record."

1970

Plymouth's Spartan muscle car did continue its traditional use of the same basic Belvedere body for 1970, although with a new sheet metal skin. There were again three models: coupe, two-door hardtop and convertible. Standard

■ *New for '69 was the 440 Six-Pack V-8 that rumbles this Road Runner down the avenue. It churned up 390 hp at 4700 rpm and 490 lbs.-ft. of torque at 3200 rpm. The designation indicated three two-barrel carbs.* Jerry Heasley

■ *This Ohio-based '69 Road Runner two-door sedan is powered by the base 383-cid V-8. It used a Carter AVS four-barrel carb and a 10.0:1 compression ratio to help it produce 335 hp at 4600 rpm.* Phil Kunz

equipment included front and rear armrests, a cigar lighter, a glove box light, a "beep-beep" horn, a high-performance hood, front bumper guards, a 150-mph speedometer, Road Runner emblems, F70-14 White Line tires on wide safety rim wheels, three-speed windshield wipers, roof-drip rail and upper door-frame moldings and heavy-duty shock absorbers all around.

By this time, there were so many different muscle cars on the market that it was hard to tell the pavement pounders from the "lick-'em-stick-'em" variety. To help buyers understand its product offering, Plymouth started a network called the Rapid Transit System that made it easy for its customers to interface with the factory and local dealers to get the hardware they needed to win the race, whether it was a "stoplight grand prix" or a run at the local dragstrip.

Plymouth's "beep-beep" bomb was an integral part of the network, though to a degree it did seem that Plymouth was gradually losing sight of the Road Runner's original concept. It had started out as a "real" muscle car with a low price tag, but when Plymouth replaced the standard four-speed gearbox with a three-speed and gave the Hemi hydraulic lifters, eyebrows were raised.

■ *Interior items included a dashboard nameplate, a fake walnut shift knob, back-up lights and a deluxe steering wheel, but front bucket seats were an extra-cost option.*

Jerry Heasley

■ *According to Warner Brothers cartoonist Chuck Jones, characters like the Road Runner were actually inspired by the bosses that the cartoonists worked for at the studio.*

Jerry Heasley

■ *Standard no-nonsense Road Runner features like an unsilenced air cleaner, a four-speed gearbox and a Hurst gear shifter made the Road Runner 440 Six Pack an "I-mean-business" super car.*
Jerry Heasley

■ *On this Ivy Green Metallic finished car, the churning legs of the Road Runner cartoon bird have a lighter orange color. The "road runner" name is done in all lower-case letters.*
Jerry Heasley

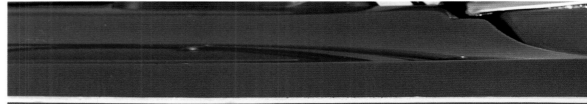

"It's no longer just a stripped down Belvedere with a big engine and heavy suspension," A. B. Shuman said in *Motor Trend*.

While enthusiasts and industry observers noticed the Road Runner getting a few more creature comforts each year to widen its market niche, the underhood hardware remained impressive, as did the performance. In addition toi a base 383-cid/335-hp V-8, power train options included a 375-hp 440 four-barrel V-8, a 440 "Six-Pak" V-8 with 390 hp and the 426-cid/425-hp Hemi. The 440 could nail down 6.6-second 0-to-60 runs and a 14.4 second quarter at 99 mph. The Hemi was even faster, of course.

A brand new Road Runner Superbird was the final volley in a battle of musclecar aerodynamics. With stock car associations imposing a 7.0-liter-engine limit, the carmakers turned to wind-cheating body designs. The Superbird—and its Dodge Daytona cousin—were designed for use on the NASCAR Grand National superspeedways. They featured a special long, peaked nose and a high airfoil on struts above the rear deck.

■ *The Air Grabber hood was standard equipment with the extra-cost Hemi V-8 and optional with other '69 models as long as the car didn't have A/C or automatic speed control.* Jerry Heasley

■ *The Model RM23 Road Runner two-door hardtop was marketed with a base price of $3,083 and weighed in at 3,450 lbs. Interest is cross-border, as this Ontario, Canada-based car proves.* Doug Mitchel

"The Superbird in concept is a vehicle for the raw competition of NASCAR tracks," suggested *Road Test* magazine. "But in street versions, it is also a fun car when you get used to being stared at." Rules in 1970 called for manufacturers had to build one car for each dealer make them "legal" for racing. Experts believe that a total of 1,971 Superbirds were built on this basis.

Though similar in concept, the Superbird and the '69 Dodge Daytona shared very few custom parts. The noses, airfoil and the basic sheet metal of the Charger and Road Runner two-door hardtops differed.

The engine used most often in the Superbird was the 375-hp/440-cid Super Commando V-8 with a single four-barrel carburetor. It was used in 1,120 cars. An additional 716 cars were equipped with the 440-cid/390-hp V-8 with three two-barrel carburetors. The Street Hemi went in 135 cars (77 with automatic transmission and 58 with four-speed manual transmission).

Racing cars used the Race Hemi and the Hemi Superbird was big enough bait to lure Richard Petty back to Plymouth, after a year of piloting NASCAR Fords. Petty Engineering hired Pete Hamilton to run a second Superbird at selected events in 1970. Hamilton promptly won the Daytona 500.

With the performance market shrinking and budgets for racing being shifted to meeting Federal safety and emission standards, there was no follow-up to the one-year-only Superbird. No wonder it's so collectible today.

"The Superbird in concept is a vehicle for the raw competition of NASCAR tracks."
— Road Test magazine

■ *The special nose added 19 inches to the car. The spoiler reached two feet high in the air, which allowed Superbird owners to open their trunks. Though it looked like part of a spaceship crashed on the car, the wing gave it hardly any aerodynamic advantage at lower speeds.* Mike Mueller

■ *You didn't need flashy "high-impact" paint colors to have people staring in amazement when you drove a Superbird in 1970. It looks pretty wild even in Spinnaker White.* Phil Kunz

■ Though similar in concept, the Superbird and the '69 Dodge Daytona shared very few custom parts. The noses, airfoil and the basic sheet metal of the Charger and Road Runner two-door hardtops differed.

Mike Mueller

■ *The '70 Road Runner two-door hardtop listed for $3,034. The vinyl top retailed for $95.70. Moulon Rouge paint, code FM3, was a real eye catcher.*   Jerry Heasley

1971

The muscle car era didn't go away suddenly. Enthusiasts wanted the cars and Plymouth wanted to build them. Uncle Sam and the insurance underwriters (undertakers?) had different ideas. Thanks to the push-and-pull between the two factions, the cars were phased out a little slower. The Road Runner got another year of life in '71, but in its hardtop format only.

■ *Violet Metallic was one of the optional ($14.05) "High Impact" paint colors offered in 1970. Lower and upper body paint codes are stamped on the body number plate. The code for this color on a Plymouth is FC7.*   Jerry Heasley

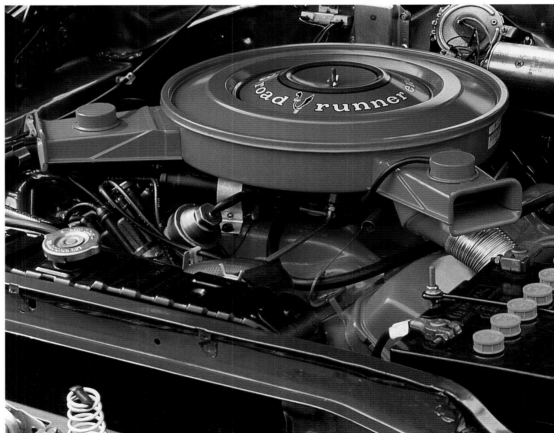

■ *This coupe has the base 383-cid/335-hp V-8, which offered plenty of snort for most buyers. Such a car could probably fly from 0 to 60 mph in 6.5 seconds and do the quarter in 14.5 seconds. 383s did get a power dome hood.* Tom Glatch

■ *The Hemi Orange dual snorkel air cleaner used with the 383 carried the Road Runner name and Warner Brothers cartoon character on it. Plymouth left lots of room for enthusiasts to twist out spark plugs.*

Tom Glatch

The totally redesigned "beeper" had a new "big boom box" front end and a cigar-shaped body with a smoother, rounder look. Acceleration, high speed and handling were still part of the package. "When the performance-minded think Plymouth they think Road Runner," said *Road Test* magazine, which selected the '71 model as its "U.S. Car of the Year." That's always a good way to get a few extra Chrysler ads, but in this case the honors were earned.

With the pricey GTX still around, the Road Runner represented the low-priced muscle car offering with its trick "beep-beep" horn, hot graphics

■ *Vinyl-trimmed high-back front bucket seats added $100.25 to the price of a '70 Road Runner. The black-and-white interior codes were XX and XW. G31 right-hand outside rearview mirror was just a $6.85 add-on.*

Jerry Heasley

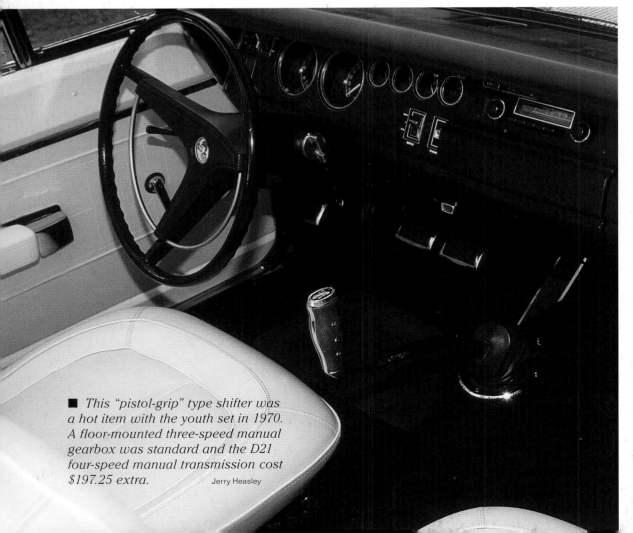

■ *This "pistol-grip" type shifter was a hot item with the youth set in 1970. A floor-mounted three-speed manual gearbox was standard and the D21 four-speed manual transmission cost $197.25 extra.*

Jerry Heasley

■ *Standard engine in the '70 Road Runner was the E63 four-barrel version of the 383 big-block V-8. You could substitute a 440 Six-Pack ($249.55) or Hemi ($841.05) if the need for speed took over.*

Jerry Heasley

■ *The owner probably saved enough by buying the coupe to splurge $250 extra to add the Six-Packed 440. He still had to pay for the Air Grabber, though—it only came free with the Hemi.* Jerry Heasley

■ *"440 SIX-BARREL" is what it actually said on the huge Hemi Orange air cleaner/hood scoop. The body tag on right-hand fender ahead of hood hinge is a good way to document the originality of a car.*
Jerry Heasley

Road Runner 1968-1974

■ It was pretty easy to spot '71 Road Runners with the 440 Six-Pack V-8 below the hood. Bold engine call-outs decorated the air scoops so everyone knew what you were running when you cruised the drive-in.
Jerry Heasley

and gobs of go power. Standard under the hood was a 300-hp version of the trusty 383-cid V-8. Other basic ingredients included a floor-shifted three-speed manual gearbox, heavy-duty underpinnings, deep-pile carpets, rallye cluster instrumentation, a performance hood, low-restriction dual exhausts, heavy-duty brakes, F70-14 whitewalls and all-vinyl bench seats with foam front cushions.

Engine options started with the 385-hp 440 "Six Pack" V-8. The 425-hp Hemi also made it back—for its last appearance—as an $884 option. Other interesting extras included an "Air Grabber" hood scoop and a rear spoiler. Considering all the pressure against muscle, the Road Runner's production total of 14,218 units was not that bad. The Hemi went in only 55 of those cars.

1972

It was the "last dance" for the muscle car crowd in '72. You either made your move and bought one or you watched the last of a legendary breed leave the dance floor with somebody else. When that final slow dance ended, there would be only slow cars left. You would still be able hop around in a tape-striped, hood-pinned, blacked-out buggy, but feel like a draft horse was pulling it, rather than a spirited pony.

■ The 425-hp Hemi also made it back for one last time in 1971. It was a slightly pricier option with a new $884 price tag. Other interesting bolt-on items included the "Air Grabber" hood scoop and a rear spoiler seen on this car. Tom Glatch

■ A floor-mounted shifter was standard in '71 Road Runners. The Code XV Black and Orange interior was one of a dozen options. The S83 woodgrain Rim-Blow steering wheel cost $20.10 or $30.50, depending on whether the car had the custom trim option or the décor package. Tom Glatch

■ An orange-painted "Certi-Tag" on the inner sheet metal, just to the rear of the battery, is Mopar's version of a Protect-O-Plate. Information tags can be used to help authenticate original features of Chrysler products. Tom Glatch

■ *The '72 Road Runner hardtop looked like a '71 with minor cosmetic alterations. The grille had a vertical fin in its center. The psychedelic body colors of the past few years were dropped.*
Jerry Heasley

The '72 Road Runner hardtop looked like a '71 with minor cosmetic alterations. The grille had a vertical fin in its center. The psychedelic body colors of the past few years were dropped. Standard equipment was mostly the same as in 1971, but the body graphics were of a new design and the engine was completely different. A 400-cid four-barrel V-8 was now used.

The 400 produced about 280 net hp at 4800 rpm and 375 net lbs.-ft. of torque at 3200 rpm. A 440 four-barrel V-8 was optional, but you had to add either a four-speed or TorqueFlite to get it. An "Air-Grabber" hood scoop was optional and required a different extra-cost tape stripe treatment.

■ *A 340-cid/240-hp small-block V-8 was now offered in Road Runners for 1972. It went from a standing start to 60 miles per hour in 7.8 seconds. The quarter-mile was eaten up in 15.5 seconds at 90 mph.*

Jerry Heasley

■ *This Red Road Runner GTX is 440-powered. To order this engine, you had to add either a four-speed or TorqueFlite. The hood scoops still said "440," but "Six-Pack" was obviously missing.*

Jerry Heasley

Plymouth made a 3.23:1 axle standard. Options included a 2.76:1 that came with the 340- and 400-cid four-barrel V-8s only. A performance axle package included a Sure Grip differential, a heavy-duty 3.55:1 rear axle, a seven-blade torque fan, a 26-inch high performance radiator and a fan shroud. A Track Pack option included all these, but the axle was a Dana model with a 3.54:1 ratio. You couldn't team the Track Pack with air conditioning.

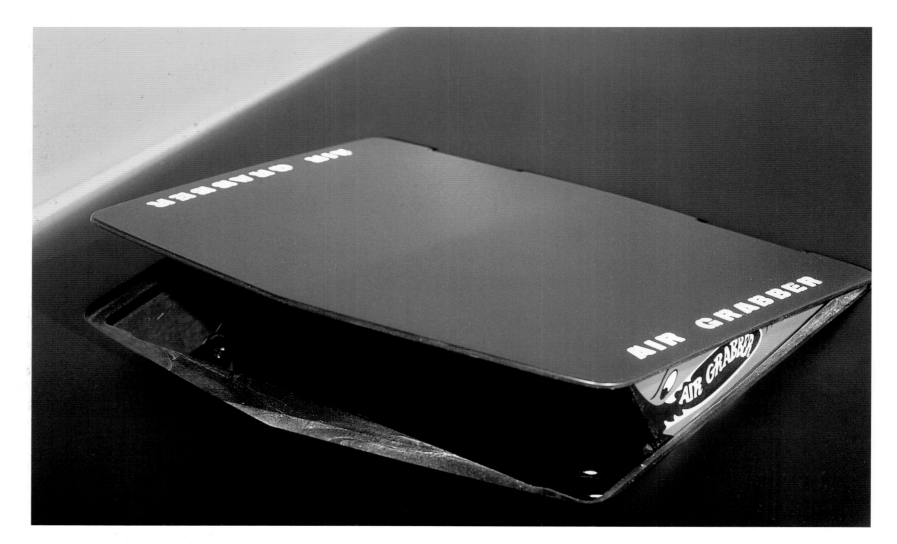

■ *An "Air-Grabber" hood scoop was optional and required a different extra-cost tape stripe treatment. It cost $67.40 and it was not available with air conditioning or on California cars with the 400-cid two- or four-barrel V-8s.* Jerry Heasley

Performance numbers were published for the '72 Road Runner with the 340-cid 240-hp V-8. It went from a standing start to 60 mph in 7.8 seconds. The quarter-mile took 15.5 seconds at 90 mph. No wonder production dropped nearly 50 percent to 7,628 cars.

1973

Yes, Virginia, there was a '73 Road Runner. It used the same body as the previous model, but with a more conventional style grille that was supposed to withstand a 5-mph impact. (That doesn't mean you should drive your car into a wall to test it). New front and rear suspensions were designed to isolate the car from just about all road feel. Handling wasn't in the same bracket that it used to be in.

The worst news was in what was under the hood – which still featured a hairy, power-blister look. The base engine was a 318-cid small-block with —get this—a two-barrel carburetor. And the exhaust system was changed to make the car quieter (even though it couldn't have been that noisy to start with).

Also less exciting was the options list. The extra-cost engine selections were a 240-hp 340, a 255-hp 400 (for buyers outside California only) or a 280-hp 440. All carried four-barrel carburetors. Gone was the Air Grabber option. A heavy-duty three-speed was base gearbox, but a four-speed was available, except with the 440. TorqueFlight was available, too—and with all engines.

Ironically, Plymouth was able to sell more '73 Road Runners than '72 models. In fact, production more than doubled at 19,056.

■ *This is the '72 Plymouth Road Runner's optional 440 Super Commando V-8. This engine came with a single four-barrel carburetor and sold for only $152.70. It was not available in three-speed cars.* Jerry Heasley

■ *Bucket seats cost $119.10 extra. If you ordered them, you could add a center console for $56.35. Road Runner lettering and a cartoon bird head decorated the glove compartment.*
Jerry Heasley

1974

This was the last year for the Satellite and the Satellite-based Road Runner. A grille with a more subdued look was adopted. For identity, the Road Runner had cartoon bird emblems on the rear roof pillar. Road Runner content included the three-speed gear box, a heavy-duty suspension, heavy-duty brakes, front and rear sway bars, a Rally gauge cluster, dual exhausts and F70-14 white-letter tires. Engine choices were about the same as in 1973. With the addition of many options, you could still get the factory to build you a relatively hot Road Runner, but it sure wasn't a "cheap and basic" muscle machine anymore. The world had changed and that skinny, speedy desert bird just wasn't fast enough to outrun the new age.

ROAD RUNNER YEAR-BY-YEAR SPEC'S

1968

Engine	Bore/Str.	Comp. Ratio	CID	BHP	WT.	W.B.	O.L.	Width	HT
V-8	4.25 x 3.38	10.00	383	335 @ 5200	3,390	116.0	202.7	76.4	53.1
V-8 Hemi	4.25 x 3.75	10.25	426	425 @ 5000	3,390	116.0	202.7	76.4	53.1

1969

Engine	Bore/Str.	Comp. Ratio	CID	BHP	WT.	W.B.	O.L.	Width	HT
V-8	4.25 x 3.38	10.00	383	335 @ 5200	3,435	116.0	202.7	76.4	53.1
V-8	4.32 x 3.75	10.10	440	375 @ 4600	3,435	116.0	202.7	76.4	53.1
V-8 6Pak	4.32 x 3.75	10.50	440	390 @ 4700	3,435	116.0	202.7	76.4	53.1
V-8 Hemi	4.25 x 3.75	10.25	426	425 @ 5000	3,435	116.0	202.7	76.4	53.1

1970

Engine	Bore/Str.	Comp. Ratio	CID	BHP	WT.	W.B.	O.L.	Width	HT
V-8	4.25 x 3.38	10.00	383	335 @ 5200	3,450	116.0	204.0	76.4	53.0
V-8	4.32 x 3.75	10.10	440	375 @ 4600	3,450	116.0	204.0	76.4	53.0
V-8 6Pak	4.32 x 3.75	10.50	440	390 @ 4700	3,450	116.0	204.0	76.4	53.0
V-8 Hemi	4.25 x 3.75	10.25	426	425 @ 5000	3,450	116.0	204.0	76.4	53.0

1971

Engine	Bore/Str.	Comp. Ratio	CID	BHP	WT.	W.B.	O.L.	Width	HT
V-8	4.25 x 3.38	08.50	383	300 @ 4800	3,640	115.0	204.0	80.0	53.0
V-8	4.32 x 3.75	09.50	440	370 @ 4600	3,640	115.0	204.0	80.0	53.0
V-8 6Pak	4.32 x 3.75	10.30	440	385 @ 4700	3,640	115.0	204.0	80.0	53.0
V-8 Hemi	4.25 x 3.75	10.20	426	425 @ 5000	3,640	115.0	204.0	80.0	53.0

1972

Engine	Bore/Str.	Comp. Ratio	CID	BHP	WT.	W.B.	O.L.	Width	HT
V-8	4.04 x 3.31	08.50	340	240 @ 4800	3,495	115.0	203.0	80.0	53.0
V-8	4.34 x 3.38	08.20	400	255 @ 4800	3,495	115.0	203.0	80.0	53.0
V-8	4.32 x 3.75	08.20	440	280 @ 4800	3,495	115.0	203.0	80.0	53.0
V-8 6Pak	4.32 x 3.75	10.30	440	330 @ 4800	3,495	115.0	203.0	80.0	53.0

Note: Net horsepower ratings

1973

Engine	Bore/Str.	Comp. Ratio	CID	BHP	WT.	W.B.	O.L.	Width	HT
V-8	3.91 x 3.31	08.60	318	150 @ 4000	3,525	115.0	210.8	80.0	53.0
V-8	4.04 x 3.31	08.50	340	240 @ 4800	3,525	115.0	210.8	80.0	53.0
V-8	4.34 x 3.38	08.20	400	255 @ 4800	3,525	115.0	210.8	80.0	53.0
V-8	4.32 x 3.75	08.20	440	280 @ 4800	3,525	115.0	210.8	80.0	53.0
V-8 6Pak	4.32 x 3.75	10.30	440	330 @ 4800	3,525	115.0	210.8	80.0	53.0

Note: Net horsepower ratings

1973

Engine	Bore/Str.	Comp. Ratio	CID	BHP	WT.	W.B.	O.L.	Width	HT
V-8	3.91 x 3.31	08.60	318	170 @ 4000	3,525	115.0	213.0	80.0	53.0
V-8	4.00 x 3.58	08.40	340	245 @ 4800	3,525	115.0	213.0	80.0	53.0
V-8	4.34 x 3.38	08.20	400	255 @ 4800	3,525	115.0	213.0	80.0	53.0
V-8	4.32 x 3.75	08.20	440	280 @ 4800	3,525	115.0	213.0	80.0	53.0
V-8 6Pak	4.32 x 3.75	10.30	440	330 @ 4800	3,525	115.0	213.0	80.0	53.0

Note: Net horsepower ratings

"The world had changed and that skinny, speedy desert bird just wasn't fast enough to outrun the new age."

PRODUCTION STATISTICS AND BREAKOUTS

■ *Red Stripe tires were considered "standard equipment," but the White Stripe style was a no-extra-cost substitution. Fancy wheels seem to clash with the car's image, and even hubcaps can be done away with.*
Jerry Heasley

1968 ROAD RUNNER

Year	Body Code	Body Type	Engine Type	MSP Price	Model Yr. Prod.
68	21	2CP	V-8	$2,896	30,353
68	23	2HT	V-8	$3,034	15,701
TOTAL					46,054

1969 ROAD RUNNER

Year	Body Code	Body Type	Engine Type	MSP Price	Model Yr. Prod.
69	21	2CP	V-8	$2,945	33,743
69	23	2HT	V-8	$3,083	48,549
69	27	2CV	V-8	$3,313	2,128
TOTAL					84,420

1970 ROAD RUNNER

Year	Body Code	Body Type	Engine Type	MSP Price	Model Yr. Prod.
ROAD RUNNER					
70	21	2CP	V-8	$2,896	15,716
70	23	2HT	V-8	$3,034	24,944
70	27	2CV	V-8	$3,289	824
ROAD RUNNER SUPERBIRD					
70	23	2HT	V-8	$4,298	1,920
TOTAL					43,404

1971 ROAD RUNNER

Year	Body Code	Body Type	Engine Type	MSP Price	Model Yr. Prod.
71	23	2CP	V-8	$3,147	14,218
TOTAL					14,218

1972 ROAD RUNNER

Year	Body Code	Body Type	Engine Type	MSP Price	Model Yr. Prod.
72	23	2CP	V-8	$3,080	7,628
TOTAL					7,628

1973 ROAD RUNNER

Year	Body Code	Body Type	Engine Type	MSP Price	Model Yr. Prod.
73	23	2CP	V-8	$3,115	19,058
TOTAL					19,058

1974 ROAD RUNNER

Year	Body Code	Body Type	Engine Type	MSP Price	Model Yr. Prod.
73	23	2CP	V-8	$3,545	11,555
TOTAL					11,555

■ *The Superbird was the final word in musclecar aerodynamics. It was designed for use on NASCAR superspeedways. A special long, peaked nose and a high airfoil perched on struts were the eye catchers.* Jerry Heasley

PRICE GUIDE

Vehicle Condition Scale

6 — Parts car:
May or may not be running, but is weathered, wrecked and/or stripped to the point of being useful primarily for parts.

5 — Restorable:
Needs complete restoration of body, chassis and interior. May or may not be running, but isn't weathered, wrecked or stripped to the point of being useful only for parts.

4 — Good:
A driveable vehicle needing no or only minor work to be functional. Also, a deteriorated restoration or a very poor amateur restoration. All components may need restoration to be "excellent," but the car is mostly useable "as is."

3 — Very Good:
Complete operable original or older restoration. Also, a very good amateur restoration, all presentable and serviceable inside and out. Plus, a combination of well-done restoration and good operable components or a partially restored car with all parts necessary to compete and/or valuable NOS parts.

2 — Fine:
Well-restored or a combination of superior restoration and excellent original parts. Also, extremely well-maintained original vehicle showing minimal wear.

1 — Excellent:
Restored to current maximum professional standards of quality in every area, or perfect original with components operating and apearing as new. A 95-plus point show car that is not driven.

1968 Road Runner

	6	5	4	3	2	1
2d Cpe	1,320	3,960	6,600	14,850	23,100	33,000
2d HT	1,400	4,200	7,000	15,750	24,500	35,000

NOTE: Item-equipped cars, value inestimable.

1969 Road Runner

	6	5	4	3	2	1
2d Sed	1,280	3,840	6,400	14,400	22,400	32,000
2d HT	1,400	4,200	7,000	15,750	24,500	35,000
2d Conv	1,800	5,400	9,000	20,250	31,500	45,000

NOTE: Item-equipped cars, value inestimable.

1970 Road Runner

	6	5	4	3	2	1
2d Cpe	1,160	3,480	5,800	13,050	20,300	29,000
2d HT	1,280	3,840	6,400	14,400	22,400	32,000
Superbird 2nd	4,000	12,000	20,000	45,000	70,000	100,000
2d Conv	1,760	5,280	8,800	19,800	30,800	44,000

NOTE: Item-equipped cars, value inestimable.

1971 Road Runner

	6	5	4	3	2	1
2d HT	1,020	3,060	5,100	11,480	17,850	25,500

NOTE: Item-equipped cars, value inestimable.

1972 Road Runner

	6	5	4	3	2	1
2d HT	960	2,880	4,800	10,800	16,800	24,000

NOTE: Add 25 percent for GTX Package.

1973 Road Runner

	6	5	4	3	2	1
2d Cpe	720	2,160	3,600	8,100	12,600	18,000

NOTE: Add 25 percent for GTX Package.

1974 Road Runner

	6	5	4	3	2	1
2d Cpe	664	1,992	3,320	7,470	11,620	16,600

NOTE: Add 25 percent for GTX Package.